Democratic Socialism

Democratic Socialism

The Mass Left in Advanced Industrial Societies

EDITED BY
BOGDAN DENITCH

Allanheld, Osmun
MONTCLAIR

ALLANHELD, OSMUN & CO., PUBLISHERS, INC.

Published in the United States of America in 1981
by Allanheld, Osmun & Co., Publishers, Inc.
(A Division of Littlefield, Adams & Company)
81 Adams Drive, Totowa, New Jersey 07512

The editor is happy to acknowledge the aid of the Institute
for Democratic Socialism in the preparation of this volume.

Library of Congress Cataloging in Publication Data
Main entry under title:

Democratic socialism.

  Includes bibliographical references and index.
  1. Socialism in Europe—Addresses, essays,
lectures. 2. Socialist parties—Europe—Addresses,
essays, lectures. 3. Europe—Politics and government—1945-   —Addresses, essays, lectures.
I. Denitch, Bogdan Denis.
HX238.5.D45   320.5'315   81-65021
ISBN 0-86598-015-2   AACR1

Printed in the United States of America

Contents

Table and Figures

Foreword

MICHAEL HARRINGTON

In the late seventies, the press in the United States and Europe was filled with articles on Eurocommunism. The evolution of the Italian Communist Party in the direction of democratic socialism, somewhat similar tendencies in Spain, and a much, much more muted trend in France were at the center of all of this journalistic excitement.

By 1980, the French Communist Party had retreated to its ghetto and once more had become a reliable agency of Soviet foreign policy, the Spaniards had become somewhat more ambivalent, and the Italians continued on their exceedingly difficult voyage of redefinition. My point is not to go into those developments in European Communism but to note that, while they were dramatic, the Eurosocialist movement was much more important in numbers, in political influence, and in potential for radicalizing the economic, social, and political structures of the continent. Even more to the point of this important volume, the Eurosocialist parties were, and are, going through a series of changes that are more significant, though less journalistically obvious, than those of the Eurocommunists.

First, consider the relative importance of the two movements. The Eurocommunists are a major force in two and a half countries: Italy, France, and Spain (Spain is the half). In France, the socialist vote is greater than the communist and any hope for a government of the Left must focus on the former, not the latter. In Spain, the Socialist Workers Party (PSOE) is the major opposition, much larger than the Communists, and will almost certainly form the first government of the Left since the death of Francisco Franco. In Italy, the Italian Socialist Party (PSI) has had a certain revival but still remains smaller than the Communists. In every other European country, the socialists are either the governing party (Austria, West Germany, Denmark, Norway) or the alternative government.

It can be rightly argued that such electoral statistics do not define political importance. If, as the Communists sometimes argue, the Eurosocialists are simply traditional social democrats, their election to office (not power) merely marks a routine alteration of "ins" and "outs" within the system and has no importance in terms of radical change. But that is most certainly not the case, as even the most cursory look at the recent history of Eurosocialism will show.

By and large, Eurosocialism reappeared after World War II as a left-moving phenomenon, at least as the "left" was defined in the thirties. The

vii

French socialist party of Guy Mallet, later to become the classic "governmental" party of the Fourth Republic, declared itself to be Marxist; the British Labour Party carried through every single plank of its 1945 campaign during the first Attlee government; the Italian PSI united with the Communists; and so on. But then there was a wave of socialist revisionism in the 1950s, when almost all of these parties rewrote their programs in response to the new economic, social (class) and political situation of relative prosperity and Cold War. In symbolic terms this was clearly a move to the "right," i.e. the German SPD removed all references to Marxism from the party program at their Bad Godesberg Congress in 1959. But it also involved a modernization of structures and political ideology: all these parties sought to appeal to nonproletarian strata among the educated employees, a force with considerable importance in the postwar class structure. At the same time there were some extremely important legislative developments that did not have the journalistic drama to become major topics of discussion like Eurocommunism. The Swedish socialists' bitter, and successful, struggle to use pension funds for social investment is an example.

Then, as the Cold War ameliorated and Europe assumed a new economic stature, there was a whole series of political and ideological changes. In France, François Mitterand succeeded in utterly transforming the position of socialism, uniting once warring factions in a new French Socialist Party (PSF) and overtaking the Communists in both votes and influence. Indeed, if the Communists had not destroyed the Union of the Left in 1977–78, Mitterand would have become the first socialist prime minister since Leon Blum with the power and the will to change the nation. In West Germany, the socialists did not simply become the normal governing party (first under Brandt, then under Schmidt) but also saw the development of a revitalized left wing, particularly among the young. In Sweden, Holland and Denmark, there were new proposals for "collective profit sharing," which offered the possibility of an incremental, but unmistakable, shift in the ownership of the decisive means of production. In Austria, Bruno Kreisky presided over the only Western government not to suffer from simultaneous inflation and unemployment.

These political developments had their ideological analogues. Throughout the Eurosocialist movement, and most dramatically in France, there was a renewal of commitment to "self-managed" socialism, with an emphasis upon factory and community control. In France, the once Christian union federation CFDT (formally CFTC) became one of the most significant elements in the move toward a socialism of self-management. All of this is not to suggest for a moment that the traditional social democratic ideology, with its emphasis upon the welfare state, the centralized nationalization of industry and the like, had disappeared. In some countries, such as West Germany, that trend was obviously dominant within the socialist party; in others, such as France, the socialists commanded a majority among the activists.

But the point is that, even in those countries where the more traditional social democrats remained in the ascendancy, there was a vitality, a ferment in the entire party. In this context, *all* of the Eurosocialists were infinitely more interesting in terms of new ideas than the French Communists, one of the most ideologically old-fashioned institutions in the modern world. Moreover, in a country such as Spain, where Felipe Gonzalez is patterned more on the Helmut Schmidt model of leadership than that of Mitterand or Palme, the party is the scene of serious and significant debate.

The Eurosocialist shift on international questions is even more dramatic and less ambiguous. The Socialist International had been reconstituted at Frankfort in 1949 at the very height of the Cold War. Almost all the socialist parties in that period supported, more or less critically, the West; some of them were locked in bitter struggles with the Communists in their own country. The International reflected that mood throughout the fifties. But at the Amsterdam Congress of 1963, held at the time of the Moscow Test Ban Treaty, there were signs of change. Paul Henri Spaak, one-time Secretary General of NATO, noted that new possibilities were opening up, that the compromises of the Cold War era were no longer necessary. By the 1969 Congress in England, Pietro Nenni, the PSI leader who had shocked his comrades by his electoral alliance with the Communists after World War II, was elected a vice president of the International (he had decisively broken with the Communists by the mid-fifties).

But the truly critical turning point occurred at the Geneva Congress of the International in 1976, when Willy Brandt was elected its president. Brandt accepted the office on two conditions: that the major leaders of the Eurosocialist parties would personally and actively participate in the International's work, and that there would be a concerted attempt to reach out to the Third World, to free democratic socialism from its European ghetto. In the years since then, Brandt and the International have delivered on these promises: missions to South Africa and Japan; active support for the Patriotic Front of Zimbabwe and the Sandinistas of Nicaragua; solidarity with socialists in Guatemala and Salvador who had been forced into armed struggle against American-backed governments; a major meeting in Santo Domingo; the first Congress of the International in the Western Hemisphere in a century (Vancouver, 1978); and much more.

These are just a few of the reasons why this book is so timely and important. Edited by one of the leading scholar-activists in the field and gathering together major contributions from different parts of the Eurosocialist world, it is not likely to become a reference point for cocktail conversations, not the least because it is much more serious than that. It describes major political developments which are still in progress and which may well have a tremendous impact on the rest of this century and the beginnings of the next.

Acknowledgements

The editor acknowledges with gratitude the cooperation and help of the *Research Institute for International Change* of Columbia University in New York, and especially its director, Professor Seweryn Bialer, in preparing this volume. Many of the issues raised in this book came into sharper focus during the years I have spent as Senior Fellow in the Institute; and Professor Lowenthal's article as well as my own piece on Left-Wing Socialism, later considerably expanded, first appeared as papers in October 1976 at the Conference on Democratic Socialism, sponsored by the Institute. It was the Institute director's kind proposal that I prepare this volume that resulted in the additional work and the present result. The Lowenthal and Denitch chapters appear with the permission of the Institute; the other chapters were obtained individually from the authors, with the exception of the Himmelstrand essay that was adapted, with his permission, from an original article appearing in *Dissent,* Winter 1979.

Bogdan Denitch

1 Prospects and Dilemmas of the Socialist Left in Europe

BOGDAN DENITCH

Background and Introduction

From their very formation, socialist movements in Europe experienced an internal tension and duality in their theory and organizational practice. This duality of socialist tradition can be expressed both as socialism from above versus socialism from below and as bureaucratic versus spontaneous organizational theories. Until the success of the Bolsheviks in the Russian Revolution, a loose Left-Right division existed within the socialist international, often leading to splits and intense internal factionalism. One can think of the anarchist, Left populist, guild socialist, and syndicalist traditions as precursors of today's socialist Left in Europe.

A second general cleavage, coinciding at times but not always with the first, centered on one's attitude toward the existing social order and political system and one's estimate of its openness to fundamental reforms. That particular dimension, loosely speaking, is the one between reformism and revolutionary socialism.

Both of these major cleavages were still further complicated by the tendency of socialists to distinguish between the maximal goals of the movements and immediate strategies and tactics. Maximal goals were often stated in cataclysmic terms by sections of the socialist movement that were in practice committed to day-to-day struggles for reform and the building of trade unions, cooperatives, and workers' educational institutions. This was nicely illustrated in the Italian socialist movement around the time of World War I, where a compromise between the left and right wings was institutionalized by the adoption of both programs. The left-wing program was designated as the maximum, the right-wing as the minimum program of the party.

In practice, of course, it was the minimum program that guided the day-to-day work and organizational life of the party. The maximum program was reserved for passionate May Day speeches and acted — if anything — as a barrier to a serious adoption of the minimal program since, while not immediately related to political practice, it did manage to frighten off potential middle-class supporters of socialism. This role of maximalism long continued as a barrier to the establishment of stable majorities supporting socialist parties, since masses of voters attracted to the day-to-day reality of socialist politics were often frightened off by a potentially revolutionary future. Maximalism is seen today as a burden by most of the social

1

democratic parties, and in the post–World War II period a number of the socialist and social democratic parties shed programmatic maximalism in order to become mass parties of social reform without explicit transformational goals. Historically, Edward Bernstein had won the ideological battle in European social democracy, which has in practice adopted his statement "The final goal is nothing, the movement is everything."

Today, socialist parties attract several different groups of supporters. Some are attracted primarily to the Fabian task of reforming, alleviating, and humanizing the existing social order, while others are attracted to the vision of an egalitarian, classless society representing a sharp discontinuity from the existing social order. Therefore, both left- and right-wing socialism are endemic tendencies in the socialist movement. Left wings rearise phoenixlike in the mass socialist parties despite their historic tendency to split away and form alternate parties and institutions, and despite the existing bureaucratic and organizational constraints in a number of the social democratic parties in Europe.

A major focus of socialist left wings has traditionally been the youth organizations of the socialist parties. Generation after generation of socialist youth seems to rediscover the themes and the politics of the socialist Left, often without much of a historic sense of continuity with long-established traditions, and therefore often repeating the fate of the former socialist Lefts—splintering factions followed by a breakaway, and an attempt to set up "purer," more principled versions of the socialist movement.

Historically, these left-wing splits, with the major exception of the Communist-socialist split, have been doomed to sectarian isolation and generally have later sought reentry into the socialist party. Workers, who form the main organizational and social base of socialist parties, tend to be tenaciously conservative in their organizational attachments and intensely loyal to whatever is the primary workers' party in their country. Thus, splits from socialist parties have rarely affected the mass base of those parties. The classic dilemma of the socialist Left was that its program, which presumably filled the needs of the industrial working-class base of the party, attracted more young intellectuals and ideologues than socialist workers. To split, one had to assume, it was easier to attract workers to a radical or left-wing socialist program from outside the existing socialist parties and institutions rather than through a struggle for a majority. There are two conditions that could lead a left wing to form a separate organization: there might be masses of unorganized radical workers and others to the left of the existing socialist parties who would respond to the formation of a new organization, or the party might be so internally blocked by bureaucratic restraints that one had to subordinate the conservative majority. While the second may often have been the case in practice (except perhaps for the period immediately following the Bolshevik Revolution), the first had never really occurred. The political climate to the left of the existing mass working-class parties appears amorphous and more suited to small transitory factions and sects than to the formation of a new mass party aspiring to win a majority within the working class.

The Communist-Socialist Split

The Bolshevik Revolution transformed the nature of Left-Right dispute by providing a specific example of a victorious revolution in a backward country, an apparently exportable organizational model: a disciplined party, committed to the revolutionary overthrow of the bourgeois social order, that sharply broke with the tradition of economism and reformism. This is why the early Communist movement attracted such diverse followers in the various European countries, ranging from revolutionary syndicalists and small groups of Marxist sectarians to traditional maximalists, left-wing socialist youth, and the more radical trade-union bureaucrats. What provided a stability, such as it was, for the early Communist movements and gave them some legitimacy was their tie with the revolutionary center in Moscow and the increasingly active role of Moscow as an internal organizational arbiter in the parties.

The cement that held together the socialist and social democratic parties was a massive electoral and organizational base of those parties; the cement that held the Communists together was loyalty to the Bolshevik Revolution as institutionalized in the Communist International and the new Soviet state. Both the Communist and socialist parties had built-in constraints to discourage those in programmatic disagreement from breaking off and setting up their own independent organizations: in one case, isolation from the mass socialist base and trade unions; in the other, isolation and rejection by Moscow. Thus organizational stability and continuity was assured to both.

This neat division between revolutionary socialists, organized in the early Communist parties, and reformist social democrats was not to continue, however, for a number of reasons. To begin with, in several countries the new Communist parties did not manage to obtain a substantial organizational base. Second, the mechanical transfer of Russian practices into the early Communist parties turned a number of them into sects that had little relevance to the politics of their own countries. Third, and more important, by the mid-twenties and certainly by the thirties the reality of the Soviet experience began to look less and less attractive, creating both splits within the Communist movement and an increasing reluctance to join the Communist parties. The socialist Left in the thirties tended to be attracted to the splinter groups that had emerged from the Communist parties, to set up their own institutions, or to work as factions within the existing socialist parties. The onslaught of fascism in World War II transformed the scene, and the failure of independent leftist parties or Trotskyist groups to establish organizational bases doomed them to the life of agitational sects.

The Post–World War II Left
and the Cold War Period

The post–World War II situation was drastically different from the prewar scene. During the period from 1945 to the late 1950s, the Cold War was the central foreign-policy issue, and the Communist parties, with the exception of the Italian party, were rigidly isolated domestically.

The Cold War had two major impacts: on the one hand, the disillusionment with Soviet reality and the exported models of Soviet socialism in Eastern Europe and, on the other hand, the dependence of much of Western Europe on an alliance with the United States, with the implicit limitations that this alliance imposed on domestic policies. Europe, immediately after World War II, desperately needed Marshall Plan aid and American credits and seemed to need the NATO shield for its very self-preservation. The prospects for radical transformation of the capitalist order were thus limited in two important respects: measures that would antagonize the United States to a point of cutting off credits and aid were unlikely to be undertaken by any government, social democratic or other; and the alliance with the United States millitarily stabilized the external and internal status quo.

The isolation of the communists from normal political processes in France and Italy made a Left majority impossible and guaranteed a continuation of centrist or conservative governments. This helped domesticate the social democratic parties and turned them into coalition partners with nonsocialist parties. The effect was to limit sharply the range of options for social democracy in Europe. This, combined with the growing prosperity of Europe in the 1950s, moved the social democratic parties theoretically and programmatically to the right. German social democracy in 1949 removed the emphasis on class struggle and the class base of the party from its program, formalizing what was the reality for the Socialist International in Europe as a whole.

During this period the socialists appeared to be committed to no more than the creation of extensive welfare states on the Swedish model and the role of junior partners in an anti-Soviet Western alliance. Within that framework, several strands of the post–World War II socialist Left emerged. The most significant, perhaps, were the Bevanites of the British Labour Party, a group whose continuity was assured by the journal the *Tribune,* and a base consisting of traditional radical trade unionists, socialist youth, and some middle-class Left socialist intellectuals.

The Bevanites concentrated on a critique of the moderate domestic program of the British Labour Party and the foreign-policy alliance with the United States. They argued that the welfare state in Great Britain, although undoubtedly a major achievement, maintained the basic class structure of British society and, in effect, helped to stabilize British capitalism by nationalizing those sectors of the economy that were financially unattractive and were losing money. The British Labour Government assured the remaining private sector of cheap transportation and energy with the taxpayers subsidizing the losses, while releasing the capital from those sectors to be reinvested in the more lucrative ones.

The Bevanites revived the debate about nationalization. State ownership of the means of production and exchange can be proposed for several reasons. One stresses the conception that socialization of industry is necessary for efficient production and planning and that the gradual nationalization of industry can be made acceptable to a majority of the population, primarily through proof of its efficiency. From this perspective, the services indispensable to the entire economy should be nationalized, and a nationalized industry should be run in a hierarchical manner not particularly distinctive from the methods of the private economy. The major difference, presumably, is that there are no profits to be paid to shareholders. In Britain this was hardly a problem, since the industry taken over had been chronically undercapitalized and had been losing money. This argument, associated with the Fabians and the Labour Party right wing, characterized the policy of the Labour Government.

The left wing approached and approaches the problem from a sharply divergent point of view. Disliking the pragmatic rationale for nationalization, the Bevanites argued from the basically egalitarian aspect of socialist thought. One nationalizes in order to strip the ruling capitalist minority of its economic and social base of power. What is required is the massive socialist takeover of the economy, which would, whether compensating the former owners or not, deprive them of the major levers of economic and political power that they hold. Therefore, one would nationalize the major industries, whether they are losing or gaining financially, to equalize the distribution of power in society. The social order would be transformed from one dominated by a capitalist minority to one in which social and political groups would compete more or less as political equals. The industrial hierarchy would be reorganized to place authority in the hands of elected public bodies. The Bevanites and their successors were never quite clear as to the degree of worker control in the economy that they envisaged. What they did say was that the practice of the Labour Government of appointing retired admirals and generals to head the nationalized industries, while pleasing the middle-class moderates, perpetuated the hierarchical and upper-class domination of British industry in the nationalized sector. In foreign policy, the Bevanites and their allies tended to deemphasize the ties with NATO, seeking to replace it with the looser defensive alliance. They wanted on the one hand to loosen the ties with the United States and NATO, and on the other were unwilling to expand the British military capacity to a point where such a dependence would seem unnecessary. They also differed from the official Labourites in paying greater attention to the movement toward national independence in the colonies and in the closer and more sympathetic ties that they had with the various African and Asian anticolonial movements. In France, the post–World War II socialist Left had firmer ideological roots, particularly in the large Federation of Seine, dominated by the ideas of Marcel Pivert, but its milieu was quite different. To begin with, in post–World War II France, the Communist Party of France (PCF) rather than the Socialist Party (SFIO) was the larger and more cohesive workers' party. The French socialists, while participating in most of the governments between the end of World War II and de Gaulle's advent to power, which ended the Fourth Republic, never had a dominant role or the power of the British Labourites.

Since most of the unions were dominated or controlled by the CP, the French socialists kept losing their working-class base and becoming a party of lower functionaries of the government and small-town reformers in the South. They found themselves with a policy antagonistic to that of the bulk of organized labor and participated in governments that had embarked on a series of bitter colonial wars crowned with defeat after defeat. Thus, the French socialists had to share in the responsibility for the war in Indochina and the prolonged agony of the war in Algiers. The lines between the Left and the Right were therefore a great deal sharper, and the tendency to break away from the SFIO led to repeated attempts to set up independent socialist parties ranging from the RDR, which included Sartre and a number of left-wing intellectuals, to the PSU, which is an almost classic socialist party of its type.

The ideology of the French Left had to be more sharply defined in relation to the Communists because of the massive French CP and because of the greater attention to ideological and programmatic questions in the French movement. Thus, unlike their British and Scandinavian comrades, the socialists of the French Left developed an analysis of the Soviet Union describing it either as "state capitalism," (i.e., nonsocialist state) or, borrowing from the Trotskyist tradition, as a degenerated workers' state or as some new type of exploitative social order. In general, they criticized the Communist Party in France from the left, attacking it for internal bureaucracy, caution, and lack of a meaningful domestic program. However, the French Left tended to fracture and fission; even the PSU by the 1960s had several highly organized antagonistic factions, and it did not really emerge as a significant force until the revitalization of the French Socialist Party under Mitterrand in the period of the Communist-socialist electoral alliance.

Convergence Theories and the European Left

The end of the post–World War II period follows the development of polycentric tendencies in the Communist world and the disillusionment of many Communist activists and trade unionists following the Russian suppression of the Hungarian revolt. The development of polycentrism over an entire decade led to a thaw of the frozen political scene in European left-wing politics. By the late 1960s several factors had changed the strategic milieu of the socialist and Communist parties in Europe. The primary factors were the stabilization of the Cold War and the increasing lack of the perception of Russia and its bloc as an active military threat to Western Europe. Other important factors were the development of independent regimes in the Third World and the growth of neutralism and nonalignment; the polycentric breakdown of the Soviet bloc into a number of competing and divergent models of Communism—Russia, China, Yugoslavia, Cuba, and so on; the gradual emergence of the Italian and French Communists from the enforced political ghetto of the Cold War; and the reemergence of class cleavages in European politics. This last was in many ways of most immediate importance for the revival of a socialist Left with defined programmatic and political goals.

Throughout the period of the 1950s, the unprecedented prosperity and apparent success of the welfare states in stabilizing the economic cycles led to a growth of "postideological" analyses of the European and American societies. These American and European analysts celebrated the death of ideology with the concomitant death of cleavage-based politics, rooted in an orientation of class conflict. The very class structure of modern industrial society that had given rise to the mass socialist movements was now assumed to be in flux; and middle-class life-styles and values would become the norms for the majority of the population. The working class was slowly losing its class identity and militance and was merging into the middle class, co-opted and corrupted by the growing consumerist temptations of an increasingly prosperous and stable Europe. Europe was, in short, being Americanized, and European parties were presumably going to respond to the new reality by becoming less ideological and more prone to consensus. They would differ only in nuances about how a welfare state was to be run. Eurocrats and technocrats would continue depoliticizing issues and reducing them to matters of technical expertise and competence.

This convergence theory was not restricted to the non-Communist advanced industrial polities. The more daring theorists saw it as a historic, worldwide phenomenon in which the bureaucratic despotisms of the Communist bloc would also begin to behave more and more like all modern advanced industrial polities. Liberalized Communist states would become increasingly technocratic, and in the golden era of East European liberalization of the 1960s East European experts increasingly echoed their West European colleagues. Class conflict was a thing of the past, modern efficient management would assure undreamt-of prosperity, and radical social transformation in the Communist bloc would lead to a similar evolution to modernity.

In the Third World, too, expertise, good will, and stability would assure that the path of modernization and political development, whether undertaken by Communists, leftist nationalists, or conservatives, would reach goals similar to those of Europe and the United States.

In that optimistic milieu where crude developmental models resembling a type of bastard Marxism were dominant, the prospects for a socialist Left appeared marginal at best. Post- and neo-Marxist theorists, of both the neo-Frankfurt-school variety and their equivalent in Eastern Europe, the *Praxis* group in Yugoslavia, tended to reduce their critique of the existing social order to attacks on bureaucratic drives which they saw as endemic to the modern industrial order. Alienation was the most acute form of exploitation — not the alienation in the process of production central to Marx, but rather the alienation of the Promethean intellectuals and youth.

The intellectual socialist Left was largely student-based, rallying around British journals such as the *New Left Review* and including American student movements of the 1960s. However, with few exceptions, they were concerned with the poor and the lumpenproletariat rather than with a working class defined as corrupted and co-opted. They tacitly shared many of the assumptions of the theorists of mass society; the difference was that instead of hailing this process they deplored it. A socialist intellectual Left around student activists grew throughout the 1960s, with few or no ties with the working class and, if anything, with an antagonistic attitude toward the trade unions and the economic demands of the workers.

During this period hostility to the United States grew continually because of its seemingly endless involvement in the Indo-Chinese war. The revived theories of imperialism saw the United States as an imperial power devoted not to progress and modernization but to the maintenance of a world status quo that increasingly doomed the nations of the Third World to poverty and dictatorial rule. However, the rebellion of the students of the 1960s was also a revolt againt the complacency of their own societies, combined with a drop in the prestige of the intellectual professions for which the students were being prepared. Here at last there were seemingly broad and growing strata "to the left" of the organized radical movements on which some type of left-wing politics could be based. Most of the student organizations of the 1960s and the entire milieu in which they operated were profoundly antiorganizational, and when organizations did arise out of the student Left they tended throughout the world to resemble the familiar Left sects and splinters of the past.

New poles of attraction had developed for radical dissidents in modern industrial societies: on the one hand, the abstraction known as the Third World, on the other Communist China. Both had enormous appeal because, since they were relatively unknown, one could project one's private utopia onto these unknown potential saviors of socialism. China and the Third World, for the student Left independent of the Communist and socialist parties, played much the same role as the then-unknown Soviet Union had for an earlier generation of European leftists in the 1920s and 1930s. However, no equivalent organizational focus was provided, and this particular leftism therefore began disintegrating and was reduced to little more than a mood or style by the middle 1970s. What remained were the mass workers' parties, and around them new programs began to form.

New Theories and Programs:
the New Working Class and Workers' Control

Several theoretical developments occurred in the middle 1960s that affect the present strategies and programs of Left socialists today. The first, developed in France focused primarily on the socialist transformation of advanced industrial societies, taking into account the shifts in occupational structure after World War II. Serge Mallet, in agreement with a number of American and European sociologists, saw that the large number of white-collar workers and professionals that had developed within the socioeconomic structure of welfare states constituted a growing sector in modern economies. Instead of foreseeing an expansion of the middle class, which would threaten the parties of the Left, he saw this "new working class" as an intellectual salaried class but subject to factorylike conditions and hierarchical discipline, within the increasingly bureaucratized sectors of the economy and society.

The new working class is the natural ally of the working class and the trade-union movement. Their conditions of work are uncreative within hierarchical and impersonal settings, leading them to organize collectively, and this is a key element in Mallet's analysis. Their skills and training make hierarchical authority especially irrational, since it is precisely they and not the management who have the skills necessary to a modern economy. This new working class has nothing to fear from social ownership and control of the economy and tends to link its particular demands to those of industrial workers, for they have skills that are indispensable for workers' control of the economy.

Mallet argued that the masses of professionals and technicians would be driven by their life condition to organize as industrial workers had and that both could unite against the owners and the capitalist order. He pointed out that in France unions of professionals and technicians tended to be more militant than blue-collar workers in raising issues about control of the work process, and that their organizations, outside of the CGT and FO unions, tended to press for a more aggressive industrial strategy, influencing the socialist and Communist trade unionists.

The teachers and technicians had been organized in the Christian and independent unions in France. These federations, dominated by a peculiar amalgam of left-wing socialists and left-wing Catholics, adopted a program stressing self-management, equality, and radical social transformation. This development in France was paralleled by similar ones among left-wing Catholics in Spain and Belgium and formed a new "objective basis" for the revival of a socialist Left. A more conservative version of the new working-class doctrine adopted by the majority in the socialist party in France gives it a radical technocratic bent that makes it attractive as a focus for the rallying of middle-class radicals and professionals. It probably has a good deal to do with the organizational growth of Mitterrand's socialists in the 1970s.

Mallet's theory also provides a theoretically useful way for socialists to analyze student radicalism and discontent. Rather than being purely ideological, it can be seen as reflecting the discontent of the future members of a new exploited class being formed in the universities. The training the students receive presumably enables them to generalize about their social condition and makes them more volatile once they enter into the work process. The significant aspect of student radicalism is therefore the radicalization of the younger professionals who provide the class-based organization of socialists with indispensable technical cadres for the running of a modern economy.

The second development affecting Left socialists today has been the growing interest in workers' control, as distinct from various participation schemes within the European labor movement. In Scandinavia, France, Spain, Portugal, Italy, and even among some German trade unions there has been a revival of interest in various forms of workers' control. This particular strategic concept has been brought into focus by the prolonged and relatively successful Yugoslav experiment in self-management as well as by the reaction to the bureaucratization of industry and society.

Demands for workers' control represent a synthesis of left-wing socialism because they presuppose a far more radical reordering of society than does mere nationalization, while stressing workers' direct participation and control of the economy and society. Thus, workers' control is the link between the ideas of the French socialist Left, the rank-and-file and left-wing movements in the BLP, the German *Jusos* (Young Socialists), and currents within some Communist parties of the West. It revives classic Marxist and early Bolshevik themes but it does so under circumstances in which a far more educated working class exists, in which the material conditions for workers' control are evidently superior to those in a relatively underdeveloped Yugoslavia.

The whole issue of workers' control raises difficult tactical points about relations of workers' councils to trade unions and of the council structure to centralized planning. Centralized planning remains for many Left socialists a major article of faith. This is why the existence of a nonutopian working model of workers' councils in Yugoslavia is bound to have a continued impact on both Left socialists and Euro-Communist politics.

A third set of themes leading to a revival of left-wing socialist politics has been influenced by the growth of multinational corporations in European economies. Theorists of neocapitalism within the socialist movement tend to stress the supranational character of the capitalist system and the difficulty of coping with it strategically within the framework of a nation-state. The tendency is, therefore, to think in terms of Europe-wide strategies or, rather, first Western Europe–wide and then Europe-wide strategies, to prevent individual socialist governments from being penalized by the flight of capital and to carry out transnational trade-union actions that are dictated by the fact that corporations can now shift production, for example, from England to Germany or from Italy to France when faced by workers' militancy in a single country.

Left-wing socialists argue that even the traditional trade-union strategies favored by right-wing socialists now require international cooperation by trade unions and socialist parties and, in countries where there are Communist as well as socialist parties, socialist-Communist cooperation. The implication here, of course, is that class politics are again assuming primacy and that, in a period of unemployment and inflation, radical class cleavages have been reached in a number of European countries. The socialist Left is more involved with policy issues of a broader cultural character than are the majority social democrats. It has supported demands to open up the universities and democratize education and has begun to stress women's rights. In part this is a generational question within the socialist movement, which has always been connected with movements demanding economic and political equality for women; the younger left socialists, however, also raise cultural feminist issues.

Euro-Communism and Strategic Opportunities for the Left

Generally, the socialist Left in Europe has gained from the distintegration of a monolithic Communist bloc. The growing independence of the Communist parties of Western Europe makes possible coalitions and left-wing majorities in France, Italy, and Spain and possibly even in Greece, Portugal, and Iceland. The very fact that such majorities exist makes a debate over programmatic alternatives assume a reality and urgency they did not have in the past. With the Left united, at least electorally, the tendency of socialists in France and Italy to participate in centrist governments is discouraged. The development of Euro-Communism opens up prospects for social transformation in Western Europe, while the difficulties within the East European state-socialist polities make the bloc appear less threatening externally, and the prospect of class conflicts based on a new large industrial working class in Eastern Europe may transform those societies internally.

The major single gain for the socialist Left that arises out of the developments in the Communist world lies in the freezing of the working-class movements of Europe from identification with the Soviet "model." It was the identification of European Communists and, to a lesser extent, of European socialists with the Soviet experience that frightened off many potential supporters of the Left. Today no working-class parties in Europe find it necessary to defend the Soviet Union. This means that it will be increasingly on the basis of their own programs and their own politics that they will be judged.

The difficulties that the classic social democratic parties in Britain and Germany have had in maintaining a degree of enthusiasm and support among younger workers encourages sections of those parties to move to the left. They can do so now, free of the fear of involvement with Moscow on the one hand and of the real or imagined threats of American intervention on the other. Therefore, European socialism is now autonomous in terms of domestic politics, and under those circumstances the normal Left-Right dimensions will reassert themselves within the socialist movement.

The Contemporary Socialist Left in Western Europe

This discussion will concentrate on left-wing socialist programs that are generated within the mass socialist and social democratic parties or in independent socialist parties that are allied electorally with the above. This is not to say that the cultural ferment of the late 1960s and early 1970s, focused as it was primarily on student and poststudent radicals, has not left an important residue of ideas, moods, and programs that influence the more substantial organized Left.

The development of a New Left in the 1960s made several contributions to the traditional workers' parties assume some importance. One was a systematic revival of Marxist and neo-Marxist thought, emphasizing primarily the theories of the young Marx, Gramsci, and some of the post-Trotsky Trotskyists such as Ernst Mandel. The second was the activation of fairly broad groups of younger intellectuals who have often graduated from their student ultraleft radicalism into the left-wings of mass parties throughout Western Europe. These act as "ginger groups" (both catalysts and activist cadres) within the parties and increasingly remain the most significant part of the New Left that is still politically engaged. In the case of a number of socialist parties, they have acted as a bridge between the

relatively antiquated party structure and cadres and the younger technicians, intellectuals, and professionals for whom the party majorities proved
arid intellectually and unimaginative programmatically.

The broader socialist left-wing today in the BLP centers around the
Tribune group and has a number of prominent spokesmen, both among the
Labour MPs and in the cabinet. Wedgewood (Tony) Benn and Michael
Foot are typical. Their particular approach can be summarized as Bev-
anism in modern dress, and it suffers from all the confusions implicit
therein. Basically, they are still wary about European solutions, and are
left-wing insofar as they feel that nationalization and social welfare
measures ought to be radically extended beyond the present Labour Party
program. They are also increasingly open to demands for workers' control.
Their insularism, however, makes them less relevant for the European
socialist strategies.

By the late seventies, a much more cohesive socialist Left current began
to emerge within the labor parties. It is a current that has been met with an
almost hysterical reaction by the Labour Party right wing and one that
poses a serious challenge to the Labour Party procedures in the local
organizations. This is the group centered around the militant Trotskyist
current that has maintained an entryist position vis-à-vis the Labour Party
for two decades. The entryist line has been recurrently present among the
Trotskyist splinter groups in Western Europe and has been pursued with
varying degrees of success in a number of social democratic parties. The
assumption here is that the mass social democratic or labor parties are
working-class parties with an adequate leadership and that the job of
revolutionary Marxists (Trotskyists) is not to try to build a separate and
distinct revolutionary party but to work within the broad parties to turn
them to the left and to develop within those parties a self-conscious Marxist
wing.

The British Trotskyists, while themselves fragmented, are one of the few
examples of the relative success of such a line. They appear to control, and
have controlled for over half a decade, the official youth section of the
Labour Party and are a force in a number of local electoral clubs. There
have been repeated cries of alarm about their presence, including an in-
vestigation of their role by the National Executive Committee. However, it
is unclear what they are doing that is illegitimate, since caucuses, even
caucuses organized around political journals, have never been outlawed in
the British Labour Party. In matters of ideology, while the Trotskyists in
the Labour Party still have a sentimental affair with Leninism and the
heritage of the Bolshevik Revolution, they are far more critical of the Soviet
Union and of the general violation of human and working class rights in
Eastern Europe than a number of "broad" Labour Party leftists who have
retained a sentimental attachment to the Soviet and East European states.

The most significant development in the British Labour Party, however,
is the emergence of a broad leftist consensus around Wedgewood Benn,
which seriously challenges the existing leadership. This broad Left has
strength both in the parliamentary party and in the trade unions, and probably has a majority of the active party members. It is committed to an ex-

tension of social ownership and the introduction of some elements of workers' control in the nationalized industries. Since the Labour Party lost the last election, the existence of a Conservative Government has tended to drive the Labour Party to the left. The further fact that the Conservatives under Margaret Thatcher are engaged in a wholesale assault on the welfare state and a confrontation with the trade unions tends to polarize British politics and may well result in a Labour Party committed to going beyond the mere extension of the welfare state in the next round.

The French Left today is a potpourri, drawing on numerous strands of thought. Two major ones are those of the neo-Marxists, former independent Marxist intellectuals including Debray, and elements formerly from the PSU who, in turn, drew both on radical Catholic and Marxist traditions. Characteristic of the French Left is its stress on self-management and workers' control, which they have managed to get the party itself to adopt programmatically.

French leftists differ from Mitterrand in several interesting respects. To begin with, they do not support Atlanticism and NATO, and would instead have France — a socialist France, that is — orient toward the formation of a socialist Mediterranean bloc that would in turn develop ties with the nonaligned bloc and the Third World. Insofar as they do have a defense policy (and it is not clear that they do), they support the concept of *defense in depth,* or general "people's" defense. In practice this means defense policies based on the Swedish and Yugoslav model: a powerful independent deterrent (short of atomic weapons) calculated to increase the costs of any invasion to a prohibitive level but outside of formal systems of alliances.

Their argument about internal French development centers on the need to break up the highly bureaucratized centralism of the French state, which they see as the major prop for the continuance of a French capitalism. The French state bureaucracy is understood as explicitly political and an obstacle to any radical social change. The social and economic differences are among the greatest, while the privileged strata are more compact and powerful in France than in the rest of Western Europe. Therefore, left-wing socialists argue, rapid extension of social ownership in the French economy would be more broadly acceptable than in the northern countries, but given the experiences with state-run industry, that extension cannot maintain popular support unless it is coupled with workers' councils. This places them in conflict with the Communist Party, which is suspicious of worker-control schemes and which stresses centralized state control and planning.

French left-wing intellectuals and professionals and more ideologically radical than their British and Scandinavian counterparts. There is, after all, a revolutionary tradition in French political and social thought that is quite distinct from the pragmatism of the British. British democratic institutions evolved gradually under mass pressure, with the extension of citizenship taking place without a drastic rupture. The French tradition is Jacobin and more accustomed to conceptualizing drastic discontinuities, a sharp confrontation of programmatically defined class parties.

A critical factor in considering any socialist program in France is that only in that country in Europe at this point does there appear to exist a viable Left majority, one that goes beyond traditional social democracy. In that lies both a temptation and a promise. Since the French Left coalition already probably has more than 51 percent of the electorate, concessions toward middle-class parties are unlikely, and no partner in the Left coalition thinks in terms of an Italian-type historical compromise. Therefore the program of a French leftist government is likely to be more radical than any of the proposals put forward in Italy by the Communist Party. On the other hand, the French establishment is both more homogeneous and powerful and more prone to extralegal solutions than its Italian equivalent. The problem of a transition in France, therefore, is more acute than in Italy.

Socialist strategy in France is further complicated by one key difference between the French Communist Party and the Italian and Spanish parties. The French party (PCF) supports an alliance of itself and socialists, provided that the PCF maintains its hegemony within the working class. Put in a different way, the PCF concedes the desirability of a socialist government made up of a number of parties only when the other parties represent groups other than workers. Within the proletariat the PCF sees one party as representing the "legitimate" interests of the workers — itself. The Italian and Spanish parties, on the other hand, not only see the coalition historically as including non-working-class parties but also accept, at least theoretically, the possibility of there being several "legitimate" working-class parties. The French Communists see the socialists as representing the petite bourgeoisie, intellectuals, or misguided workers with false consciousness.

Specifically, what the French socialist Left will contribute to a unified Left in France is a stress on the migrant workers, a Mediterranean orientation, and an emphasis on workers' councils and decentralization. All of these themes resonate in sectors of the French electorate and therefore give the French socialist Left a potential mass base outside of the traditional trade unions and party militants. The weakness, however, is that the emphasis of the French Left almost guarantees its predominantly intellectual and middle-class composition, with possible exceptions in the movements for regional autonomy in France. A critical question in France is what the reaction of the Right would be to a Left socialist program, and the history of the French military after World War II is hardly reassuring to those who would press for drastic social transformations without armed struggle.

A complicating factor for the socialist Left in France remains the recalcitrant nature of the French Communist Party. Not only did the French Communist Party assure the defeat of the unified Left in the 1978 elections, but it has all but guaranteed that such a unified Left will not be reconstructed in the foreseeable future. The French Communists, when forced to choose between a minority role in a unified socialist-led Left government and the maintenance of their dominant position with the traditional working class, chose the second. They chose to confront the socialists when it appeared that the Socialist Party under Mitterrand was wresting away from the Communist Party the hegemony of the Left and, above all, when it began to threaten the Communists by making serious inroads in the trade-union movement and the working class.

The problem for the Socialist Party as a whole, however, is that it remains mathematically impossible to create a Left majority without either the Communist Party itself or a large segment of that party, which retains the allegiance of more than 20 percent of the French electorate. As a consequence, the present disputes within the French Socialist Party between the Rocard and Mitterrand wings are reflections of this dilemma and posit different strategic alternatives to it. The organized Marxist Left in the French Socialist Party, the CERES group primarily centered in Paris, has in practice merged with the Mitterrand wing. The issue appears disarmingly simple. If a Left majority is not possible, and the Left is not to remain in permanent opposition in a ghetto, one option remains: a Center-Left or a Left-Center coalition, a prospect not at all unattractive to the centrist currents backing the present French president but one which, while providing the Socialists with some ministerial responsibilities, would probably shatter the party and reduce it to its pre-Mitterrand shell. It would certainly drive the Left out and, retroactively, prove that the Communists had been right all along about the tendency of socialists to make compromises with centrist and bourgeois parties.

Mitterrand's own option is to continue calling for a unified Left on the electoral plane, forcing the onus of this unity onto the PCF and hoping for one of several alternatives. The most obvious one would be a shift in the policy of the French Communist Party toward a line resembling that of their Italian comrades, and there are indeed powerful currents with such politics within the French party. However intransigent the present Communist Party appears to be, and however willing to make common cause with the Soviet Union on specific foreign-policy issues when it suits its purpose, the previous iron discipline has broken down and the party leadership seems incapable of reasserting a degree of centralism that would shut off internal debate.

The second alternative which the broad Socialist Party majority could look forward to would be the possibility of a massive defection from the Communists, and the creation of a party having hegemony on the Left. While that is unlikely, it is not impossible, and maintaining the present Socialist Party position encourages such a development.

The third possibility would be for the Socialist Party to make major inroads toward both the center and the left and thus to force the present Communist leadership back into a coalition to avoid complete marginalization.

Given the present line of the Socialist Party, however, the Left socialist currents as a part of that majority tend to lose their distinctiveness. Their specific role appears to be to pay more attention to ideology, to be more combative within the trade unions, and to continue stressing the somewhat verbal and symbolic distinction between the French Socialist Party and the European social democracies.

The program of the Swedish social democratic party had been considerably affected by a left wing that may well become more powerful as a result of the electoral defeat of the party. Basically, what is involved is a critique of the Scandinavian welfare states, which are seen as maintaining gross class inequality through the control of the economy by a relatively small number of corporations. Scandinavian welfare states are often described by left-wing socialists as tending increasingly to neocorporatism rather than socialism. The emphasis of the social democratic governments in taxing income rather than attacking ownership has in their view created resentment on the part of middle strata and even the more skilled workers about high tax rates, without decisively attacking the major strongholds of class power, which still exist in the privately owned major corporate sector. In Sweden, for example, they argue that there is far less social ownership of the economy than in France or Italy. To advance further, they propose to extend workers' control and to effect a progressive transfer of ownership to the councils throughout the present private sector.

The left-wing socialists criticize social democratic gradualism on the grounds that it neither mobilizes the traditional working-class base nor draws younger middle-class and intellectual elements into the movement. They stress the need for a more drastic discontinuity, which alone could make the workers' councils effective and rally enthusiastic support for the Left. In other words, if the workers' councils are gradually extended into the economy, they will be perceived by the workers as yet one more bureaucratic trade-union operation limited to activists and to the already committed. Therefore, the establishment of workers' control must be dramatic and must occur parallel to and outside of the formal trade-union structure.

Like their British counterparts, the Scandinavians — even the Scandinavian leftists — tend to be programmatic rather than ideological and to be constrained by criteria of efficiency and consensus. They are more involved in nontraditional issues than the majority of social democrats, supporting feminist, student, and anti-imperialist issues. They thus inject a more radical tone into the movement. However, the left-wing socialists not only are more radical than the social democratic parties but seek to make changes that would have the effect of decisively tipping the social power in their countries beyond the point of no return. Their growing influence is likely to sharpen class and political cleavages in Scandinavia, and since they attract disproportionately the younger and newer supporters of the parties, they appear to be the ascendant wing.

In Germany, the *Jusos,* or young Socialists, form a substantial sector of the party. Based on former students and some middle-class professionals, they are influential in a few major unions. They represent an increasing problem for the party leadership, since it is their presence as a growing sector of the party membership, though not necessarily of the electorate, that is used by the Christian Democrats to frighten off middle-class voters. The *Jusos,* unlike their British and Scandinavian counterparts, are ideologically coherent and explicitly Marxist. In this, of course, they are merely reflecting an older tradition in the German labor movement that has paid more systematic attention to theory than their European partners. The *Jusos* developed in part because of what can only be called the extraordinarily cautious and moderate program of the majority Social Democrats.

All the necessary conditions for the existence of a socialist Left exist in

Germany: major class differences, an economy firmly dominated by the private sector, a welfare state that has made no major advances in a decade, and a Germany that plays all too obviously the role of the major U.S. ally in Europe. In addition to these classic sources of discontent, there are two that give the German Left a special character: the massive presence of immigrant workers who occupy the bottom of the class ladder and who are, to all appearances, a permanent factor in German society, and the strength and prosperity of German capitalism, which create more options for drastic economic and social surgery than is available to stagnant economies such as those of Britain and Italy.

The *Jusos* join their leftist counterparts in other parties by demanding workers' control and pushing for a major extension of social ownership. Their arguments for workers' control are more ideologically cohesive and detailed than those of the British and Scandinavians, and they distinguish workers' councils and workers' control from the present workers' participation schemes in Germany. What they are about, of course, is the classic problem of control rather than co-optation and encapsulation of the trade unions and workers as junior partners in an economy that remains in private hands.

There is a classic dilemma in the strategic calculation involved. As a social democratic party moves toward respectability, it makes limited gains from traditional middle-class voters who, in any case, tend to prefer centrist and conservative parties. The new middle class, or Mallet's new working class, tends to be, if anything, more radical than the party itself. The domestication of a social democratic party, however, encourages passivity and inactivity among workers and sharply limits the ability of the party to mobilize massive enthusiasm for its program. If it is seen merely as a more humane, welfare-state alternative to the status quo, its gains to the right may be offset by indifference and passivity in its traditional electoral base.

Welfare-state measures of the classic social democratic type tend to reach their limits relatively early, and they do not deal effectively with the type of economic difficulties that have characterized the European economy in the recent period. They neither generate more work nor cope effectively with inflation, both of which require more drastic restructuring and redistributive measures. A move to the left, however, has its own attendant risks, and one of the major distinctions between left- and right-wing socialists is in how they estimate this calculus. The *Jusos,* for example, believe that a breakthrough is possible through a radical socialist program that would mobilize the traditional support of social democracy and extend it among the younger voters who are not as yet integrated into the value nexus of the capitalist system. The German social democracy, they argue, is too established to be viewed as a vehicle of social change, and that explains its inability to advance politically today. In foreign policy, the *Jusos* are not dissimilar to the Italian Communists. They look forward to a socialist Europe, independent and acting as an alternative to the Russian and American blocs, and while they are ambivalent about the necessity of maintaining a NATO shield, at least for the time being, they are clear about their Europeanism — that is, their assumption that socialist developments in Western Europe will facilitate progressive social change in Eastern Europe. They are for an extension and a deepening of the *Ostpolitik*, assuming that increasing ties with East European countries will help liberalize those regimes and that, within a liberalized East European Communism, class politics will push toward an extension of workers' power against the Communist bureaucracies.

The maximalist tradition of the Italian Socialist Party and local alliances with the Communist Party of Italy (PCI) have always provided a more hospitable soil for Marxist Left socialist currents within the party. More than any other current in Italy, they raise demands for workers' control and a radical restructuring of the Italian economy and society. Thus they view themselves as being to the left of both the majority socialists and the PCI today. Their other characteristic is that they pay greater attention to social and cultural questions that would democratize Italian society and free it from clerical domination. Thus they are among the most active supporters of women's movements, demands to democratize Italian education, and decentralization. They have been the major political group in Italy supporting the right to divorce and the right to abortion, sometimes embarrassing the Italian Communists over these issues.

Summary: Prospects and Programs

Out of a number of different sources, a left-wing socialism has been reborn within European social democracy and on its left fringes. The roots of this rebirth can be seen in the economic crisis that shook up the two decades of uninterrupted prosperity and economic expansion, the disillusionment with U.S. leadership in world affairs, a sensitivity to the problems of the Third World, and a general feeling that social change is again realistically on the agenda. The background factors were aided by the development of Euro-Communism and the prospect of the development of a Mediterranean bloc in which Communist and socialist coalitions could dominate. But, perhaps, a major organizational factor can be found in the exhaustion of social democratic reformism whose rightward drift in the 1950s and early 1960s was not substantially reversed. The welfare state is taken for granted. The question is what lies beyond. The present majority response in the socialist movement is more of the same, and while that appeared to be a solution in a Europe seen as stable, prosperous, and politically immobile, it is inadequate today when faith in the present system has been severely shaken up and a new generation of young intellectuals and worker activists is emerging.

The revival of harsh East-West polemics and the near Cold War atmosphere has the tendency to force the socialist and social democratic parties in Europe to emphasize their autonomy from the United States as the leader of the Western bloc. Since the Afghan invasion, the European socialist Left has found itself moving even closer to a de facto alliance with the major independent Communist Party in Europe—the Italian. In practice, this is related by the common resolutions in voting in the European parliament and by the ever-growing distance between the Italian and French Communists. The assertion of autonomy within the Western alliance by the major socialist parties, and even by unanimous vote of the Socialist International's leading body, tend to mute the disagreements between the socialist left wings and the party majority leaderships. They also, however, urgently pose the problem of developing new alternate strategies outside of a framework of an Atlantic consensus.

The prolonged European economic crisis has had a polarizing effect that deemphasizes the consensual role played by the moderate social democrats and welfare states. The welfare state itself is under attack, as is the powerful position of the trade unions within the European economies. The obvious bankruptcy of Keynesianism reopens scenarios of a far more drastic and radical transformation. If there is to be austerity, clearly it can either be imposed on a recalcitrant working class, with great difficulty since it will resist, or be the product of a government that assures that the sacrifices are not disproportionately borne by the workers. That can only be a government either controlled or dominated by working-class parties. This is all the more so since most nonsocialist theories about how to get out of this crisis emphasize broad cutbacks in the social sectors and increasing profits for the investors in order to encourage capital formation.

But capital formation can occur under different conditions and be directed for sharply divergent class aims. Since the purpose of growth is not to produce a gradual secular increase in the living conditions of the workers, redistribution is far back on the agenda. The moderate social democrats, in effect, are subject to the same crisis of faith and purpose as the liberal economists and politicians. As a consequence, socialist left-wing currents assume a greater relevance and have better prospects within their respective parties than they have had since the early thirties. In addition to these factors, there is a general feeling within the European socialist and social democratic Left that a major historical opportunity for a breakthrough to the left has been lost in the mid-seventies. A sharp debate about the causes of this failure is now on the agenda. One factor seems to be the inability of the traditional social democratic programs to attract the enthusiasm and active support of the new highly educated technical- and skilled-worker strata and of the young issue-oriented constituencies, which, as a consequence, often vote for marginal protest single-issue parties such as the "Greens" (ecologists) or the Radicals in Italy. Regaining the organizational élan and momentum is a major necessity for the parties of the Left if they are to win. To do this, they must offer a convincing and reasonably dramatic alternative to the status quo. That, however, is done more substantively and convincingly by the socialist left wings than by the present party majorities. Thus, in order to survive, the mass parties of the European working class will probably move to the left in the decade of the eighties.

2 The Postwar Transformation of European Social Democracy

RICHARD LOWENTHAL

This chapter aims neither at a comparative documentary study of successive party programs adopted by the governing, or potentially governing, social democratic parties of Northern and Central Europe nor at a history, however sketchy, of the policies pursued by each of them in the last three decades. It aims, instead, to present what appear to be the most significant trends in their outlook and practice. Illustrations will be taken chiefly from the development of the German SPD, because it is most closely known to the author, but comparative glances will also be cast at the British Labour Party and the social democratic parties of Scandinavia.

The Post-Keynesian Change in "Reformism"

In the social democratic movement before World War I it was usual to distinguish a "revolutionary" from a "reformist" tendency: the dividing line was the attitude toward the existing state. Reformist acceptance of functioning within the given constitutional framework generally prevailed in those Western democracies where government was responsible to democratic control and where the principle of equal suffrage was fully or approximately applied (at least for men). Revolutionary preparation for the overthrow of the political system was a matter of course under Czarist despotism in Russia and in some of the Balkan countries. In Central Europe, where the German and Austrian empires combined the ultimate power of the monarch with free elections to a parliament of limited influence and with considerable scope for trade-union activity, the dominant outlook among the social democrats was a combination of revolutionary rhetoric with reformist practice, with "revisionist" or "Left radical" minorities calling for greater consistency in one or the other direction.

After the formation of the Communist International, most of the revolutionary wing joined it and became formally committed to the revolutionary overthrow of "bourgeois democracy" and the goal of party dictatorship. The remaining democratic socialist parties became reformist defenders of the old and new democratic states, and many of them repeatedly joined coalition governments with nonsocialist parties or, like the British Labour Party, formed minority governments that depended on nonsocialist toleration. "Reformism" in practice could only have meant piecemeal social improvements of the situation of the working class, though most of the party programs retained as a definition of the socialist goal the nationalization of the large corporations at least in key industries and banking.

The world economic crisis of 1929–32 became the starting point for a major change. On the one hand, a policy of pure defense of the social achievements of labor proved impossible in these conditions, as the fate of the German Social Democrats demonstrated most dramatically. On the other, in Sweden, where a brilliant school of economists had developed Keynesian ideas independently and indeed ahead of Keynes, the Social Democrats won a majority in 1932 with a program calling for state intervention of a primarily fiscal and monetary type to overcome the crisis and restore full employment. The Social Democrats thus acquired a control of the Swedish government that was to last, practically without interruption, for 44 years. Franklin D. Roosevelt's electoral victory that same year was also followed by a broadly successful, though very imperfectly conceived, policy of "priming the pump." By contrast, in Germany, where the Social Democrats had rejected the advice of trade-union economists to adopt a program similar to Sweden's, the desperate demand for a strong, active government to create work contributed to the collapse of democracy and to the rise of Hitler's dictatorship — and it was the Nazi regime that created full employment, within the framework of massive rearmament.

The negative lesson of Germany and the positive example of Sweden caused a number of social democratic parties to adopt programs of "planning for full employment" in the following years. For the Norwegian party (which had once belonged to the Communist International and had retained dogmatic Marxist traditions long after it left the International in 1923), the adoption of such a full-employment plan became in 1934 the occasion for the party's emancipation from dogma, for its return to the Socialist International, and, in 1935, for the formation of a long-lasting labor government. In Britain, the adoption of Keynesian ideas by the Labour Party was first advocated by John Strachey in 1939 and was incorporated into Labour's postwar election program by Herbert Morrison. Backed by the national experience of prolonged mass unemployment in the 1920s and 1930s and followed by full employment in wartime, the adoption of Keynesian ideas contributed vitally to Labour's victory in 1945.

Commitment to planning for full employment and steady growth thus became a central part of the social democratic program on an international scale. But that meant a change in the nature of "reformism" as hitherto conceived: the improvement of the workers' lot by piecemeal reforms, while still important, now took second place to a deliberate attempt to change immediately the dynamics of the capitalist economy as a whole. This macroeconomic policy could well be described as a synthesis of the earlier "reformist" and "revolutionary" concepts, accompanied as it was by the nationalization of key industries under the first Labour majority government, and also under the postwar government of France in which the socialists participated. At the same time, it was combined with a continued firm commitment to the Western type of pluralistic democracy under the rule of law and to its defense against all internal subversion and external pressure on the part of the Communist parties and powers — all of which became defining characteristics of the democratic socialist parties.

Autarkic Austerity Planning — or Growth in a Worldwide Framework?

Both in England and in Germany, though not in Sweden, the transition to full employment policies had first been made in a war economy — by Hitler before the war and by the British coalition government during it. In both cases, it had thus been born amid critical shortages of foreign exchange and foreign supplies. Hence the concept of planning seemed to comprise not only monetary and fiscal planning of the total volume of economic activity but such physical planning for austerity as the limitation of imports, the rationing of food, and the allocation of raw materials. In Britain, because of the massive loss of foreign assets, such austerity conditions continued for some years after the war. In defeated and destroyed Germany with its worthless currency, austerity conditions continued up to the currency reform and the beginning of the Marshall Plan.

When primary necessities are scarce, rationing on the basis of equality is indeed the alternative to the injustice of "rationing by the purse"; hence in the early postwar years both the British and German socialists came to see austerity planning as a necessary part of social justice, and therefore as a necessary part of socialist planning. The German Social Democrats opposed Ludwig Erhard's 1948 decision to dismantle the rationing and allocation regulations, which proved an immense success; and the British Labour Party continued many wartime regulations longer than the people thought necessary. More than that, both the British and the German parties long continued to hold a concept of planning as primarily *national* planning. This concept was based on the memory of planning measures that had emerged as a means of national self-protection in the face of the collapse of the international currency and credit system during the world crisis. It was based also on the memory of the role of such measures in the fair distribution of later shortages. This association of socialist planning with national sovereignty was the basic reason for the German Social Democrats' initial opposition to the creation of the European Coal and Steel Community in a capitalist framework, and for the prolonged opposition of British Labour to the European Economic Community.

Yet, in fact, a policy of full employment and steady growth proved compatible with the abandonment of autarky planning, the restoration of a functioning credit network, and an intensive division of labor among the industrially advanced democracies. This was so thanks to three interrelated postwar developments: (1) the adoption of a high-employment and growth policy (however imperfectly executed at the time) by the leading Western economic power, the United States; (2) the creation of a new, flexible world currency system at Bretton Woods; and (3) the initial American policy of granting massive credits for international reconstruction, notably the Marshall Plan. The combined effect of these policies was the unparalleled quarter century of high employment and steady growth that followed the end of World War II. This period of increasing affluence and social security could not have been brought about by a pure capitalist free-market economy, as some of its ideological defenders maintained, nor by socialistic national planning for austerity, but only by the actually practiced methods of monetary and fiscal planning for high employment and steady growth operating in a worldwide market economy.

The Scandinavian Social Democrats have never been addicted to the doctrine that the fair distribution of shortages, however inevitable at certain times, was something inherently socialist. The German Social Democrats were gradually cured of it by experience, without adopting the opposite doctrine of a free-market economy defended by their domestic opponents. This enabled them in 1966–67, when the absence of a well-planned high-employment policy produced a recession in the Federal Republic, to enter the Grant Coalition government with a Keynesian plan that proved successful and helped to pave the way for the Social Democratic victories of 1969 and 1972. The British Labour Party, operating in a country where periodic balance-of-payments crises brought about for other reasons permitted no steady growth, has never completely overcome the belief of many of its intellectuals and trade-union leaders that Britain could do better if more physical controls were imposed, and that this would somehow be more socialistic. That is one of the principal reasons for the continuing gulf between the party's leadership in government on one side and the majorities at its party congresses on the other.

The Gradualization of the Old Issues

The abandonment of the belief in detailed physical planning by the social democratic parties (with the partial exception of British Labour) and the acceptance of the need for Keynesian global planning by most nonsocialist parties (including since 1967 those of the Federal Republic) have greatly diminished the traditional difference between socialists and nonsocialists in the field of general economic policy. Of course, practical differences remain on many concrete economic decisions, but it has become difficult to formulate them in terms of general ideological principles. They are differences of degree, of priorities, and of group interests—not of concepts of the economic system. The same applies to the achievements of the welfare state, which have largely been the handiwork of the democratic socialist parties; the "bourgeois" parties have generally accepted them as part of the given economic and social landscape, and only criticize specific defects in their operation (defects to which the democratic socialists are not insensitive, either).

A similar development has taken place with regard to the issue of nationalization. The nationalized industries in Britain and France—not to mention those in the Soviet bloc—have not been felt by their workers to be different in style of management from privately owned capitalist industries. From the workers' point of view, they continue to represent an alien power. (The growing importance of demands by the workers or their representatives for a share in the management of both the private and nationalized enterprises is the reverse side of the disappointment.) Neither have these nationalized industries generally shown superior efficiency. While many of the complaints about the inefficiency of nationalized enterprises are partisan exaggerations, referring to industries that suffer from such structural handicaps as those that afflict the coal mines and railways of Britain, the fact remains that nationalization has not generally been able to overcome such handicaps. Finally, the belief that nationalization would give the government an additional level for steering the economy as a whole — for example, by direct decisions to make or postpone investments at a given time — has also been eroded as the financial complications of such decisions have become apparent.

As a result, the British Labour leadership generally has not bowed to the pressure of its left-wingers for new measures of nationalization, notably of the banks and insurance companies, even when such demands have commanded a majority at party congresses. The German Social Democrats regard nationalization as a weapon of last resort rather than an important part of their program. The Social Democrats of Scandinavia have built up a number of new industries and mines that are state-owned, but in their decades of government have not nationalized any existing enterprises. Today the issue, on the whole, is barely alive.

Finally, there are now hardly any differences of principle between democratic socialists and their opponents on foreign policy and defense. Within three years after the end of the war, Soviet suppression, persecution, and "forced fusion" of the democratic socialist parties of Eastern Europe succeeded in uniting the Western social democrats in the realization that their very existence would be threatened by any further Soviet advance. Accordingly, they have supported Western unity on such constructive programs as the Marshall Plan, but also on resistance to such Soviet encroachments as Stalin's Berlin blockade, the Soviet-supported Korean War, and Khrushchev's Berlin ultimatum and his Cuban missile crisis. Attitudes to defense have varied in accordance with national situations: the Austrian, Swedish, and Swiss social democrats have joined most other parties in their countries in affirming their neutrality and, of course, the Finns had no choice. But in the NATO countries the social democrats have generally supported NATO; the one important temporary exception — the initial opposition of the German SPD to a West German "defense contribution" — was based on specific wishes for American military assurances and specific hopes for German reunification by four-power negotiation, not on any pacifist or neutralist principles. In fact, the opting by the German Social Democrats for Western democracy has been clear from the early days of Kurt Schumacher and Ernst Reuter.

Differences between social democrats and other parties have of course existed, and continue to exist, on concrete questions of diplomatic policy and military expenditure. Social democratic leaders have generally argued, not always convincingly, that they could negotiate with the Soviets to better effect than their opponents, and that they could reduce the burdens and diminish the risks of competitive armaments. But these, again, have been generally questions of degree, with the notable exception of the dramatic controversy over the *Ostpolitik* of the German Social Democrats. However, even that policy has been conducted within the framework of a general Western, and particularly American, policy of détente. It has resulted in removing some specifically German territorial disputes that the Western powers had no inclination to make their own, in improving security, and in diminishing the causes of friction in Berlin.

One issue about which social democrats in many countries have been more critical of American policy than have their opponents has been the war in Vietnam. But even this has had no influence on the practical policy of social democratic governments, except in neutral Sweden. Here, however, we are approaching a policy area in which consensus is generally less developed—that of relations with the Third World, to be discussed later.

We have described the gradualization of old party conflicts in such vital areas as economic planning, nationalization, foreign policy, and defense. By the early 1960s, the apparent weakening of differences between the major parties of Left and Right in the Western democracies had become a general topic of discussion among political analysts. The Godesberg program of the German Social Democrats, adopted in 1959, and their subsequent explicit acceptance of the policy of Western integration initiated by their Christian Democratic opponents, which paved the way for the Grand Coalition of 1966–69, are viewed as the classic examples of this more general process. However, since then a number of new, divisive issues have increasingly come to the fore, greatly influencing the policies and programs of the democratic socialist parties. These are the issues of equality by redistribution and equalization of chances by educational reforms; of participation by the workers in management, and of democratization in general; of the control of inflation and the role of the trade unions in it; of the adaptation of planning to the new awareness of environmental problems and limits of growth; and of the changing relationship between the industrially advanced democracies and the poor, less developed countries.

From Equality by Redistribution
To Equality by Education

In a book on socialist theory published during the 1950s, the late British Foreign Secretary Anthony Crosland stated categorically that "socialism is about equality." According to this view, the primary difference between the democratic socialists and their conservative opponents did not concern such structural economic questions as the degree of planning or the share of nationalized ownership of the means of production, but the struggle to overcome or maintain the social gulf between the classes—a gulf that had always been felt particularly deeply in Britain.

Most democratic socialists understood that an approach to economic equality that relied on raising directly the share of wage incomes within the national income or on reducing directly the income differentials between the wage-earning and salaried occupations would be severely limited by economic laws. The latter attempt would also be severely limited by the resistance of trade unions and professional associations. Hence economic egalitarianism had to rely in the main on a secondary redistribution of income and (as far as possible) of capital ownership, by taxes on one side and social security benefits on the other. The effort at such a secondary redistribution by progressive taxation of income, social services including free medical treatment and public old-age pensions, public provision of low-cost housing for the lower income groups, and other measures was greatly facilitated throughout the postwar quarter century by the steady increase in total national income. This increase generally permitted an upward equalization in which the lower income groups benefited absolutely and relatively, while the higher groups lost only relatively. The approach achieved its greatest successes in Sweden, where it had been practiced for the longest period, but it began to reach a saturation point there in recent years as the tax progression came to be resented as excessive by a growing part of the electorate. It had its most dramatic postwar start in Britain with the introduction of National Health Service and the housing policy conceived by Aneurin Bevan, but part of the gains were lost there in later years as economic growth under both Labour and Conservative governments continued to lag behind that of other advanced Western countries and as new forms of marginal poverty emerged. It also made considerable progress in West Germany during the long period of nonsocialist rule, but in part under the pressure of the strong Social Democratic opposition, which shared in framing the housing law and in passing the introduction of "dynamic" (index-based) old-age pensions. That process has continued under socialist-led governments even during the recent recession.

Results in the redistribution of capital ownership by taxation have generally been far less substantial, despite such measures as English death duties and West German introduction of "capital-forming savings" as an addition to workers' wages. The basic problem here is to find ways to transfer a share of capital ownership to wage earners without discouraging investment. Plans for putting a growing share of capital in the workers' hands through legislation, as has been achieved in America by tariff agreements about pension funds, have played a growing role in West German and Swedish public discussion in recent years, but have not yet passed into law.

In addition to efforts to achieve greater equality through redistribution, democratic socialists have always known that essential equality of individual chances depends to a large extent on the structure of public education. They have always fought, not only for free elementary education, but for free secondary and finally tertiary education for all those whose parents could not afford to pay. The expansion of scholarships to grammar schools and universities in postwar Britain—and the corresponding expansion in the number of universities—has in fact caused a major change in the social composition of the educated classes.

A new concept of the way to equalize educational chances, which was adopted by the British, Swedish, and West German social democrats in the postwar period, was the idea of the "comprehensive school." Under this system, children of all social classes should be taught together for the first five or six years and then be sorted out for different branches of the educational road according to their natural talents and efforts, as measured by general results in class or by an examination. As a principle of social justice this idea has come to be widely accepted. In practice, however, there have been a number of failures where the system was introduced before enough comprehensive schools had been built and enough teachers trained for them. There have also been many complaints about the psychological pressures created among children by the approach of the examination.

Before the new system could be consolidated in England or Sweden, and indeed before it was at all widely introduced in Germany, the struggle for its introduction and consolidation was overtaken and complicated by the impact of a new didactic ideology. According to this ideology, what had been regarded as differences of natural talent had also to be largely attributed to the different family environment in which children grow up; hence the task of the school, from an egalitarian point of view, was not to open the better career to the more talented, but to equalize the natural inequality by special efforts for the less gifted pupils, even at the risk of slowing down the more gifted ones. This prescription, however questionable in its consequences, could be understood in the special context of dealing with disadvantaged racial minorities in the United States, where it had partly originated. In the different context of Western Europe, it had only ideological zeal to recommend it and was likely to do serious harm to the general level of school education. Moreover, the combination of the introduction of the comprehensive school with experiments in the new didactics exposed the former to the criticism that it was conceived as an instrument not for the equalization of opportunity, which was widely popular, but for the equalization of results, which is clearly rejected as an ideological fad by the majority everywhere in Europe.

Inside the social democratic parties, the struggle about this new concept of equality has not yet been concluded. In a number of cases, social democrats have favored experiments on the basis of equality of results. However, the reaction of the electorate is likely to force them back to the more limited concept of equality of opportunity, a concept that is clearly more appropriate for a society that depends on the maximum performance of its citizens in international competition.

Participation and Democratization

One of the principal new themes introduced into social democratic discussions during the postwar era has been that of the participation of the workers—or rather of their representatives—in management (codetermination or *Mitbestimmung*). This concept arose as a goal for West German trade unions as a result of their early role on the boards set up by the Anglo-American authorities for the management of the "decartellized" enterprises of the coal and steel industries of the Ruhr and as a result of the West German Social Democrats' failure to achieve the nationalization of those enterprises and the introduction of a socialist planned economy, either under occupational rule (when General Lucius Clay vetoed a "premature" decision on nationalization) or after the creation of the Federal Republic, when they had no majority. As a result of both developments, the West German trade unions began to regard their own generalized representation on the boards of all major West German corporations as a substitute for socialist planning by the government.

A second root of the international debate on workers' participation was the introduction in Tito's Yugoslavia in 1950, two years after the break with Stalin, of a system described as "workers' self-management." Under this system, the "management committees" elected by the workers' councils of nationalized enterprises could elect the director, subject to the agreement of local and national authorities, and share with him in the running of the enterprise. The workers also reaped a share of the profits.

A more general reason for the spreading interest in the idea of workers' participation in management, also underlying the Titoist experiment, was the spreading disappointment with the fruits of nationalization for the workers of both East and West. By the time the demand of the German trade unions was actively taken up by the German Social Democrats as part of their immediate program, it was no longer regarded as a substitute for nationalization but was considered preferable to it. The Social Democratic leaders probably had no illusions that enterprises with 50 percent or slightly fewer trade unionists on their board would be necessarily easier to control by government directives. But they welcomed the idea of strengthening the direct interest of the workers, and specifically the trade unions, in the prosperity of the economy. This argument gradually made the idea also more acceptable to other West German parties and finally led to its application, in modified form, beyond the coal and steel industries to all enterprises employing more than 2,000 people. The German law falls short of the union demand for a 50 percent share by reserving one of the seats on the workers' side of the board to salaried executives. It also seeks to combine the right of the workers to direct election of their representatives with the eligibility of "outsiders" (trade-union officials), which had been opposed by the nonsocialist parties.

Since then, the German example has led to widespread discussions about the desirability of imitating it in other West European countries, prompted more by the example of "social peace" in West Germany than by militant trade-union pressure. The British trade unions in particular are still largely opposed to what many of them, like their American colleagues, regard as involvement on the employers' side of the negotiating table, while the most militant French confederation, the independent but pro-Socialist CFDT, is committed to more far-reaching demands for *autogestion* or workers' self-management.

The rise of more radical demands among the French Left is, in fact, part of a general upsurge, beginning with the students' revolt of the middle 1960s, of demands for democratization transcending both the institutions of political democracy and the field of industrial democracy. This participatory upsurge, expressed in demands for the democratization of universities and schools, news media, and churches as well as in the mushrooming of local "citizens' initiatives," is based on the general argument that parliamentary democracy combined with bureaucratic administration has become too remote to be relevant to the issues that really concern people. It should therefore be at least supplemented by the democratic self-government of all concerned in those various places — if not replaced, as the more radical groups have argued, by an idealized type of council (Soviet) democracy.

The social democrats have generally tried to channel this upsurge — in Germany by adopting the formula that democracy should be "extended to wider fields of social activity" — without yielding the prerogatives of the elected parliament and of the government based on it to autonomous decisions of those concerned. In the process, they have in several countries — notably in parts of West Germany, in Denmark, and in the Netherlands — accepted forms of democratization of the educational system that are clearly in conflict with its function for society as a whole, and that have combined with the didactic egalitarianism discussed above to lower the standards of many of those institutions. More recently, the impact of experience has led to the partial correction of such measures. At the same time, the shock of the participatory upsurge may have led to a healthy increase in the sensitivity of politicians in general and social democratic politicians in particular to the need for timely consultation with those locally affected by central administrative decisions.

The Struggle Against Inflation and the Role of Concerted Action

Experience has shown and economic theory explained that the combination of full or nearly full employment with free price formation in the market and free trade unions is inseparable from at least a moderate inflation. The growing share of the populations of advanced countries engaged in such postindustrial activities as government, education, and health care, in which the share of wage costs in total costs is far above average and the growth of productivity far below it, has been diagnosed as another permanent inflationary factor. Democratic socialists have generally agreed with the majority of expert opinion that such a moderate inflation — in Western Europe for two decades an average of 2 to 3 percent per year — is not too high a price to pay for the benefits of full employment, steady growth, and improving social services.

However, the problem became far more serious when inflation began to accelerate in the middle 1960s under the impact of the increasingly negative American balance of payments, caused in part by the Vietnam War and in part by inflationary forms of capital export, infecting the world economy because of the dollar's privileged position in the Bretton Woods system. Accelerating inflation not only interferes seriously with the calculations of investors and leads to harmful waste of capital; it also embitters the distributive struggle, particularly between the part of the working population that is sufficiently well organized to force regular adjustments of its income to the rising price level and the receivers of fixed incomes and the small savers. Because this period of accelerating inflation preceded and continued into a worldwide recession, the distributive struggle was further sharpened.

In these circumstances, it was natural that a general search for methods to control that struggle, and specifically to achieve a moderation of wage demands, should begin in the advanced Western countries. Methods proposed, and partly tried, have ranged from imposed wage and price controls to suggestions for institutionalizing the major interest groups in a kind of corporative chamber so as to bring them under government discipline and also to the now familiar methods of concerted action—voluntary regular consultation by the government of the major interest groups on the state of the economy and on a desirable economic policy. The social democrats, linked as they are to the trade-union movement, generally have advocated sticking to the voluntary method—apparently the least drastic remedy.

In practice, the creation of quasi-corporative institutions has not been tried in any democratic country. The method of imposed price and wage limits has been tried with little effect in the United States, and has failed dramatically under the British Conservative Government, whose resistance to massive wage increases was broken by equally massive strike action.

By contrast, the method of voluntary consultation or concerted action, when practiced by social democratic governments close to the unions, has proved remarkably successful. It has limited inflation in Sweden to a level there regarded as tolerable and reduced it to a much lower level—by now 4 percent—in the Federal Republic. Most dramatic has been the case of Britain, where a Labour Government, coming to power when the situation was completely out of hand following the unions' victory over its Conservative predecessor, at first allowed the inflation rate to increase even further, until the unions themselves had to face the fact that recovery from threatening national catastrophe depended on them alone. At this point, the government proceeded from consultation to actual extraparliamentary negotiation, obtaining the vital consent of the unions to wage restraint in return for the pledge of specific changes in taxation. It seems likely that this pathbreaking example, known as the social contract, may be followed in future crises and in other countries, turning the big organized interest groups not into corporative institutions but into a recognized part of the constitutional reality, even while they retain their independence.

Environmental Protection, Limits of Growth, and the Need for Structural Planning

The critical years since the late sixties have also brought a new awareness both of the dangers of the despoliation of the environment and of the limits of growth throughout the advanced industrial world. The common characteristics of both problems are that they point to the destructive aspects of the recent unparalleled unleashing of our productive forces and that they cannot be solved by the automatism of the market alone.

The damage caused to our natural environment by modern techniques of production has assumed proportions that make preventive and remedial action imperative. Preventive action involves the transfer to the polluter of communal costs caused by pollution and the imposition of conditions or outright bans on methods of production shown to be inevitably or even potentially harmful. In other words, it requires that public policy no longer confine itself to regulating the total rate of investment by monetary and fiscal measures but influence the direction of investment by means of taxes or conditional subsidies, imposed safety measures, or outright bans.

The limits of growth, which in general are not absolute limits but foreseeable dangers of the exhaustion of specific raw materials or sources of energy, require similar action, because the market is apt to react with price increases only when much of the damage has already been done. Again, public policy—and more likely than not international public policy—will have to take responsibility for timely action to stop or slow down the growth of production lines and techniques that are wasteful of potentially scarce and at the moment irreplaceable materials and to encourage lines and techniques that are material-saving or energy-saving. And again, such action, even if it makes the least possible use of bureaucratic regulation and the greatest possible use of monetary incentives and disincentives on the market, amounts to a critical step in the transition from purely global planning of the volume of investment to structural planning of its direction.

Such conclusions will hardly find a congenial reception among political parties closely tied to specific interests that may be negatively affected, or among parties wedded to a doctrinaire belief in a free-market economy. Conversely, these conclusions are likely to be accepted as natural by proponents of democratic socialist thought. In fact, internal discussion in the German Social Democratic Party in recent years has largely revolved around the issue of investment control, with the party's Young Socialist left wing (the *Jusos*) stressing the need for new institutions to enforce control by making major investments dependent on specific permission. At the same time, moderate leaders are warning against the danger of wasteful bureaucratic methods approaching those of Soviet planning, and they are stressing the need for primary reliance on monetary incentives and disincentives that would work through the market rather than trying to replace it. With this cautionary provision, the principle of investment control or structural planning has indeed been incorporated into the 15-year program adopted by the Mannheim party congress in 1975.

Although they acknowledge that control of the direction of investment in light of the need for long-term conservation of resources is likely to imply a slowdown of economic growth, the Social Democrats have resolutely turned down the concept of zero growth advocated by some leftists. Zero growth is not considered inevitable, and it is unacceptable not only because of its likely consequences for the internal distributive struggle but also because of the vital interest of the poor and underdeveloped countries in further growth.

Relations with the Less Developed Countries

One of the great new problems for the industrially advanced democracies is the dangerous deterioration of their relations with most of the less developed countries (LDCs). This tendency, dramatized by the oil crisis and by a number of debates and votes in the United Nations, is welcomed by the Communist powers. Yet it is due in the main not to their diplomacy and propaganda, but to the serious worsening in the economic situation of a majority of LDCs over a prolonged period.

On the one hand, the total amount of development aid offered from all sources—private and public, Western and Eastern—has always been insufficient; and none of the major powers has come near to meeting the standard of allocating 1 percent of its national income for that purpose. On the other hand, the price relation between the raw materials exported by many of those countries and the industrial machinery imported by all of them has been extremely unstable. Moreover, during most of the postwar period—except for the Korean and Vietnam war booms and the immediate aftermath of the oil boycott—this price relation has tended to change heavily to the disadvantage of the raw-material producers. The result has been that many of the LDCs have lost more on the commodity markets than they have gained from development aid. Their indebtedness has increased to the point where many can no longer bear the burden.

Beginning with the first session of the United Nations Conference on Trade and Development in 1964, a steadily increasing number of LDCs have therefore united in more and more specific demands for what they call a "New Economic Order." They have concentrated on proposals for indexing or other forms of stabilization of raw-material prices, and for preferences for the sale of the products of their light industries in the markets of the advanced countries. Prior to the oil crisis, these demands found very little echo among the rich nations; since then, the need for negotiations on these matters has come to be generally recognized, but progress continues to be exceedingly slow.

It is, therefore, an important fact that the social democratic parties of some of the smaller rich countries, notably Sweden and the Netherlands, have shown an early sympathetic understanding for the plight of the LDCs, and that their example has begun to influence party opinion in some of the bigger Western democracies. The small nations, under social democratic leadership, have advocated, on grounds of distributive justice and not merely diplomatic expediency, a search for ways to meet the demands for raw-material price stabilization in substance. While they recognize the argument of leading Western economists that some specific proposals, such as the tying of commodity prices to an index of prices for industrial machinery, are impracticable and would be highly inflationary if put into practice, they insist that such arguments are no alibi for doing nothing, and that the burden rests on the West to find better ways of meeting the real grievances of the poor nations.

The real cause of the resistance of some of the rich countries, strongly resented by the poor, is, of course, that any effective measures along this line would amount to some substantial international redistribution from the rich to the poor—a course that is prima facie unlikely to recommend itself to the electorate of the rich countries. A second obstacle is that the most practicable measures, such as price stabilization by means of international buffer stocks for raw materials, would be contrary to the received doctrine of a free world market. All the more important, therefore, is the initiative of the social democrats of some of the smaller countries and their growing influence on opinion in some of the bigger parties, such as the German SPD. It may be said that the latter party has by now been officially converted to the need for a serious effort to meet the demands of the poor countries, even though the West German coalition government, under the influence of its liberal Minister of Economics, was until recently a major opponent of such measures.

Conclusion: The Question of Relevance

First of all, democratic socialist parties are parties committed to Western democracy. Some of them, such as the German, Austrian, and Norwegian parties, had to overcome the ambiguities of a powerful Marxist tradition to become fully conscious of that commitment, although it had long been implicit in their practice. Others, such as the Danish and Swedish parties, have never had such a tradition, while the British Labour Party experienced a substantial irruption of Marxist ideas as late as the 1930s but was able to digest it. But all of them have had an important share in the broadening or in the very creation of democratic institutions in their countries, and all of them have been most consistent defenders of those institutions when they were threatened from within (as in Germany and Austria in the 1930s) or from without (as by Hitler during and by Stalin after World War II).

Second, democratic socialists are committed to socialist values. These values may be variously defined. The German Social Democrats speak of "freedom, justice, and solidarity." But it must be understood that the socialist concept of justice implies more equality and social security, and the socialist concept of solidarity greater emphasis on communal needs, than the automatism of a market would produce by itself, just as the socialist concept of freedom implies the active participation of the citizen and not only his right to be left in peace. Also, democratic socialists believe in the universality of those values; and this implies an international solidarity that cannot be indifferent to the absence of freedom and justice anywhere, including the injustice of international distribution.

But values may be interpreted in two ways in political debate. They may be seen as a guide to an ideal society, to a utopia where they are fully realized or maximized; or they may be viewed as criteria for choice in dealing with practical problems as they arise. The first approach is that of the ideologist who, because of his youth or his specialization, is remote from practical experience. The second is that of the practical politician who despite his pragmatism has not renounced a commitment to his basic values. A living socialist party needs both types. Without the ideologist, it ceases to produce cohesion and commitment among its members and followers; without the pragmatist, it ceases to be relevant to the political issues of the day.

The foregoing analysis has given examples both of issues where democratic socialist parties have been and are extremely relevant to the ma-

jor problems of our time, and of issues where, misled by one-sided experience or lack of experience and building ideological programs on that
basis, they were not. The early Keynesianism of the Swedish Social
Democrats was extremely relevant to the problems of the world economic
crisis; the failure of the German Social Democrats to adopt a comparable
program in time made them irrelevant to the crisis that led to the rise of
Hitler. Again, the Labour Party's commitment to wartime planning and to
immediate postwar austerity was extremely relevant to the survival of British
democracy; but the ideological fixation on national austerity planning as if it
were a socialist goal made them largely irrelevant to the postwar development of Western Europe. The struggle of the social democratic parties to
achieve greater equality and social security by secondary redistribution was
extremely relevant, and so was the struggle for equal opportunity in education; but both, and particularly the latter, were damaged by irrelevant
ideological concepts of a utopian kind of equality. The concept of worker's
participation in management has proved relevant both to the individual
worker's status and conditions of work and to continuity of production and
social peace, and so has the development of concerted action into a
mechanism of actual negotiation between democratic government and the
great, organized interest groups. Together, these innovations may become
as central to the coming period of Western development as the welfare state
was for the quarter century after the war. Yet ideological experiments in
democratization of functional institutions seem to have proved irrelevant
and harmful. I believe that the struggle for extending public control of the
direction of investment so as to take the limits of growth into account will be
as vitally relevant as the ideological formula of zero growth is irrelevant.
And I am convinced of the urgent relevance of negotiating a fairer deal for
the poor, underdeveloped countries — despite the irrelevance and uto-
pianism of some of these countries' concrete ideas.

Finally, there is one vital issue for the future of the industrially advanced
democracies where the socialist outlook may have a contribution to offer:
the need for greater international cooperation, and indeed for international
institutions with powers of decision. The struggle against inflation and
recession would have utterly failed if each of the major industrial nations,
instead of seeking a common way out, had tried to save itself by "beggar-
my-neighbor" policies (as was done with disastrous effect in the world crisis
of 1929–32). The struggle will not be finally won until a new world currency system is established under the management of an international institution. The control of investment with due regard to the limits of growth cannot be effectively undertaken by any one industrial country, if its competitors continue to approach these limits heedlessly. The negotiation with
the poor countries has to be conducted by the advanced countries with a
common policy, not in order to negotiate from strength like a cartel, but
because no single country can make the necessary sacrifices unless its competitors join in. Democratic socialists are, of course, as much tied to national interests, and as liable to nationalist blinkers, as are other people; but
their basic commitment to universal values and an internationalist outlook
should enable their more farsighted leaders to cast aside the blinkers and

look beyond a narrow conception of their national interest. If, by accomplishing that, they can help to improve our international cooperation and to establish the international mechanisms of decision we need, and gradually to develop forms of democratic control for them, that might be the most relevant task of all.

3 *Waiting for Lefty:*
The Capitalist Genesis of Socialist Man

ROBERT E. LANE

> What we have here to deal with is a communist society, not as it has *developed* on
> its own foundation, but, on the contrary, as it *emerges* from capitalist society;
> which is thus in every respect, economically, morally and intellectually, still
> stamped with the birthmarks of the old society from whose womb it emerges.
>
> Karl Marx

While a self-destructive economic system might be transformed into an efficient and equitable set of working institutions by a new socialist regime, it
is unlikely that a population damaged by its experiences with capitalism (if
that were the case) would be prepared for such a transformation. What this
implies is that at least two parallel processes — economic and
psychological — are required for change in a socialist direction. But these
may not be in harmony with one another. In the earlier Marxist version the
two processes were sequential and harmonious: the economic process
leading to breakdown was immanent in the capitalist system and came first;
the psychological process leading to the regeneration of man followed upon
his release from the repressive, alienating, humanly destructive influences
of capitalism. The later incrementalist views of democratic socialism correct the Marxist economics but retain much of its psychology, indeed
elaborate upon it. But nothing in contemporary psychological research or
historical experience reveals a capacity for such rapid human change as
these psychologies imply; they represent too plastic a view of human
nature. The more nearly correct the analysis of capitalist destruction of
human capacities and values, the more certainly wrong the hope of easy
and rapid transformation.

We are here concerned with what has come to be called the
"environment-personality fit,"[1] as this may develop under capitalism,
preparing or failing to prepare people for a different environment-
personality fit under socialism. This is, of course, only a special case of the
more general problem that all changing societies experience, whether consciously or not. The analysis and prognosis, therefore, must borrow from
some aspects of the general theory: the nature of human needs, their
plasticity, and the sources and tensions of change and of a poor fit.

The extreme case of lack of plasticity, indeed of a perverse fixity, is
represented by Freud's view that, because of men's aggressive instincts,

I wish to acknowledge the clarifying help received from the Yale Institution for Social and
Policy Studies seminar on the market-oriented society and personality, although the views expressed in this paper are dissonant with those of many of its members.

society developed and perhaps had to develop ethical commands that, when internalized, were the sources of chronic and almost unrelievable unhappiness. This led him to ask, "Would not the diagnosis be justified that many systems of civilization — or epochs of it — possibly even the whole of humanity — have become 'neurotic' under the pressure of civilizing tendencies?"[2] There is a little hope in relaxing these ethical commands, to the extent compatible with man's aggressiveness, and adjusting men's attitudes toward property, but not much. There is no room for real human liberation in the Marxian sense here.

The extreme, but long-term, case for human plasticity in the face of institutional requirements is offered by a Darwinian view of the process of adjustment. Robert LeVine's evolutionary selection theory, for example, achieves this equilibrium between personality and environment by means of three mechanisms: autonomous institutional variation, selective rewards for the human qualities most compatible with these variants, and selective socialization of the young to endow them with the qualities demanded.[3] Strain is reduced by making individuals want to do what they have to do, thus harnessing their energies for system requirements.[4]

If one were to accept this view, the long-term prospects for socialism would be favorable, but the transition we have in mind might be difficult, for not only would capitalist man be fitted for capitalist, not socialist, requirements, but he would have learned to prefer them. He would not then be an agent for change, and capitalism would go on reproducing itself.

Between the theory that there is a fixed and powerful set of human needs that require institutional control and the theory that institutions require the adjustment of these needs to serve institutional demands, there is a third position that we will adopt. There are certain (fragile) human needs that prompt people to resist domination by unfriendly institutions, and that, therefore, serve as agents of change. For the socialist cause, the character of these needs is obviously crucial.

What is more or less "new" in contemporary psychology is the development of theories of at least two benign needs. One of them, of course, is Maslow's theory of the "instinctoid" need for self-fulfillment, for personality growth and self-actualization.[5] This is particularly congenial to the socialists' cause, for it posits a "need hierarchy" such that when people have satisfied their more basic economic needs, then (but only then) will they naturally move toward gratifying higher needs, the highest being an insatiable need for self-actualization or personality development and fulfillment. It is favorable because it suggests a psychogenic force for changing economic institutions in ways congenial to many of the socialists' proposals, and it favors an easy transition because the higher needs would be exerting their pressure before and during the transition; they are not dependent on the new environment.

The second "new" instinct is called a drive for competence or "effectance" and represents the inherent need for a sense of mastery of one's own environment, control over what happens to oneself.[6] It is congenial to and has been elaborated upon by various cognitive theories of "attribution" of causal force (to self or to something external to the self), and, again in contrast to

Freud's two instincts, it is generally regarded as a benign instinct, favoring personality development, congruent with democratic theory, and supportive of socialist views of man. It is also thought to lie behind human preferences for intrinsic rewards — those that come from the doing of the act itself — as contrasted to extrinsic rewards controlled in some measure by others.[7] We shall see below how the operations of these two needs are favorable to possible transitions to socialism.

Finally, the maturational theories of genetically programmed cognitive development, associated with Piaget and Bruner,[8] have been applied to societal development, where research shows that as societies develop and as education becomes more widespread, the level of cognitive complexity among the members of a society increases.[9] With cognitive complexity comes the possibility of greater moral development, a decline in the rule-boundedness of authoritarianism, and a capacity to imagine situations contrary to fact, hence to entertain alternatives to any status quo.

The research on these two instincts and on the extension of the instinct-based cognitive maturation theories to societal change is impressive. With the exception of the Maslow need hierarchy, which seems actually to be a two-level rather than a multilevel hierarchy, the underlying conceptions (if not the instinctual character, which is hard to prove) are reasonably well confirmed by research.[10] Leaning gingerly upon them, then, one might expect to see pressures to fit institutions to these personality needs and cognitive capacities, along with economic pressures to fit personality characteristics to meet institutional demands. And this seems to be what is happening in late capitalism. A simple illustration of what we shall explore later is the change in theories of industrial management, from Taylor's "scientific management," adjusting the worker to the work and relying on a single monetary incentive, to the human-relations movement based on simple theories of worker morale, to the job-enrichment theories of tailoring work to meet needs for challenge and fulfillment.

The Mismatching of Economic Demands and Personality Needs

But if one were to expect these benign forces automatically or quickly to shape social institutions to meet human needs, one would be disappointed with many, perhaps most, societies. The Dobu survived for many generations without recognized leadership or law, holding the belief that one man's welfare could only be wrung from the suffering of an opponent; the Alorese devised a child-care system in which the mother of the young child was absent in the fields and, because no one was responsible for the child, he never received nurturant care; among the Indians of British Columbia some tribes' borrowings from others left them with an uncoordinated hodgepodge of myth and custom that failed to give coherence to their own culture; the Tepoztecans lived in a world of mutual suspicion and jealousy that prevented them from reciprocal farm help; and thirty years ago the people of Plainville, U.S.A. suffered the sexual frigidity and impotence inherited from two thousand years of Christian prudishness and sanctioned denial.[11]

Yet there are better and worse fits, and to some observers it seems that eighteenth-century precapitalist society was better and that the introduction of the self-regulating market made things worse. While there may be elements of nostalgia in this view, it is nevertheless true that market is a very imperfect mechanism for fitting the variety of human needs to the demands of economic institutions. For all its claim that the market maximizes satisfaction, some contemporary estimates of sources of satisfaction state that, giving them monetary values, five-sixths of these satisfcations escape the market mechanism.[12] The satisfactions that contribute most to an overall sense of well-being rank family and leisure above standard of living; and friendship and freedom from stress contribute more than income.[13] Further, with their command over resources, the agents of the market may confuse people about the things that give them their greatest satisfactions, leading them to prefer commodities, for example, over more enduring, ego-syntonic satisfactions. In short, while we cannot easily make a comparative statement, it seems unlikely that the claim that a transaction-based system maximizes satisfaction implies that it maximizes the satisfaction of human needs, and therefore that it is a superior instrument for devising a better environment-personality fit.

Most theories of social character or basic personality hold that the two primary socializing agencies fitting character to economic institutions are occupations, which provide for people's livelihood, and the family, which serves as the agent of society in preparing children for the occupations they will enter as adults. Within this model there are several opportunities for slippage. First, much research now points to the fact that occupations by themselves rarely shape personality; rather, for an occupation to have this effect it must be embraced by a community—a culture carrier—as is the case in a mining village or in a profession.[14] After all the work of the world is done, there may still be disjunction between economic demands and personalities—which, perhaps, is just as well. Second, increasingly it seems that occupations are not the center of a person's life; leisure is more important. Thus, with less strain, one may continue in uncongenial occupations, never learning, never adapting, and more important for the theory, never teaching one's children what one has not oneself learned.[15] Third, if the working parent is obsolescent, if he or she dislikes the work, if, as is usual, the work is done away from the home and is abstract and unrelated to a child's immature concerns, there will be slippage.[16]

But if the occupation fails to shape the worker's personality the family may equally fail as "the agent of society" for two important reasons. First, it has other business to do, may follow the lead of the church, as in the Plainville example above, may suffer from a "generation gap" created by changing mores that make parental guidance appear obsolete to the child, and may suffer parental disagreements, as so often happens in a working-class family where the mother tries to teach middle-class values in opposition to the father's own internalized norms.[17]

Second, the disintegration of the family and the failure to provide substitute source of nourishment and socialization may wreak havoc on any systemic meeting of the child's needs. In the United States the number of single-parent families is high and growing: almost always headed by females, single-parent families now serve as the home unit for about a sixth of American children. Further, over half of the mothers of children under six are working, most of them full-time. Since provision of day-care centers is minimal (with places for about 19 percent of the children of working mothers), many are, like the children of Alor, left with no care at all during part of the day; they are "latchkey children."[18] These problems are more distinctively American than capitalist, but one cannot help wondering whether the individualism that denigrates familism, the emphasis on income as the measure of worth, and the consumer culture that stimulates commodity wants but not devotion to children do not serve to destroy the family, while the capitlist fear of government prevents the development of alternative institutions, which alone could repair the damage.

Within modern capitalist cultures, the impact of technological change and hence of occupational obsolescence, of migrations from, for example, peasant cultures to industrial cultures, the competing claims of institutions for loyalty and belief, as may be the case where advertising inspires a hedonistic way of life and industry requires thrift and dedicated work, the discrepancies between moral injunctions and economic practices all create casualties in the environment-personality fit — as well as niches for personality variants. Under these conditions the fragile forces abetting the human needs mentioned above cannot easily change economic institutions. It would be as plausible, therefore, to expect the deterioration of human personality under capitalism as to expect its growth and development; and there are many who claim that this deterioration is well under way.

Before turning to the evidence, however, we will examine three historical cases of the mismatching of institutional requirements and personality dispositions. After World War II a team from the Harvard Russian Research Center interviewed over 300 Russian displaced persons (51 of them "clinically") who had remained in Germany. Although these Russians had been socialized under the Soviet system, the interviewers found a number of areas where it seemed to them that the institutions of the regime and the personalities of the sample were indeed mismatched. "Virtually all aspects of the Soviet regime's pattern of operation," said these scholars, "seem calculated to interfere with the satisfaction of the Russians' need for affiliation. The regime has placed great strain on friendship relations. . . . Many of the primary face-to-face organizations most important to the individual were attacked or even destroyed by the regime. The break-up of the old village community and its replacement by the more formal, bureaucratic, and impersonal collective farm is perhaps the most outstanding example." The team found the Russians marked by needs for oral gratification and emotional expressiveness, but the regime was seen as having "orally depriving, niggardly, non-nurturant leadership . . . [which] emphasized and rewarded control, formality, and lack of feeling in relations." The former Soviet citizens were found to have profound ambivalences regarding the degree of trust to put in others and the regime, which "seemed always to talk support and yet to mete out harsh treatment." The individuals in the Russian sample were characterized by a more "passively accomodative" posture toward striving than those in a comparable American sample; hence, when the regime made great demands on them for constant hard work, long-range planning and deferred gratification, it encountered great resistance and created personal strain.

The regime sought to shame its citizens into more efficient and effective performance, but for these citizens the proper basis of shame was not efficiency but moral delinquency, where, turning the tables, they found the regime shameful. In short, the poor institutional-personality fit was not due only to the repressiveness of the regime; it was equally due to the regime's appeal to incentives and moral standards that were incongruent with those of their citizens and to the destruction of institutions which, over time, had been worn to fit the needs of the public.[19]

In 1936 and again in 1951 another Harvard team studied the "value orientations" of five communities in the American Southwest: Zuni, Navaho, Latin-American, Texan Presbyterian, and Mormon. The value orientations, which are taken to be elements both of personality and of culture, deal with concepts of man (good-bad, fixed-plastic), the relationship of man to nature (subjugated to nature, mastery over nature), time orientation (past, present, future), activity orientation (being-doing), and relational, in the sense of appropriate authority relations (lineal, collateral, and individualistic). The dominant culture of the Texans and Mormons embraced concepts of mixed good-bad but educable human nature, mastery over nature, future orientation, and individualism. These were described as fitting the economic requirements of the farming, herding, and various other employment opportunities of the region — what we have called institutional demands. The Spanish Americans, on the other hand, were discovered to have shifted in the period from 1936 to 1951 toward an individualistic orientation, but to retain their present time orientation, a sense of subjugation by nature, and a being, as contrasted to a striving-doing, orientation toward work. They lived a marginal existence, saw no reason to do more work than the present situation required, did not save but rather spent their money on immediately gratifying purchases (including alcohol), and lived in a decaying community compensated, if at all, only by recreational and religious activities. They had, of course, been exposed to (and subjugated by) the Anglo-American culture since the incorporation of the territory in 1846, but the culture-personality change over most of that period was very slow. Within the fifteen years covered by the study, "the acculturation process among these people [was] progressing at a speed hitherto unknown," but only very slight shifts from the being orientation to the doing orientation were noticeable, there had been a change from present toward future time orientation, but it was not yet dominant, and while shifting from a lineal, dependency orientation toward authority, "the shift [had] not been easy for a majority." On the whole, "the changes to be noted [were] . . . the superficial ones made necessary by the demands of adaptation, and they [had] as yet scarcely touched the deeper convictions of the people." The prospect is for continued slow acculturation, if the economy makes room for them, or "a fairly thoroughgoing disorganization both for the group as a whole and for personalities within the group."[20]

A third case of the mismatching of personality and institutions is suggested by Fromm's analysis of the weak hold of democratic and socialist ideas in the German working class during the Weimar period:

The vast majority of German workers before Hitler's coming into power voted for the Socialist or Communist Parties and believed in the ideas of those parties; that is the *range* of these ideas among the working class was extremely wide. The *weight* of these ideas, however, was in no proportion to their range. The onslaught of Naziism did not meet with political opponents, the majority of whom were ready to fight for their ideas. Many of the adherents of the leftist parties, although they believed in their party programs as long as their parties had authority, were ready to resign when the hour of crisis arrived. . . . A great number of them were of a personality type that has many of the traits of what we have described as the authoritarian character. They had a deep-seated respect and longing for established authority. The emphasis of socialism on individual independence versus authority, on solidarity versus individualistic seclusion, was not what these workers really wanted on the basis of their personality structure.[21]

If the Russians, after perhaps 25 years of intensive conditioning, found the morality, the incentive system, the human relations of the Soviet regime so unpersuasive; if the Spanish Americans after over 100 years of exposure to the American economic culture still found it alien; and if German workers espousing communist or socialist programs were so easily dislodged from their beliefs by an alternative but authoritative voice, how very easy might it be for socialists come to power to assume an idealism, a collectivist orientation, a posture toward authority in the work place that was not there, perhaps reading it off an election record that did not mean that at all? Would a capitalist population, for all its growth and competence motives and cognitive development, be prepared for a new socialist economy?

Capitalist Man, Socialist Man

One way to enter this problem is to compare the idealized versions of man in the two societies, on the grounds that these are but heightened versions of what the systems require or will require. Although Marx himself was partially (but not totally) reticent about the nature of socialist man once the constraints and abuses of the capitalist economy had been removed, there is no dearth of interpreters on this ideal in the current literature. Thus Trotsky, in a lyrical moment, believed that socialist man "will become immeasurably stronger, wiser, and subtler, his movements more rhythmic, his voice more musical. . . . The average human type will rise to the heights of an Aristotle, a Goethe, a Marx."[22] Marek Fritzhand, a Polish writer, interprets Marxian socialist man to be one who loves others "as a natural phenomenon of human life. . . . He feels the welfare of others as his very own."[23] Bhikhu Parekh, a British interpreter, believes that socialist man will, in accepting the "human brotherhood," also accept his own powers and talents "as a social trust" with the implied "social responsibility for the well-being of [others]," and will work cooperatively, not competitively, for the welfare of all.[24] Erich Fromm, a neopsychoanalytically oriented writer, develops and endorses Marx's view of man's potentials which would come to flower in a socialist system. Man, in this scheme, is above all self-realizing, in the sense that he has within him creative powers, wide-ranging talents and curiosities, desires and capacities for autonomous self-regulation and self-expression, and naturally seeks mutual and cooperative relations with his fellow men.[25] These and many similar interpretations of man under socialism may lack veridical, even sober, properties, but they all reveal one basic point: man is naturally (in his "essence," says Marx) a good and wonderful creature, stunted by the institutions of the market. Socialist institutions will set him free.

The same cannot be said of the idealized version, such as it is, of man in capitalist society. Of course, in talking about a future society, the socialist is unrestrained by concrete observations or immediate, practical requirements (and when Marx talks about these, he reverts to an incentive system not unlike the capitalist one), but even in a like situation, before the "triumph" of capitalism, its defenders had more to say about restraining the passions, channeling self-interest, balancing antisocial tendencies, than about liberating a benign essence.[26] Except, perhaps, for Montesquieu's favorable opinion of "the spirit of commerce," and some Scottish Enlightenment views on promoting the market men's "personal independence," its apologists viewed the self-regulating market as a way of harnessing man's selfishness, rather than as a way of expressing his better qualities. Adam Smith, for example, had this to say about the "disadvantages" of the commercial spirit: "The minds of men are contracted, and rendered incapable of elevation. Education is despised, or at least neglected, and the heroic spirit is almost utterly extinguished."[27]

It is true that Herbert Spencer defended his "first principle," embracing all the commercial freedoms along with others, on the grounds that only through the exercise of this principle could men develop all their faculties, and that William Graham Sumner and others believed that capitalism nurtured the virtues of self-reliance, but the weight is on the other side. In comparison to "the democratic character,"[28] for example, "the capitalist character" has no moral standing, and the "marketing personality" and the "organization man" are despised. Capitalist man is a necessity; socialist man is a fulfillment. Capitalist man grows in spite of the economy that nurtures him; socialist man grows because of the economic institutions that foster his growth. And this gives us a clue to the major problem of the environment-personality fit under socialism: the socialists require a great deal more from the human personality than do the capitalists.

But these are figments; they tell us little about real persons or even about the requirements and possibilities of the two economic systems.

The Functional Requirements of Two Economies

What motives, values, self-concepts, causal attributions, postures toward authority, interpersonal relations, and concepts of equity are required to work the two economic systems? If they were, in fact, no different the problem of transition mentioned earlier would be a simple matter but the socialist disappointment would be very great, for the very purpose of socialism, in both its contemporary "humanist socialism" and its Marxian versions, is not so much justice and equality as the change in character that socialism is thought to make possible. For Marx, says Fromm, "the aim of socialism was the development of the individual personality."[29] And, in many respects they are different, even in the moderate versions currently advanced.

The central differences may be briefly set forth as follows.

Incentive. The incentive system of a market economy makes no great demands upon men's altruism, concern for others, empathy, or recognition of the brotherhood of man. Rather it employs a durable, reliable, primitive (in the sense of easily taught and understood) motivation based on self-interest. Although there are doubts about the way the system actually works, it is seen to offer its rewards contingent upon effort, skill, and contribution, in good Skinnerian fashion. This makes reinforcement of the desired acts prompt and automatic, thus inducing the learning that makes the system work.

The incentive systems in a socialist economy must rely on similar self-interests, too, but there are more demands upon individuals for other motives, and rhetorically, a chorus of voices raised against what is called "selfishness." Owen called it "immoral," Fourier a "perversion," Marx thought it worthy only of an animal, William Morris equated it with "hell," Mao calls it "poison," Castro "the beast instinct."[30] Marx hoped that in true communism men would be guided by the principle "from each according to his ability, to each according to his needs." But setting aside the rhetoric, the socialist principle of an enlarged domain of free goods, the "socialistic" principle of a guaranteed income, the extension of the progressive income tax to equalize incomes (changing the effort/reward contingency relationships), within the bureaucracies common to both systems the extension of civil service security to those previously vulnerable to unemployment, and the enlarged participatory demands made by "worker self-management"—all these institutional changes also alter the incentive system to dilute the clear contingency reinforcement system of the market. Socialism is more demanding in two senses: (1) it offers the possibilities of rewards without commensurate effort (ironically, the very criticism socialists once leveled at the leisure class of capitalism) and of effort without commensurate rewards, and (2) it requires that collective advantage serve as a motivating consideration for the individual in the same way in which self-interest narrowly defined motivates him in the market society.

Innovation. The market creates incentives for invention and, more important perhaps, for implementing invention and discovery; it provides access to capital for innovators and multiple decision centers for experimentation, with varied risk preferences thus distributed throughout the economy. It creates penalties for failure to innovate. It further encourages innovation by exempting the innovating firms from the social costs of human obsolescence or redundancy, cultural disamenities, community dislocation, and the destruction of valued traditions, thrusting these costs onto individuals and governments. Thus it institutionalizes protections against human tendencies to prefer the familiar, to protect the established status hierarchies and interpersonal relations; it forces men to review and revise their routines. By rewarding innovators it creates them.

Socialism, by reducing the number of autonomous decision centers, by changing the magnitude of rewards for adopting innovative processes or products and hence the risk/gain-loss calculations, by centralizing investment decisions, by its very protection of amenity and human costs, and by vesting authority in security-conscious worker self-management teams, alters the calculations that favor innovation. There is no compelling reason to believe that socialist firms or societies must be risk-averse or conservative; the counterexamples of innovation by the military (currently, if not historically, a socialized sector of the economy) and by the National Aeronautics and Space Agency (it was a mixed enterprise that put a man on the moon), the high growth rates of partially socialized economies on the European continent and Israel, and the higher productivity increases (compared to the United States) of countries moving in a socialist direction all foreclose any argument regarding the necessary economic conservatism of socialist tendencies. But the change in incentives and institutions make demands upon the persons in charge of socialist destinies. *They* must be innovative when their institutions do not require it of them.

Authority. To some extent the market economy separates governmental and economic power — more, at least, than does a socialist or partially socialized society. Further, within the private sector, power is decentralized, either by competition or by countervailing power. Authority over what shall be produced is vested in some uncertain balance between producers (producer sovereignty) and consumers (consumer sovereignty). Authority over whom to employ and what wages to offer is divided among employers constrained by efficiency (nonparticularistic) considerations, government regulations, and union power. Thus, to some degree at least, power is dispersed, constraints are institutionalized. And to that extent the constraint on power does not depend upon the conscience or values of the powerful. Nor does it depend upon the volunteered, socially motivated attendance or vigilance or participation of the subjects of industrial power: if workers have little voice, they have the option of "exit" — they can find another employer. Thus control of power in a capitalist economy, however, adequate or inadequate, makes fewer demands on the personal qualities of either the powerful or the less powerful; it is institutionalized.

A socialist system, even if it decentralizes, even if it creates participant citizen and worker institutions, must, in order to implement its policies of planning and intelligent social guidance, have more power at the center. In the end, the boards of trustees, the minister of planning, the agency that controls investments, and the members of the councils on culture and the arts will be appointed officials, for if these boards and officials are not responsible to the central government, they cannot coordinate and cannot be coordinated, and planning loses its point. Furthermore, the demand upon these planners goes beyond the resistance of temptation to corruption and abuse of power; because the criteria are vaguer and broader than profitability, something close to "wisdom" will also be demanded of them.

The exception of this concentration of power lies in the arrangements for worker self-management within firms, private or public, but this requires volunteered vigilance, willingness to confront authority, and balanced judgment at or near the bottom of the status hierarchy. In both cases, in the case of the institutionally less constrained central officials who must have internalized controls and interpret "the public interest" and in the case of the worker self-managers who must have strengths of character to deal with authority without tension, the demands upon the individual personality are substantial.

These three considerations — work incentives, innovation, and control of authority — represent the basic areas of risk for the socialist society. Without solving these problems the socialist or socializing system cannot maintain its standard of living and freedom. But socialists want more than that; they want a system that is more equal, a system where men treat each other as brothers, as ends and not means, in cooperative rather than competitive fashion, and a system where all human beings seek fruitfully to fulfill themselves. These represent the opportunities of socialism. In this chapter, I shall treat predominantly the risks — the areas where, should the socialists fail to solve their problems, all else would also fail. It is a biased treatment in the sense that it fails to unfold the promise of socialism, but it is a first step.

Intelligent central planning designed to foster human development, combined with industrial democracy extending a person's power over the circumstances of his own life, is both the hope and the risk of socialism. Socialism, potentially at least, is therefore a high-gain, high-risk system. And the gains and the risks depend to a great extent on the character of the people who seek to work the system. Let us examine this high-gain high-risk concept.

A socialist or socializing system may be less efficient than a capitalist system, or it may be more efficient. Those who would argue for its inherent tendencies toward inefficiency might follow Okun's argument that there is a tradeoff between equality and efficiency implying that socialist egalitarianism is bought at the expense of efficiency in the ways he suggests.[31] They would employ the characterizations of economists regarding the market/nonmarket distinction: in market economies "efficiency considerations tend to predominate over welfare and noneconomic considerations," while nonmarket economies are "predisposed toward consumption and welfare and/or satisfaction of noneconomic goals (e.g., conquest or defense; support of political power or social status; advancement of religious, moral, or ideological principles; etc.) including investment required for them." Market economies compared to nonmarket economies, say these analysts, have higher rates of technological and managerial innovation, more competition, and expand with productivity increases. (The market/nonmarket distinction is used to explain Britain's economic decline.)[32] In the United States, but not in Britain, the proponents of this view would contrast the publicly owned post office with the "privately" owned telephone company. They would point to the "low productivity" of municipal and state administration, supporting this with studies of the great variability in their per-unit costs and qualities of service among these noncompetitive units. But above all they would argue deductively from the logic of the two situations.

Their opponents, defending socialist efficiency, would point to the empirical nonrelationship between security of employment and productivity (as in Japan), the nonrelationship (or positive relationship) between welfare-state effort and productivity: among twenty-two OECD countries, Austria, Germany, and Belgium were at the top of the welfare-state GNP ranking and Australia, the United States, and Japan were at the bottom (omitting Israel), with the East European Communist countries in the middle.[33] In answer to the use of the market/nonmarket distinction to explain Great Britain's decline, they would point to the higher productivity gains in Britain than in the United States in the 1950–73 period.[34] In answer to Okun, they would point to the higher productivity gains in Europe of countries more egalitarian than the United States. The experience of the guaranteed-income experiment in New Jersey in the late sixties would help their case,[35] as would experience with worker self-management councils in Germany and the Scandinavian countries. Capitalism, they would say, relies on a scarcity psychology that the capitalist system itself has made obsolete. But, like the defenders of market efficiency, they, too, would argue deductively from the necessary wastes of the market and the benefits of central planning. It is an indeterminate argument.

Nor is the issue of the abuse of power clearly resolved in favor of either side. Within those countries which have experienced democratic regimes for a generation or more, the empirical evidence of any association between equality or security of income, welfare-state effort (proportion of GNP going to various social security measures), or workers' councils, on the one hand, and abuse of power, on the other, is totally missing; indeed, considering the control of private power in employment by workers' councils, the evidence of protections against abuse of power seems to favor the socializing regimes, or, if one prefers, those with the most developed welfare states and the largest public sectors. But the world's experience is geographically broader and historically deeper than that. The deductive arguments of the Milton Friedmans and the Friedrich von Hayeks, the experience with government bureaucracy and with trade-union oligarchies, all command respect for the plea for alternatives, for multiple units with autonomous power, offering choice as to employer, producer, product, and spokesman.

In the absence of clearly superior argument or evidence favoring either the efficiency or the control of power in one system compared to the other, and in the presence of historical experience with capitalism, we have settled for a conceptualization reflecting these considerations: the socialists offer more risks and opportunities; the capitalists offer fewer of both, that is, more certainties.

The two systems may be graphed in summary form, as in Figure 3.1, recognizing that separate graphs of the efficiency dimension (work incentives and innovation), the control-of-power dimension (bureaucratic tyranny and industrial democracy), and the various moral and self-development

Figure 3.1　Risks and Opportunities for Socialism and Capitalism

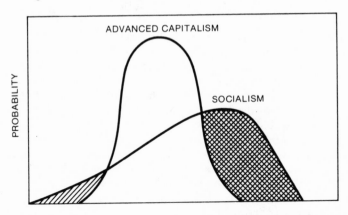

Bad outcomes: poverty, stasis, abuse of power, impersonal relations, gross inequality, impoverished personal development

Good outcomes: affluence, technological progress, greater democracy, more equality, brotherhood and community self-fulfillment

dimensions would clarify the risks and the opportunities in more detail.[36]

In this schematized form, it is clear that even though the probabilities for a better society are greater under socialism or socializing tendencies, many would prefer the safety of the lesser-risk society, especially since, for some, *any* increased risk of poverty, and for others *any* risk of decreased freedom, make the socialist alternative unattractive, all the more so if they do not know or care about the possibilities for human development that a socialist society may open up. The capitalist solution is a maximin option, for it cuts one's possibilities of loss and so protects against regret, but does not offer much more.

The portrait of possibilities and risks has a special bearing on the psychological readiness of a society for socialism, for, as has been argued, socialism not only promises to create more psychological mature and developed personalities but also requires these mature personal qualities to work the system. If it were the case, as will be argued, that many of these qualities are in fact developed by advanced capitalist systems, then the probability of loss, the shaded portion of the graph, would shrink in size, and the probability of gain, cross-hatched in the graph, would swell. But, if capitalist institutions progressively destroy the qualities we have said are necessary for socialist institutions, the socialist curve shifts to the left, increasing the probability of loss. The implications for the timing of socialist change in this course of human development are clear: premature efforts to implement socialist practices are excessively risky.

The reader will not fail to have noted the paradox here: the reliance of collectivist socialism upon *individualistic* restraints and the reliance of individualistic capitalism on *social* restraints.

The Capitalist Genesis of Socialist Man?

Given the requirements of a socialist system for appropriate work motivation, for internalized preferences for innovation and control of authority, has capitalist modernity prepared its members for these requirements? Would there be a decent environment-personality fit?

Work incentives. Work under socialism would be voluntaristic in two senses: it would take place under circumstances of security such that it would not be an economic necessity (he who did not work *would* eat); and it would be positively attractive in itself, offering intrinsic satisfactions, challenges, and opportunities to grow, thus enlisting voluntary effort. Further, to a larger extent than under capitalism, individual performance and reward would be separated, partly through rewarding collective or group effort and partly through deemphasizing monetary reward itself. Rewards would be more egalitarian because of floors and ceilings on income. The system would elicit cooperative behavior more than competitive behavior, but also (and the requirements may be incompatible) each person would have more control over his own work, more autonomy, and more responsibility. Workers would participate in more of the decisions affecting their lives, and the work place itself would constitute a kind of community. Finally, productivity would have to be high; no (or few) socialist proposals envisage an economically poorer society.

By and large capitalist society has prepared men well for work in the institutions of democratic socialism as described, but there are certain caveats and certain inconsistencies in the demands themselves that signal problems. Assuming that socialist work will thrust responsibility and initiative back down the (inevitable) hierarchy to the individual worker, or to work groups that can show initiative only if the individuals are so disposed, the system requires high levels of individual initiative at the work place. The characterological history of the quality of independence or initiative is interesting. Hunting and fishing societies have the quality more than agricultural ones, which tend to be more passive and accepting of routine. Commercial societies, then, had to revive this quality, but early industrialism probably eroded it again among the manual work force. Advanced industrial society revived it again, with its demands for better-educated workers to fill positions requiring more discretion, and the use of automation to take over many routine jobs.[37] All the relevant measures of "field independence," "internal locus of control," and independence from custom and authority reveal advanced technological societies as possessing more of these qualities than the less advanced societies.[38] And so far as we can tell, these tendencies are still accelerating under advanced capitalism, for qualities of initiative seem to be increasingly demanded by management facing conditions of great technological and organizational complexity. If there were any socialist disposition to believe that brotherhood, or collateral authority relationships (as Kluckhohn and Strodtbeck term it) would improve productivity more than individual initiative, a glance at the Zuni and Navaho economies, where collateral relationships prevail, would destroy that disposition; they are well prepared for archaic herding, but not for modern socialism.

Because socialists propose to establish conditions under which people are secure in their jobs, or securely attached to a minimal income whether or not they have jobs, they must rely upon a set of work motives that embrace such concepts as the doing/striving orientation, a work ethic wherein their occupations are viewed as a moral "calling," and competition against an internalized standard of excellence—the need for achievement. Under capitalism these motives have grown and prospered, and in spite of current theories that a hedonistic, advertising-based erosion of the work ethic has taken place, the secular evidence (attitudes, absenteeism, second jobs, labor-force participation, job satisfaction) reveals the work ethic and need for achievement to be strong and thriving.[39] The content of hymns and stories stressed this achievement motive in 1960 to a degree not apparent for a hundred years.[40] The work ethic has not been eroded by social security and other welfare-state legislation (such as guaranteed annual income); it is a reliable product of capitalism, even welfare-state capitalism, available to the socialists when and if they come to power.

The idea of capitalism as fueled by competition in the sense of rivalry between known competitors has been exaggerated; it is not, even theoretically, a part of "competition" in a perfect market, where no single individual perceives his own acts as affecting those of any particular other. Market economists think of competition as choice: the competition between alternative opportunities. Furthermore, modern industry requires as much cooperation as competition; it requires men to work in groups where each depends upon the action of another. And within a firm, deliberate attempts to develop cooperative relationships among team workers are as successful as deliberate efforts to develop a "spirit of competition" between rival competitors.[41] Scarcity is more likely to breed competition than is affluence, at least in primitive societies, and there is no evidence that individuals in capitalist societies are more competitive, in the sense of rivalrous, than others. Moreover, certain kinds of prosocial (altruistic) behavior are more common in the capitalist West than in less developed countries. In spite of the attention given to it, the competition/cooperation alternative is not a problem.

But the collectivization of rewards may present problems—even if "successful." It is true that men under capitalism have developed a clear contingency expectation: reward will be individual, extrinsic, and dependent upon effort, contribution, and skill; it is the feedback that tells them their worth. While piece-rate systems rarely work, more carefully devised incentive systems sometimes do, and the entire reward structure is adjusted to these individualized perceptions and expectations.[42] By separating income from these contingencies (as above), by emphasizing collective reward for collective effort, and by equalizing rewards within a narrow range, the socialists propose to alter these expectations. This may be possible, especially if jobs and organizational climates are adjusted to increase the intrinsic rewards of work, as Herzberg and the authors of *Work in America* have proposed and as some firms have tried to do, but several caveats are in order.[43] First, all work is both an exchange of effort for satisfaction and, except in ascriptive systems, a means of establishing one's worth in one's own eyes. But it appears that praise from a supervisor, honor among co-workers, community esteem, and media recognition will serve as well. To make these other rewards serve the function of pay incentives, however, offers few advantages and the special disadvantage that they are more loosely tied to performance and that the contingency link is more easily broken; therefore, they may lose their power to motivate and may increase the sense of inequity: my benefit/effort ratio is smaller than someone else's.

Second, the collective rewards are certainly motivating, especially under the circumstances the socialists propose: participation in decisions, contribution to outcomes, sharing in the benefits.[44] But these apply to face-to-face groups, not larger collectivities. Now it is the case that building these strong face-to-face cellular units in an enterprise can increase total productivity, but it is also the case that they can reduce productivity: the stronger the cell the greater the deviance from the norm. It is by no means certain, therefore, that creating small collectively rewarded units in an enterprise will serve the cause of the larger socialist undertaking. And it is certainly true that attempting to rely upon appeals to the public interest or general societal goals, except under external threat, are ineffective. A sympathetic observer of the Cuban effort to enlist volunteer (i.e., unpaid) teams of agricultural workers noted that the effort ended in a military type dragooning of reluctant participants.[45] In sum, the capitalist *Gesellschaft* has not destroyed the possibility of small-scale *Gemeinschaft*, but neither capitalism nor any other system can prepare the socialists to convert an entire society into a working *community*.

As for the deemphasis on money, a theme in all socialist writing since Marx, one could argue that the process is already taking place. This inference follows from studies showing the rise of postmaterialist values in economically developing Western societies;[46] from studies of contributions to an overall sense of well-being by various life "domains" showing that family, friends, and nonworking activities contribute more to happiness than does income, and, incidentally, revealing the very loose relationship between actual pay and satisfaction with pay;[47] from the rising cohorts of better-educated workers seeking challenge and developmental opportunities more than pay and security in their occupational life; and from related studies showing that "interesting work" contributes more to job satisfaction than does pay. Beyond a certain level, both within nations and between nations, pay is only an indicator of achievement; it is not sought by the achievers for what it will buy but rather for what it tells them about themselves.[48] Other indicators may serve as well. The success motive, that is, is malleable, and the socialists might simply harness it for other purposes. In conformity with economic laws, capitalism, by making real money — purchasing power — more plentiful, decreases its value relative to other sources of satisfaction. But, like other economic laws, this one doesn't always work very well.

While this sketch—it is hardly a portrait—is favorable to the socialist cause, there is another major caveat to which socialists should attend: human nature is varied. Cultures are also varied. Some industrial psychologists think of their field as having three levels made up of individual characteristics, job characteristics, and organizational characteristics such as leadership style and reward structures. Their findings show great interaction among these levels: changes in organizational climates and job characteristics are congenial to some individuals and not to others. Some people want and work well with more responsibility and autonomy, but others do not: kibbutz workers are productive and have high morale in egalitarian work situations; Americans are productive and have equally high morale in informally hierarchical situations (in contrast to Yugoslav, Italian, and Austrian workers), but one could not expect the kibbutzim and the Americans to thrive in each other's circumstances.[49] If the socialists change organizational climates, incentives, and job characteristics without regard to the characters and needs of their work forces (and, indeed, their managers) they will fail. While our analysis of work motives and character under capitalism has been generally favorable, the variability and slow generational change of mankind requires a careful tailoring of work to human needs as they are, not only to what they might be.

Innovation. It is agreed that a capitalist system is innovative, but authorities differ on the causes: Weber because of the corrosive power of its rationality, Marx because of the logic of the profit system and the implications of the theory of surplus value, Schumpeter because of its creation and licensing of entrepreneurs, Habermas because of its power to break social traditions. As outlined above, the play of forces among multiple autonomous units competing for advantage institutionalizes change. This propensity for change, then, might be threatened by shifting power from these units to the government unless those who run the system have internalized qualities that make them receptive to change.

These qualities would include (1) the capacity for innovative thinking, implying cognitive complexity and the ability to imagine conditions contrary to fact; (2) an evaluative support of novelty and change implied, for example, in disagreement with the standard personality measurement question "If you try to change things very much, you will usually make them worse"; (3) characterological autonomy such that one is not at the mercy of either conventional authority or public opinion—that is, lack of conformism or an obedience orientation; (4) tolerance of ambiguity, of heterodoxy, and a willingness to entertain and "play along with" a discrepant idea; and (5) to make these capacities and attitudes and values effective, a belief in the effectiveness of one's own actions, the absence of powerlessness/helplessness syndrome.

Wherever they have been measured, these traits are stronger in modern Western societies than in traditional societies, and they seem to be the product of a Western type of education.[50] Within developing societies they are associated with exposure to modern industrial and commercial institutions;[51] within Western societies they tend to increase with education and, to some extent, with income. There is very little and conflicting evidence, however, that they are associated with any particular occupations, commercial or otherwise, except that they tend to increase with level of management in managerial hierarchies.[52]

The trend of the available data similarly represents a progressive improvement within the (American) capitalist system in generating a receptivity to change. Thus, there is direct evidence of the decline in authoritarianism, with its conventionalism and intolerance of ambiguity, as well as evidence of a decline in parental support for conformism and other-directedness, a measured increase in tolerance for heterodoxy, and scattered indications of relaxed parental and peer-group control over opinions, a process of sociological release or individuation.[53] The close relationship between education (especially college education) and cognitive complexity, internal locus of control, and preferred range of novelty suggests, with some reservations, that these have also increased. These qualities have thrived under capitalism, but there is nothing that links them to capitalist institutions per se. There is, therefore, no reason to believe that they would wither under socialism.

Further, they are generally associated with two circumstances that the socialists might even enhance: a nurturant (but also "critical") family socialization and a degree of security and perceived lack of threat (the very opposite of some hard-line views of the uses of insecurity). As noted above, the American capitalist variant is witnessing a disintegration of child care that can only be repaired by intelligent governmental policy.[54] And, for all its affluence, capitalism promotes a sense of insecurity and, as many commentators have noted, a sense of scarcity. In both respects there are reasons to believe the socialists would do better.

On the other hand, qualities of innovativeness are concentrated in the better educated, the better off, the higher management.[55] To the extent that the socialists lodge investment or other strategic decisions in workers' councils, they may create a conservative, change-resistant feature in their decision processes.

Finally, since socialism is sometimes associated (mistakenly, I think) with bureaucracy, it is useful to note first that in studies of welfare policies it is the bureaucrats, not the unions or the politicians, that have taken the lead in innovation,[56] and second, that studies of policy flexibility find that in some important respects bureaucrats are more flexible than those in other settings.[57]

The problem of innovativeness under socialism does not disappear in light of these findings; but the latter do suggest that the characterological base for innovation under socialism has been created by innovative capitalism.

Control of authority. The personal qualities that form internal restraints against the abuse of power share much in common with those that facilitate innovation, but they go beyond them.

1. The cognitively simple tend to be rule-bound and authoritarian; while often just as "intelligent" as the cognitively complex, they tend to see only one solution to a problem, usually the conventional or "authoritative"

one. Groups made up of the cognitively simple tend to be less democratic than groups of the cognitively complex; a group cannot rise above the level of its members.[58] Thus *cognitive complexity* is a protection against authoritarianism and the abuse of power. And the findings and inferences that led to the conclusion above that under modern capitalism cognitive complexity has increased offers the first hint of the capitalist genesis of this socialist (and democratic) requirement.

2. The control of power implies the capacity to stand outside the conventional morality and "law and order" mentalities which the powerful employ to justify their rule and, standing outside, to generate and employ an independent morality. This capacity is embraced in the concept of *moral reasoning,* which has recently been measured and tested under a variety of circumstances. Generally, levels of moral reasoning are higher in advanced capitalist countries than in less developed countries; the levels increase with level of formal education, with college education a condition of the higher levels. While there is no indication of historical increases in levels of moral reasoning among the working class, there is indication that middle-class levels of moral reasoning may have increased in the past generation; in one American sample, at least, the middle-class sons of middle-class fathers achieved a higher level of moral reasoning than their fathers.[59]

3. Because *authoritarianism* implies the preference of hierarchical situations in which human relations are characterized by dominance and submission, defines the world as composed of glorified in-groups and denigrated out-groups, rejects "tenderness" in favor of toughness and aggression, and is uncomfortable with democratic leadership, the measured decline in authoritarianism represents a contribution to the world the socialists hope to create.[60]

4. The "good Germans" who went along with Hitler were thought to be uniquely *obedient to authority* until Milgram showed that most normal, decent Americans would obediently give potentially lethal shocks to relatively unknown others when told to do so, not because of aggressiveness, but because they abdicated responsibility for their own acts.[61] Moreover, survey evidence revealed that when Lieutenant Calley shot old men, women, and children in a Vietnamese village under the impression that these were his orders, most Americans believed that he was justified in the shooting and said that they would have done the same thing.[62] The evidence is frightening and seems to call for further institutionalized checks against abuse of authority, not the internalized constraints the socialist scheme requires. But consider two modifying circumstances. First, the two personality qualities that restrained Milgram's subjects from "malignant obedience" were high levels of moral reasoning and low authoritarianism, which are dealt with above. Second, Milgram closes his book with this quotation from Laski: "The condition of freedom in any state is always a widespread and consistent skepticism of the canons upon which power insists." For a decade the unthinking acceptance of American institutions, including capitalist ones, has been declining;[63] the beginnings of "a widespread and consistent skepticism" may, if nurtured, temper malignant obedience.

5. Since democratic control of institutions begins with democratic interpersonal relations, Tocqueville's belief that, for the Americans, "Democracy has gradually penetrated into their customs, their opinions, and their forms of social intercourse; it is to be found in the details of their daily life as well as in the laws,"[54] offers the socialists modest hope for the one country of which they may despair. Whether or not this democratic social intercourse has persisted is hard to say; on the one hand there are documented reports of increased amoral manipulative interpersonal relations;[55] on the other hand the measures of interpersonal trust have remained constant for twenty years and (something Tocqueville would not have anticipated) there have been increases in friendships between blacks and white, as well as other evidence of increased tolerance.[66]

6. In the discussion of innovation, we discussed the sense that a person is the author of his own acts, a causal agent, the controller of his own fate. We also discussed the problem of conformity. The rise of "internality" and the decline of conformity will serve the control of power as it serves to implement change. Perhaps of all the features discussed here, this one is the most important.

7. Finally, the control of power requires active participation in power-controlling agencies: workers' councils, campaign committees, voluntary organizations of all kinds. Advanced capitalism, as reflected in the record of the United States, shows a mixed performance: a decline in proportion of the work force in unions combined with an increase, especially by the poor and disadvantaged, in voluntary organizations of all other kinds;[67] a decline in voter turnout combined with an increase in other forms of electoral participation;[68] a decline, too, in sense of political efficacy combined with an increase in political competence, as reflected in better knowledge of the relationship between issues and parties, and between ideologies and issues.[69]

But on the specific question of participation in voluntary organizations designed to modify management control of the factory, a study by John Witte of an experiment in limited worker self-management in an American plant is revealing.[70] Compared to the members of Yugoslav workers' councils, the Americans initiated more actions, spoke up more, challenged management more often, and exercised, within the modest domain allotted to them, more influence. One major reason is that in the American case there was a difference of only two years of formal education between the worker council members and management members, while in the Yugoslav plant there was a difference of eight years. Another significant finding was that in the American plant it was the ambitious workers who did not believe that they could realistically expect a promotion who took the lead in the council initiatives. A third important difference, reminiscent of Tocqueville's observation, was the historical culture of hierarchy and rank that the Yugoslavs inherited and had to transform, but that was absent in the American case.[71] Quite independent of the influence of market institutions on personality, this suggests that a high level of worker education, a democratic culture, and the availability of personal ambition for voluntaristic worker control of management activities combine to offer the socialists promise for a participatory system controlling the abuse of power.

Conclusions

Marx was quite right — it is a mistake to press socialist institutions upon a society that is not ready for them — but the "readiness" consists of the qualities of personality and character required to work a democratic socialist system and to protect it from degeneration into poverty, stasis, or the abuse of power.[72] Further, Marx may have been right about the immanent qualities of self-destruction in capitalism, but these are not economic; rather, they deal with the tendencies of advanced capitalism to create values, especially among certain portions of the professional middle class, that the system itself cannot fulfill. And, as others have argued, under these circumstances it will be the universities and not the factories that generate discontent, for, true to their mission, they rehearse for their members alternative value schemes.

There are some ironies here. Of all the qualities that seemed most central to the prosperity of the socialist cause, something close to individualism is the most important: the individual's belief that outcomes are contingent upon his own acts, his autonomy from collective pressure and authoritative command, his capacity for independent moral reasoning, and his belief in himself and his own powers. Only such "individualized individuals," generated by complex and nurturant institutions, can work a collectivist system. Further, it is affluence and security, not scarcity and threat, that create the possibility of generating such qualities. There may be other roads to socialism, such as those which the Tanzanians, the Chinese, the Cubans are embarked upon; but they will not be democratic socialisms unless these societies first create the conditions of autonomy, and then the autonomous persons themselves. Western affluence may not be necessary, but something like Western individualism (in the sense described) will be. For innovation and for the control of power the individual must have "a place to stand" outside of the collectivity.

And so to return to the original concept of the fit between institutions and personality, there is hope, but not certainty, that advanced capitalist society has shaped a personality that would fit, with transitional strain, the proposed socialist institutions.

Notes

1. See John R. P. French, Jr., Willard Rodgers, and Sidney Cobb, "Adjustment as Person-Environment Fit," in George V. Coelho, David A. Hamburg, and John E. Adams, eds., *Coping and Adaptation* (New York: Basic Books, 1974), pp. 316–33.

2. Sigmund Freud, *Civilization and Its Discontents* (London: Hogarth Press, 1951), p. 141.

3. Robert A. LeVine, *Culture, Behavior, and Personality* (Chicago: Aldine, 1973).

4. The phrase "to desire to act as he *has* to act," cited by LeVine, is Erich Fromm's. See his *Escape from Freedom* (New York: Rinehart, 1941), pp. 282–84.

5. Abraham H. Maslow, *Motivation and Personality*, 2d ed. (New York: Harper & Row, 1970).

6. Robert W. White, "Motivation Reconsidered: The Concept of Competence," *Psychological Review* 66 (1959):297–333.

7. Edward Deci, *Intrinsic Motivation* (New York: Plenum Press, 1975).

8. Jean Piaget and Barbara Inhelder, *The Psychology of the Child,* trans. Helen Weaver (New York: Basic Books, 1969); Jerome S. Bruner, "The Course of Cognitive Growth," *American Psychologist,* vol. 19 (1964); reprinted as Warner Module no. 400 (1973), pp. 1–15.

9. See, for example, O. J. Harvey, David E. Hunt, and Harold M. Schroder, *Conceptual Systems and Personality Organization* (New York: John Wiley, 1961); Philip I. Vernon, *Intelligence and Cultural Environment* (London: Methuen, 1969).

10. For modestly supportive evidence on the growth need, in addition to Maslow, see Jeanne N. Knutson, *The Human Basis of the Polity* (Chicago: Aldine-Atherton, 1972); E. L. Simpson, *Democracy's Stepchildren: A Study of Need and Belief* (San Francisco: Jossey-Bass, 1971); J. Aronoff, *Psychological Needs and Cultural Systems* (Princeton: Van Nostrand, 1967). For a more cogent and critical review, suggesting the two-stage limitation, see Edward E. Lawler III and J. Lloyd Suttle, "A Causal Correlational Test of the Need Hierarchy Concept," in Richard M. Steers and Lyman W. Porter, eds., *Motivation and Work Behavior* (New York: McGraw-Hill, 1975), pp. 39–46. The concept of competence and an effectance drive has led to work that elaborates and specifies the conditions that favor its expression. See Richard De Charms, *Personal Causation* (New York: Academic Press, 1968); for a review of the work stemming from a Rotter's concept of "locus of control" see Herbert M. Lefcourt, *Locus of Control* (New York: Erlbaum/Wiley, 1976). A review of the related concept of "ego development" is available in Stuart T. Hauser, "Loevinger's Model and Measure of Ego Development: A Critical Review," *Psychological Bulletin* 83 (1976):928–55. See also Edward Deci, *Intrinsic Motivation.*

11. The Dobu and the British Columbians are discussed by Ruth Benedict in her *Patterns of Culture* (Boston: Houghton Mifflin, 1934); the Alorese and Plainville are discussed in Abram Kardiner, with Ralph Linton, Cora du Bois and James West, *The Psychological Frontiers of Society* (New York: Columbia University Press, 1945); for the Tepoztecans, see Oscar Lewis, *Life in a Mexican Village* (Urbana: University of Illinois Press, 1963).

12. See Tibor Scitovsky, *The Joyless Economy* (New York: Oxford University Press, 1976).

13. Agnus Campbell, Philip E. Converse, and Willard L. Rodgers, *The Quality of American Life* (New York: Russell Sage, 1976), pp. 76, 368.

14. The general statement on occupations and personality is based on a literature reviewed by Kenneth Pittman, "Social Structure and Personality: The World of Work," Yale University. On the effects of community see David Lockwood, "Sources of Variation in Working-Class Images of Society," in Martin Bulmer, ed., *Working-Class Images of Society* (Boston: Routledge & Kegan Paul, 1975); Graeme Salaman, *Community and Occupation* (New York: Cambridge University Press, 1974).

15. See Robert Dubin, "Industrial Workers' Worlds," *Social Problems* 3 (1956):131–42. For an example of the effects of occupation on child training, however, see Daniel R. Miller and Guy E. Swanson, *The Changing American Parent* (New York: John Wiley, 1958).

16. On the general relationships between family and work, see Rosabeth Moss Kanter, *Work and Family in the United States* (New York: Russell Sage, 1977).

17. Ibid., pp. 65–66.

18. Advisory Committee on Child Development, National Research Council, *Toward a National Policy for Children and Families* (Washington, D.C.: National Academy of Sciences, 1976), pp. 1–2.

19. Alex Inkeles, Eugenia Hanfmann, and Helen Beier, "Modal Personality and Adjustment to the Soviet Socio-Political System," *Human Relations* 11 (1958):3–21.

20. Florence R. Kluckhohn and Fred L. Strodtbeck, *Variations in Value Orientations* (Evanston, Ill.: Row, Peterson, 1961), pp. 175–257; the quotations are from p. 257.

21. Fromm, *Escape from Freedom,* pp. 280–81.

22. Quoted in Michael Harrington, *Socialism* (New York: Bantam, 1973), p. 453.

23. "Marx's Ideal of Man," in Erich Fromm, ed., *Socialist Humanism* (Garden City, N.Y. : Doubleday/Anchor, 1966), pp. 180–81.

24. "Introduction" to Bhikhu Parekh, ed., *The Concept of Socialism* (New York: Holmes and Meier, 1975), pp. 1–13.

25. Erich Fromm, "Marx's Concept of Man," in Erich Fromm, ed., *Marx's Concept of Man* (New York: Ungar, 1961), pp. 1–69.

26. Albert O. Hirschman, *The Passions and the Interests: Political Arguments for Capitalism*

before Its Triumph (Princeton, N.J.: Princeton University Press, 1977).

27. Adam Smith, *Lectures on Justice, Police, Revenue, and Arms,* quoted in Hirschman, *The Passions and the Interests,* pp. 106-7. Compare Max Weber's mourning over the loss of "the Faustian universality of man" under the influence of rising capitalism in *The Protestant Ethic and the Spirit of Capitalism* (New York: Scribner's, 1958), p. 180.

28. See, for example, Harold D. Lasswell, "Democratic Character," in *The Political Writings of Harold D. Lasswell* (Glencoe, Ill.: Free Press, 1951); Alex Inkeles, "National Character and Modern Political Systems," in Francis L. K. Hsu, ed., *Psychological Anthropology* (Homewood, Ill.: Dorsey, 1961), pp. 195-98.

29. Fromm, *Marx's Concept of Man,* p. 38.

30. From a similar summary in Bhikhu Parekh's "Introduction," *The Concept of Socialism,* p. 5.

31. Arthur M. Okun, *Equality and Efficiency: The Big Tradeoff* (Washington, D.C.: Brookings Institution, 1975).

32. Theodore Geiger, "Using the Market/Nonmarket Distinction," *New International Realities* 2 (October 1976):18-24.

33. Harold L. Wilensky, *The Welfare State and Equality* (Berkeley: University of California Press, 1975), pp. 30-31.

34. U.S. Department of Labor, Bureau of Labor Statistics, *Current Developments in Productivity,* 1934-74, Report 436 (Washington, D.C.: Government Printing Office, 1975), p. 26.

35. See Harold W. Watts and Albert Rees, eds., *The New Jersey Income-Maintenance Experiment, Volume 2: Labor-Supply Responses* (New York: Academic Press, 1977).

36. I am indebted to David Mayhew of the Yale Political Science Department for this graphed version of the concept.

37. One of the more important responses of workers who have experienced the introduction of a new technology in their work is the feeling that they have more discretion and that the job is more challenging. See Eva Mueller, *Technological Advance in an Expanding Economy* (Ann Arbor, Mich.: Institute for Social Research, 1969). Robert Blauner proposes a curvilinear theory of work alienation due, inter alia, to low discretion: low in the craft stage, rising through the machine and assembly line stage, declining at the automation stage. See his *Alienation and Freedom* (Chicago: University of Chicago Press, 1964).

38. For some relevant cross-cultural summaries, see Barbara B. Lloyd, *Perception and Cognition: A Cross-Cultural Perspective* (Harmondsworth, U.K.: Penguin, 1972); Jacqueline Goodnow, "Cultural Variations in Cognitive Skills," in Jerome Hellmuth, ed., *Cognitive Studies,* vol. 1 (New York: Brunner/Mazel, 1970); Stephen Bochner, Richard W. Brislin, and Walter J. Lonner, eds., *Cross-Cultural Perspectives on Learning* (New York: Halsted/John Wiley, 1975), especially Harry Triandis, "Cultural Training, Cognitive Complexity and Interpersonal Relations."

39. The relevant series is available in U.S. Bureau of the Census, *Statistical Abstract of the United States, 1976* (Washington, D.C., 1976), pp. 363-64; U.S. Bureau of the Census, *Historical Statistics of the United States, Colonial Times to 1970,* Bicentennial Edition, Part 1 (Washington, D.C.: 1975), Series D., 1-10, 11-25; Party 2, Chapter W.

40. David C. McClelland, *Power: The Inner Experience* (New York: Irvington/John Wiley, 1975), p. 410.

41. Steers and Porter, *Motivation and Work Behavior,* chapters 8-10, 15.

42. Edward E. Lawler III, "Pay and Organizational Effectiveness" (New York: McGraw-Hill, 1971), summarized in Steers and Porter, *Motivation and Work Behavior,* pp. 534-48.

43. Frederick Herzberg, *Work and the Nature of Man* (New York: Mentor/New American Library, 1973); *Work in America,* Report of a Special Task Force to the Secretary of Health, Education, and Welfare (Cambridge, Mass.: MIT Press, n.d.).

44. These are the conditions that Daniel Katz says are important because then "the individual can regard the group as his, for he in fact has helped to make it." See "The Motivational Basis of Organizational Behavior," in Steers and Porter, *Motivation and Work Behavior,* p. 274.

45. René Dumont, cited in Harrington, *Socialism,* p. 291.

46. Ronald Inglehart, "The Silent Revolution in Europe: Intergenerational Changes in Post-Industrial Societies," *American Political Science Review* 65 (1971):991-1017.

47. Campbell, Converse, and Rodgers, *The Quality of American Life,* pp. 76, 304, 374.

48. David C. McClelland, "Money as a Motivator: Some Research Insights," in Steers and Porter, *Motivation and Work Behavior,* pp. 523–34.

49. Arnold S. Tannenbaum, Bogdan Kavčić, Menachem Rosner, Milo Vianello and Georg Wiesner, *Hierarchy in Organizations* (San Francisco: Jossey-Bass, 1974), pp. 210–16.

50. See notes 9 and 38, above. A very wide and scattered research generally supports these statements. Thus, in the review article cited in note 38, Jacqueline Goodnow finds that the main difference in ability "as we move away from a technological society . . . [is in] tasks where the child has to transform an event in his head, has to shift or shuffle things around by some kind of visualizing or imagining rather than by carrying out an overt series of tasks" (p. 245). On the conformity dimension, in a research report characteristic of this cross-cultural field, Shaul C. Sohlberg, in "Social Desirability Responses in Jewish and Arab Children in Israel," *Journal of Cross-Cultural Psychology* 7 (1976):301–14, finds the order of conformist responses, from most to least, to be: Arab, Israeli, American. But on this particular dimension, it should be observed that other studies have found the Americans more concerned about their popularity than, for example, Russian and English samples.

51. Alex Inkeles and David H. Smith, *Becoming Modern* (Cambridge, Mass.: Harvard University Press, 1974).

52. See note 14, above.

53. Nevitt Sanford, "Authoritarian Personality in Contemporary Perspective," in Jeanne N. Knutson, ed., *Handbook of Political Psychology* (San Francisco: Jossey-Bass, 1973), p. 165; Otis Dudley Duncan, Howard Schuman, and Beverly Duncan, *Social Change in a Metropolitan Community* (New York: Russell Sage, 1973), p. 39; James A. Davis, "Communism, Conformity, Cohorts, and Categories: American Tolerance in 1954 and 1972–73," *American Journal of Sociology* 81 (1975):491–513; Vern L. Bengsten, "Generation and Family Effects in Value Socialization," *American Sociological Review* 40 (1975):358–71.

54. The inference that working mothers necessarily enter the labor force at the expense of their children may be corrected by references to Lois Wladis Hoffman and F. Ivan Nye, *Working Mothers* (San Francisco: Jossey-Bass, 1974).

55. Lefcourt, *Locus of Control,* p. 114.

56. Hugh Heclo, *Modern Social Politics in Britain and Sweden* (New Haven: Yale University Press, 1974).

57. Melvin L. Kohn, "Bureaucratic Man: A Portrait and an Interpretation," *American Sociological Review* 36 (1971):461–74.

58. Harold M. Schroder, M. J. Driver, and S. Streufert, *Human Information Processing* (New York: Holt, Rinehart & Winston, 1967), pp. 3–41.

59. Lawrence Kohlberg and R. Kramer, "Continuities and Discontinuities in Childhood and Adult Moral Development," *Human Development* 12 (1969):103–5.

60. See note 53, above.

61. Stanley Milgram, *Obedience to Authority* (New York: Harper & Row, 1974).

62. Herbert C. Kelman and Lee Hamilton Lawrence, "Assignment of Responsibility in the Case of Lt. Calley: Preliminary Report of a National Survey," *Journal of Social Issues* 28 (1972):177–212.

63. Louis Harris for the U.S. Senate Subcommittee on Intergovernmental Relations, *Confidence and Concern: Citizens View American Government* (Cleveland: Regal Books/King's Court Communications, 1974), p. 7.

64. Alexis de Tocqueville, *Democracy in America,* edited by Phillips Bradley (New York: Knopf, 1945), vol. 1, p. 321.

65. Richard Christie and Florence Geis, *Studies in Machiavellianism* (New York: Academic Press, 1970), pp. 315–21.

66. *Political Indicator Time Series, 1952–1970* (Ann Arbor, Mich.: Center for Political Studies of the University of Michigan, 1972).

67. Herbert Hyman and Charles F. Wright, "Trends in Voluntary Association Memberships of American Adults," *American Sociological Review* 36 (1971):191–206.

68. Sidney Verba and Norman H. Nie, *Participation in America: Political Democracy and Social Equality* (New York: Harper & Row, 1972), pp. 250–52.

69. Philip E. Converse, "Public Opinion and Voting Behavior," in Fred I. Greenstein and Nelson W. Polsby, eds., *Handbook of Political Science* (Reading, Mass.: Addison-Wesley, 1975), vol. 4, pp. 98–111.

70. John Witte, *Democracy, Authority, and Alienation in Work,* unpublished doctoral dissertation, Yale University, 1977.

71. Tannenbaum and associates, *Hierarchy in Organizations,* p. 221.

72. There is an ironic historical reversal in this "correction" of Marx; according to Robert Tucker, the post-1845 Marx represented a direct translation into social terms of the concepts of self-alienation elaborated in the 1844 Paris manuscripts. Instead of the divided self we have the divided society, a sociologizing of Marx's earlier psychology. What is suggested here is a return trip. See Tucker's *Philosophy and Myth in Karl Marx* (Cambridge: Cambridge University Press, 1961).

4 Party, Class, and State: A Leninist and a Non-Leninist View

RAYMOND S. FRANKLIN

The fundamental weakness of democratic socialism, used in its most generic sense, is its failure to grasp the kind of tactics and strategies necessary to transform Third World societies.* In a symmetrical way, the generic weakness of Leninism is its failure to appreciate the kind of tactics and strategies that are viable and appropriate in advanced democratic capitalist systems.

This essay is an attempt to make a theoretical case for a variant of socialist reformism in democratic capitalist societies, although for reasons other than those offered by reformists themselves. It is concerned with primary or first principles — that is, the essential assumptions that must be made about the nature of the capitalist state and its class domination and conflict with labor. These matters relate to the kind of political organization that is required to transform modern capitalist societies, especially when compared to what is needed to transform Third World (underdeveloped) societies. Derivative of one's position concerning first principles are those subtleties and modifications that relate to the treatment of specific issues, the development of programs, the mode of projecting alternative visions to the present system, and the question of forming coalitions. An approach to some of these derivative concerns will be briefly explored in our conclusion.

To make the case for some variant of socialist reformism, I commence with a discussion of the views of Lenin and Eugene V. Debs and what they had to say about party structure, its relationship to the working class, and the development of a revolutionary movement. Quotes are selected to represent *stylized* interpretations of these political leaders; they are not intended to imply a judgment about how they applied their own ideas or a judgment about their contribution in other spheres.

The Problem

What is the nature of the capitalist state in relation to the exigencies of reform or revolution? What kind of party is needed to build a socialist movement? How should radical intellectuals relate to the labor movement? And what is the relation between ideological work and direct action around specific issues that of themselves lack socialist content?

Sometimes these questions are put in the form of minority versus ma-

*I want to express my appreciation to Carol Brafman, Martha Ecker, Solomon Resnik, Carl Riskin, Mark Rosenblum, and Frank Warren for their helpful comments on an early draft of this essay.

joritarian socialism. In my view, the substantive and practical nature of these questions has to do with the general problem of the relationship between a minority that is intellectually committed to bringing about a radical transformation of capitalism and a larger public that is moved more by bread-and-butter issues or problems of immediate concern perceived in relative isolation from each other. While the intellectual minority's perception of the capitalist process is holistic, the public's is fragmented and uneven; while the minority has a long-run horizon, the majority has a short-run time perspective. This dichotomy poses a problem faced by every radical or socialist movement that has not learned how to sustain itself and grow in the complex and vacillating currents of American society.

Both Lenin and Debs raised the above questions and problems, but the answers they gave were radically different because of the differences in social environment in which the two functioned. For these answers to be clearly understood, it is necessary (1) to state Lenin's position on the vital matter of party organization and its relationship to class, (2) to indicate why Lenin's position as a matter of principle is not workable in the United States, (3) to show how Debs resolved the same problem that Lenin raised but in a different way, and (4) to specify the contemporary implications of the Lenin-Debs differences as they apply to the underdeveloped and modern capitalist countries. This latter concern leads to a discussion of those aspects of the advanced capitalist states which necessarily justify the development of a reformist approach to the transformation of capitalist society. Although the discussion is often couched in general terms, my main preoccupation, it should be noted, is with the United States.

The Leninist Model

Lenin had to find original answers to two general but related problems: obstacles to group thinking due to inadequate means of communication and difficulties in coordinating and controlling practical activities. Lenin believed that exigencies of the Russian environment required a highly disciplined political organization of full-time *professional* revolutionaries who would surrender themselves completely to the functioning of the party apparatus. This tremendous stress on perfection in organization and the need for absolute devotion to the party were reactions to what Lenin considered a terrible weakness in Russia. He not only called for "iron discipline," but went on to suggest that the lack of organization was a national characteristic.[1]

Such full-time professional revolutionaries as Lenin conceived of were to be drawn from the intelligentsia and the cream of the working class. The former were for the most part to be leaders and directors of the latter, although within the party there were not to be formal distinctions between intellectuals and workers. Furthermore, control of the political organization was to be concentrated in the hands of a highly centralized body of leaders from which smaller groups that operated in larger mass organizations could be effectively led. As a matter of fact, Lenin believed that the durability of the movement rested primarily upon its leaders.[2]

This distinct form of centralization also facilitated quick and efficient changes in tactics without cumbersome discussions involving large numbers; this process gave to the party a central direction. The party as a whole was an elite group consciously keeping itself from integrating with the larger and more amorphous mass organizations yet influencing these mass organizations by organizing nuclei party groups within them.[3]

In other words, Lenin insisted that the party be conceived narrowly, that strict lines be drawn between it and the masses. It was a party connected to but not controlled by organized portions of the working class or general public. This point was so fundamental to Lenin that he was willing to split the Social Democratic Party rather than yield to a compromise on this issue.

Another major but related idea running through Lenin's mind at this time involved his struggle against "economism" (a matter to which I shall return and discuss in greater depth at a later juncture), which he equated with trade-union consciousness in contrast to class or socialist consciousness. In analyzing the limited nature of the strikes of the 1890s, which were described as trade-union struggles with only immediate ends, Lenin argued that socialist and class consciousness would have to be brought to the workers from without.[4]

In sum, the Leninist model involves the following: (1) the adherence to the latter idea of "socialist consciousness from without" (a breed of dualism in which the party represents the mind or consciousness and the masses the body or material force); (2) closely guarded (if not always secretive) tactical deliberations; (3) centralized leadership; (4) full-time professional functionaries that are highly disciplined for the purpose of collective action, coordination, and adherence to party rules; and (5) the notion of party/class separation.

No doubt, adaptations of Lenin's ideas are possible in different countries, especially in underdeveloped ones where structural conditions correspond to those of Czarist Russia. However, whatever the adaptations, a Leninist believes that there should be a separation of the party (or whatever the revolutionary unit is called) from class or popular control. Because such a party necessarily involves the maintenance of strict discipline and a purity of purpose, splintering and purging are elevated to the level of sound tactical principles. Lenin's overall position—which accented the volitional, subjective side of a revolutionary possibility—was implicitly based on the assumption that the will to state power depended not so much on the conscious understanding and enlightenment of the working class or general public as a whole, but upon the use of correct strategies and flexible tactics by a cohesively organized party in the context of a convulsive societal breakdown.[5] Under such circumstances, no general effort can be made to appeal to the intelligence of the whole class. Lenin was quite emphatic on this question of acquiring socialist consciousness. Contrary to what many leftists believe, socialist or class consciousness was not seen as arising from exploitation (working hard and long hours in the factory under miserable conditions) or in "spontaneous" conflicts with bosses or the government or from general experience as a worker, but from well-spent studious leisure.

Class feeling, militancy, or anger are quite different from class consciousness, a notion that Lenin often used interchangeably with socialist
consciousness.[6]

The kind of "education" that was possible for the masses in the Russian
context, and for underdeveloped masses in general, consisted of formulating slogans and demands, developing brief programs, and dramatic
kinds of action that had immediate symbolic relevance. The problem was
less the need to identify the system's oppressiveness and inform large
numbers about their dire circumstances (this was clearly felt if not
understood), but to demonstrate a capacity to lead, to fight, and to use
issues for revolutionary purposes without letting them become ends in
themselves. The problem was to bring the masses into action from a defensive, inactive and nonparticipatory slumber associated with the combined
weight of tradition and sociopolitical repression. In essence, the cultivation
of revolutionary "thought" in a society that was basically illiterate and lacking a mass communication infrastructure required a very limited kind of
propaganda appeal and general educational effort.

Inapplicability of Leninism to the United States

The reason that Lenin's ideas are not workable in the United States lies in
the character of American society. There are four major social and political
"facts" that must be squarely faced by anyone interested in bringing the case
of some form of socialism to the American people: (1) the high percentage
of literacy and education in the working class and the population in
general; (2) universal suffrage and a stable parliamentary form of government; (3) a long history of an organized labor movement led by workers
and for workers; and (4) a tradition whereby organizations tend to be self-
directed and organizational relationships and cohesion within the organizations are primarily welded and held together by way of voluntary allegiance
and support of its members and supporting publics. While no one of the
above observations is critical in and of itself, in aggregate they represent a
qualitative contrast to the kind of society in which an elite vanguard party
with a charter from history and a monopoly on truth is appropriate.[7] But
for a class that has the potential of cultivating self-discipline, guided by its
own understanding and knowledge, to cope with and change the existing
environment, which has experience in making decisions and voting on
issues, there must be a systematic appeal to it and the general public that
socialism is the ideology that would best enable them to fulfill their needs;
that socialism is a solution for *all* segments of the population who experience the malaise and alienation specifically related to capitalism; that
the organization that expounds and cultivates that ideology is an instrument of the broader constituencies that it represents; and that socialism
provides both the means and the ends to a better life.

The Debsian Model

What did Debs have to say on this question of party organization and its relation to class? I have already indirectly suggested the answer to this in my arguments against the attempts to apply Leninism to the United States. I shall now proceed a bit further with some elaboration and documentation.

The Debsian concept of party was actually opposite to that of Lenin. Whereas Lenin argued that the party be *for* and *above* the class, Debs argued "that workers can be emancipated only by their own collective will, the power inherent in themselves as a class, and this collective will and conquering power can only be the result of education, enlightenment, and *self-imposed* discipline."[8] In other words, Debs not only conceived of a party that was for the class, but of one that was *of* and *by* and therefore *integrated* with the class.

Whereas Lenin's concept of party relied heavily upon intellectual leadership, Debs believed that

the Socialist movement is essentially a working class movement . . . and as a rule party officials and representatives, and candidates for public office, should be chosen from the ranks of the workers. The intellectuals in office should be the exception, as they are in the rank and file.[9]

Debs went on to say that the intellectuals could play a very important role for the working class and the party in other capacities.

Whereas Lenin's concept of party out of necessity endorsed a clandestine attitude, Debs argued against any tactic that involved "stealth, secrecy, and intrigue."[10]

The work of the Socialist movement must all be done in broad open light of day. Nothing can be done by stealth that can be of any advantage to this country. . . . If our locals and the members who compose them need the protection of secrecy, they are lacking in the essential revolutionary fiber which can be developed only in the play of the elements that surround them. . . . They [the workers] have got to learn to distinguish between their friends and their enemies and between what is wise and what is otherwise and until the rank and file are so educated and enlightened their weakness will sooner or later deliver them as the prey of their enemies.[11]

Whereas Lenin tended to envision leaders as fixtures in his concept of party, Debs had great fear of

officialism and bureaucracy. I am a thorough believer in the rank and file, and in ruling from the bottom up instead of being ruled from the top down. The natural tendency of officials is to become bosses. They come to imagine that they are indispensable and unconsciously shape their acts to keep themselves in office.[12]

Debs has frequently been dismissed as not being a theoretician. The observation is true in the sense that he never wrote anything that could be clearly identified as an abstract, theoretical treatise on the nature of economics or the nature of the state. Debs has often been characterized by radical socialists as a saintly, popular leader, but one who lacked a hard-nosed understanding of political organization. This is often "proved" by noting that Debs refused to go to party conventions and get involved with in-group factionalism. Perhaps Debs was negligent in this sphere. Nevertheless, there is another side to the way he chose to lead the Socialist Party.

Debs did not want to purge heterogeneities and factions in the party although he was openly critical of the direct-action, anarchistic tactics of Big Bill Haywood and the cautious middle-class reformism of Victor

Berger. Debs correctly believed that the only way a socialist movement and revolutionary perspective could survive in an environment like the United States was by providing room for all these factions, even those with which he disagreed. Debs recognized the need for the radical energy and militancy that came from the Western wing, however inapplicable its tactical principles with respect to the *whole* labor movement. He also tolerated the role of the practical men in the party, even though he saw in them signs of opportunism, and even though he himself felt the need to pursue revolutionary objectives as vital exigencies of the day. Heterogeneity of the whole labor movement required that a viable socialist party had to include both tendencies without permitting either tendency to generalize itself. This could not be accomplished by decree or purging, but only by maintaining an active dialogue on all tactical questions as they related to the conditions and needs and sentiments of the whole working class. The discipline that Debs sought was related not to the party as such but to his understanding of the working class and its central tendencies. Debs was able to do this effectively precisely because he was not drawn into factional and petty party bickering. Moreover, Debs's active noninvolvement in party factionalism freed him to concentrate on making the objectives of socialism and the class interpretation of history meaningful to large numbers. Debs's ability grew by talking and arguing with audiences who did not agree with him. He interacted and played with the hostile elements surrounding him without becoming cynical and bitter; he scolded workers for whom he had great compassion without being contemptuous of their limitations. He knew how to get ordinary people to rise above their personal preoccupations and narrow interests, and therefore how to stimulate them to struggle for longer-run objectives.

The importance of Debs rests in the fact that he understood the relationship between party and class as they specifically apply to a country like the United States with a stable parliamentary system, however such a system might be manipulated by the capitalist class. The Debsian case was essentially that of revolutionary reformist. Debs held to an uncompromising public commitment to revolutionary goals while practicing (broadly speaking) as a matter of principle reformist tactics, tactics comprehensible and viable for the whole working class and nonpropertied public. Given the low probability that the system will undergo a convulsive, dramatic breakdown in which the whole authority structure will be fractured in a moment of revolutionary truth, Debs saw the necessity of devising methods of struggle that were intuitively comprehensible as he projected revolutionary goals for immediate contemplation and sought to cultivate a class or revolutionary consciousness among those in the midst of struggle. Debs argued that tactics should not be devised to reflect individual needs or small segments of the labor movement. Seeking to avoid unnecessary stratification within the laboring classes, he argued that sound tactics must relate to the characteristics and temperament of the whole working class and thus fought against the IWW educational approach, which revolved about the "propaganda of deed."[13]

Debs went on to point out that "propaganda of the deed" in the American context was a function of weakness not strength, despair not hope. In essence Debs assumed that revolutionary goals and consciousness could be achieved, not easily and not without tremendous struggle, but without the need of violently smashing the state in the way envisioned by Lenin. In this sense, the Debsian socialist route was a theoretical and practical alternative to the bland politics of social democrats whose relationship to capitalist reform parties has been such as to destroy the social democrats' ability to inspire mass involvement in socialism and cultivate a socialist consciousness. It is an alternative to various parties of the Leninist type whose theoretical assumptions about the nature of the state were so far removed from the realities of the American environment that they avoided serious ideological work and substituted intense involvement in specific issues and the ritualistic creation of so-called transitional programs, as if issues and paper-generated programs alone could become the vehicles of a socialist takeover when capitalism collapsed in its moment of Marxist-Leninist truth.

The State in Under- and Overdeveloped Nations

The next concern is why the Leninist approach is functionally appropriate to the transformation of the Third World societies, and why a variant of the Debsian one is most relevant to the transformation of mature capitalist ones.

The social and economic exigencies in which the Third World finds itself require that it undergo political, social, and economic transformation more or less simultaneously — that is, in a relatively condensed period of historic time. The political transformation requires a violent smashing of the agencies of power embodied in the old state; the social transformation involves the removal of all kinds of social, class, ethnic, and sex barriers that define the repression and *immobilism* of the old order or its atavisms; and the economic transformation involves capital accumulation and a widespread dispersion of technical changes in the work process.

Viewed from the more affirmative vantage point of a revolutionary process in motion, the overall transformation involves creating and developing new governing agencies and forging new secular symbols of work and national pride. A successful revolution makes it possible to "harmonize" the previous disparate underprivileged segments and classes of society into a more integrated whole for the purpose of achieving the more long-term goals of social and economic development. This involves holding down consumption relative to rising expectations and needs in order to accumulate capital, introducing technological changes, altering the composition of the labor force, breaking down social barriers, and changing work habits. Revolutionary efforts involve forging new secular organizations capable of stimulating higher levels of productive effort. The rigidity and fears of the old governing elites and ruling classes (a distinction I will elaborate upon at a later juncture) make them generally incapable of developing an ideological "market" in which increases in productive effort are "exchanged," not only for goods but also for national pride and a new sense of participation.

Looking at the nature of the Third World problems from a slightly different angle, today's underdeveloped nations do not have what England and other nineteenth-century capitalist nations had from the sixteenth century to the beginning of the twentieth—that is, a relatively defenseless external source of surplus labor providing accumulation derived from "gold and silver in America, the extirpation, enslavement and entombment in mines of aboriginal population, the conquest and looting of the East Indies, [and] the turning of Africa into a warren for the commercial hunting of black-skins."[14] From this fact a general conclusion follows: the primitive accumulation of capital involving the extraction of a larger, self-sustaining surplus and its reinvestment will occur primarily through the internal exploitation of labor involving the direct use of numerous political mechanisms of the state and therefore will require political control of the labor process.[15]

The Leninist approach is functionally appropriate to the violent smashing of the old state apparatus. This state apparatus embodies the instruments of power, which maintain the barriers that prevent the development thrust. The revolutionaries who moved from the vanguard party to the vangaurd state carried with them their prerevolutionary paternalistic attitudes and their single-minded determination to forge economic development. Just as the prerevolutionary vanguard party stood above the working class and yet was related to it through operating cells, the postrevolutionary vanguard state stands above mass control while it simultaneously remains connected to the masses through functioning political agencies of the state and party. This "connectedness" to the people that is built up in the revolutionary process enables the Leninist state to acquire secular prestige and presence, cohesion, autonomy, and the power necessary to exhort labor to work harder and to generate the kind of secular push needed in the construction of a new social order, a prerequisite for the economic and technical transformation of Third World societies. The politics and sociology of Leninism, initially a unique adaptation to special Russian conditions, became an appropriate follow-up model cultivated more or less consciously by Third World revolutionaries who presently operate in an environment not too dissimilar to that of Czarist Russia.

It is for this reason that postrevolutionary processes that take development tasks seriously have been tagged by Paul Baran as "underdeveloped socialism" or have led to what others have described as "bureaucratic socialism," or what even others, namely Western development economists, have referred to as "command economies."[16] My own preference, following in the tradition of Max Weber, is for the term "administrative economies." This is not a transitional form but a genus that goes back to antiquity. While variations are, of course, possible and likely, an administrative economy is one in which a public bureaucracy administers (appropriates, allocates, collects, and redistributes) the surplus in accordance with established rules that may or may not be egalitarian. Historically such "types" have proven to be stable and long-lasting.

In any event, whatever one wishes to call the broad development of indigenously successful socialist revolutions from 1917 to the present in the underdeveloped portions of the world, there is no doubt that, as Joseph Schumpeter once wryly remarked, "history sometimes plays tricks of questionable taste."[17] Of course, the trick that has been played has been on Western Marxists and socialists, and it has led to unresolved debates about the nature of Third World socialist societies, producing considerable amounts of unproductive intrasocialist fighting. Those in the Marxist-Leninist tradition not infrequently find themselves lavishly defending the U.S.S.R. or China or Cuba in the name of socialism. Western reform socialists have frequently been obsessed with denouncing such "socialist" countries and, in fact, have denied that there is any legitimacy to the socialist label that has been employed to identify such countries. In a peculiar way, both positions in their more pristine form are untenable and stem from doctrinaire modes of thought. Marxist-Leninists end up trying to justify to their own publics a "socialist" practice that has no relevance to their own history and effort at acquiring more presence at home. In the end, they find themselves defending internal processes of another country that are totally incomprehensible to their own contemporary publics, to say nothing about the need to rationalize horror stories and avoid uncomfortable issues. Reformist socialists have devoted so much energy to denouncing Third World revolutionary socialist movements and societies that they leave their home audience, whenever they get around to discussing socialist politics and alternatives, wondering whether there is any value to any kind of socialism, including their own reformist brand.

One way out of this bind (there is no easy answer in this sphere) is to recognize that successful revolutions in Third World countries, however far from realizing Marx's original expectations about the nature of socialism, have become instruments or catalysts, if not for the creation of good and humane societies, for industrial transformations. This latter process is a necessary, although not sufficient, condition for a more civil superstructure, however different its evolution in fact will be from that which has taken place in Western Europe and North America. This makes such Third World Leninist-conceived revolutions a valid, historical process, but it is a process that the West has already experienced in a different set of circumstances and one that has been stretched out over many centuries. From such an angle of reflection, Third World revolutions do not represent the future as much as a catching up with Western industrial development. With Marxism serving as the ideology of development, it necessarily has acquired a harsh social and political edge, a fact that disorients by association the projection of socialism among its Western advocates, who are seeking to develop it in a more benign society and in the context of relative affluence. For this reason, Western socialists should neither slavishly condone nor violently condemn the burgeoning brands of Third World Marxian-guided socialisms. We should simply learn to observe these societies, advocate dealing with them on pragmatic grounds, debate their qualities without issuing static papal position papers about their worth or worthlessness, and, most importantly, get on with the business of developing our own socialist perspective as it applies to solving problems applicable to our own communities and economy.[18]

In contrast to societies with large peasant and agriculturally rooted populations that must accumulate capital from low levels, ours is one that needs to socialize the use of a capital stock that has already achieved high levels. Agriculturally dependent societies require austerity and belt-tightening to achieve objectives related to acquiring bargaining parity with developed countries and minimally decent standards of life; modern urban capitalist societies are concerned with waste, the meaning or utility of an oversized surplus, and the inability to fully use available resources and labor in productive ways because of inadequate aggregate demand. In Keynesian terms, accumulation in advanced capitalist countries is related more to increasing consumption than to increasing savings. Or, finally, as one prominent Marxist, Samir Amin, suggested, the preoccupation with extracting rather than absorbing the surplus in Third World nations means that "wages . . . emerge . . . only as a cost."[19]

Exploring the fuller implications of these numerous practical and theoretical differences between underdeveloped and advanced capitalist nations leads inevitably to the conclusion that the state apparatus in mature capitalist systems must be in a different relationship to its subordinate classes than the state apparatus in "preaccumulating" underdeveloped societies. This proposition, when examined closely, leads to the dropping of the Leninist assumption that the state must be smashed in order to achieve a revolutionary departure from the past or a basic change in the social order. This, in turn, leads to the termination of the need for a Leninist-type vanguard party as a matter of historical necessity. It forces left-wing socialists and Marxists to consider the reformist road, a road that has in fact often been traveled by them as a practical exigency, but one that has not been discussed with much theoretical clarity or seriousness due to the reliance on Leninist rhetoric and the subjective preoccupation with Leninist thought.

The Bifurcated System

Defining the nature of the state changes with the purpose for which it is being examined. The failure to understand this point is a source of considerable confusion in the discussion between the so-called revolutionists versus the reformists. For some purposes (for example, to demonstrate the state's business bias), it may be correct to portray the capitalist state, as Marxists are wont, by suggesting that it is akin to the "committee of the bourgeoisie" and that the state is concerned with reproducing the business system and the domination of the capitalist class. For other purposes (for example, the question of why the background of the elected officials is of no relevance or why the state cannot forge consistent policies), the debates that revolve about such issues as instrumentality versus autonomy, the state's conflicting functions such as accumulation versus legitimacy, its ideological role in obfuscating the class nature of issues, or its employment of specific mechanisms to exclude anticapitalist interests from state activity, are sensible and often illuminating.[20] What is lacking in much of the current debate about the state is the fact that the issues discussed are not intricately connected to questions about reformist versus revolutionary approaches and therefore do not relate various notions of the state to political models necessary to transform capitalism. In this sense, the current debate, although interesting, is relatively static. That is to say, the insights developed have little bearing on what socialists do, on the way they perceive political tactic and strategy models and the transformation of capitalism.

To correct this, the focus here is not to identify the nature of the capitalist state per se but to identify that unique aspect of it which is specifically germane to issues concerned with proper socialist tactics and strategies. Viewing the state in relation to this kind of question produces a different social statement, to repeat for emphasis, than if one were concerned, for example, with only how the state reproduces the economic system and its corresponding stratification.

Most current Marxian writers implicitly tend to assume, once having proved that the specific qualities of the state are particular to the capitalist society and its relations, that reformism is illusory. This was recently illustrated in an interesting and thoughtful article by Fred Block. Concerned with current Marxian theorizing about the state, the author reflects that it "remains in a muddle despite the recent revival of interest in the subject."[21] After a discussion of capitalism's capacity to reform itself as a result of conflicts among capitalists, workers, and state managers, after arguing persuasively that the business class does not directly control the state, after suggesting that the "ruling class is diffused, lacks class consciousness and political sophistication,"[22] after pointing to the fact that there are "structural mechanisms that make the state serve capitalist ends regardless of whether capitalists intervene directly or consciously," the author comes to the astounding conclusion that he has established a powerful argument and critique against "socialist reformism."[23] His case rests mainly on how rapidly the state comes to the rescue of capitalists when private investment declines. Since fluctuations in private investment determine much else — for example, the state's capacity to finance its own activities and perhaps existence — the state's knee-jerk reaction to a cloudy investment picture is to preserve the investment climate — that is, to give business people what they need.

While I am in agreement with Block's numerous observations, in my judgment he has made, contrary to intentions, a case *for* (not against) socialist reformism. The fact that he is unaware of this is one of the symptomatic weaknesses of the Marxian perspective about the state as it relates to conceptualizing a process concerned with socialist tactics and strategies. While it is generally valid, it fails to identify the more subtle and practical dimensions of the way political power is, over the long haul, exercised in democratic capitalist states. As a result, he, like many sophisticated Marxists, fails to cast clear light on democracy in the capitalist context[24] and the kind of political party that people must think about as political activists seeking to transform capitalism. It is for this and related reasons that we must reformulate some of our notions about the democratic capitalist state.

A former teacher of the writer, while he was stationed in England at the end of World War II, reported the following remarks made to him by a large English shipping magnate: "After the war many bad things are going to happen that will end the British civilization that I know and love. The Labour Party and workers are going to strangle Britain with all kinds of socialist programs. I, and many businessmen like me, want to stop them, but what can we businessmen do? They are so many and we are so few."

Although only an anecdote, this shipping magnate's story has several implications that warrant a more formal exploration. First, this was the statement of a man who might fight to retain his power and privilege in order to slow down the erosion of his position, but who would be unlikely to dig himself into trenches and prepare for civil war. Second, he did not see the government as belonging to him or his class. He clearly was resigned to a declining position. Yet, even as this shipping tycoon was reflecting on his declining fate, I am sure that his influence in the halls of government and those of others in similar positions were considerable. Marxists would find evidence to prove that, even when labor has political power, the government was still under the spell and influence of the business class. And they would not be wrong. To get at the peculiar implication of this problem and apparent paradox, we must understand that it has deep roots that relate to the origin of the capitalist state. The matter was put by the Marxian-socialist editors of the *Monthly Review* in the following way:

[The struggle of economic liberalism] took the form of an unremitting effort on the part of the bourgeoisie to enforce a clear-cut distinction between private and public spheres in life. The economy was assigned to the private sphere, the state to the public sphere. . . . Success in their struggle may be said to have marked the triumph of capitalism.[25]

A conceptual understanding of the origin of the capitalist state requires distinguishing between a ruling class on the one hand and a governing "class" on the other. In general, the capitalist social order involves a ruling class that does not govern, or, what reduces itself to the same difference, a governing class that does not rule. The governing class — which administrates, legislates, and adjudicates in behalf of the state — involves *public* officials who "claim to be guardians of what is public" and have "unique access to the use of legal coercive power . . . within a given territory."[26] The ruling class in a capitalist society is in the private domain and is outside the direct public purview. Since it owns the means of production and is an appropriator, accumulator, and prime allocator of society's surplus, it possesses an inordinate amount of power for its relatively small numerical size that is not directly accessible to public authorities. Whatever the nature of the interaction between the public domain and the private one, there is an institutional weakness built into the capitalist state. It was precisely this weakness that was idealized by classical liberal economists in the nineteenth century and that is lamented by present-day conservatives. It should be emphasized, moreover, that the more pluralistic is the distribution of political power (as when there are regional and local levels that do not readily mesh with centralized ones) in a state system relative to the concentration of private economic power, the weaker is the public structure's capacity to govern in the general interest relative to the private structure's capacity to rule in the private interests. This is, of course, the main institutional basis upon which Marxists criticize pluralists.[27] The other side of this political-pluralism question has to do with the degree of competition in the private sphere. The greater the degree of competition the lower the capacity of the capitalist class to exert its power as a whole through the state system. These propositions, of course, necessarily vary with the extent of labor's power as an organized class.

The implication of this bifurcation in mature capitalist societies, though it may be presently more blurred than in the nineteenth century, is the source of considerable confusion for both Marxists and pluralists as they seek to explain the relationship between the state and its policies on the one hand and the operation and influence of the private economy on the other. This bifurcation is the main reason that pluralists fail to understand the limits of state power even when that power is held by "good," independent-minded administrators, and that Marxists do not appreciate the possibility of acquiring state power legally and by degrees and then using it to "gradually" change the nature of the capitalist system.[28]

Perhaps the issues raised by this fundamental bifurcation in mature capitalist societies can be brought into a sharper focus with some con-trasting examples. Is it necessary to smash the state apparatus to forge a revolutionary change in the economic system? In answering this question, Marxist-Leninists implicitly or explicitly are prone to a certain kind of mechanistic reasoning, which, crudely stated, unfolds as follows: since no class that dominates the state can be expected to eliminate its own privileges, it is necessary to smash the state in order to effect fundamental changes in the class structure. This mechanistic reasoning, often buttressed by grandiose examples about the violent transition from slavery to feudalism, or from feudalism to capitalism, is a way of avoiding a close examination of the relationship between the class and state in ma-ture capitalist societies that have not been hospitable to Leninist modes of work.

In slave and feudal states, the ruling class is so closely connected to the state that it cannot be characterized merely in terms of class domination of those who manage the state apparatus. Because the economic and political functions tend to merge, the struggle against such states is equivalent to acts of class warfare, and, of course, acts of class warfare are confrontations with the state. Political mechanisms are closely intertwined with economic ones, an observation made by Marx.[29] In such arrangements, there is simply no way of acquiring state power without upsetting the class struc-ture.

In many presently underdeveloped countries there is a rigid class-state connection derived from precapitalist institutional atavisms. These societies are pressed, as was argued above, with the need to accumulate capital from relatively low levels of income if they are to overcome the "hump of backwardness." Modernization — or at least its self-sustaining breakthrough — requires smashing many "frozen" social and political struc-tures. The Leninist approach, again to repeat the implication of my early arguments, is viable in this context, especially so because of the absence of any strong, democratic political tradition.

But in modern capitalist societies with strong democratic traditions and institutional procedures to alter power relations, the problem is different. The main institutional contradiction and source of tension in such societies, even under the assumption that such societies have capitalist states rather than states in capitalist societies, that those who possess private power do not govern, and that therefore it has been possible, to one degree or another, for the majority or for significant segments of the population who do not own the means of production to acquire power through their own self-determined representatives; at least the potential is there if not always the actuality. However, acquiring governing power does not automatically affect private relations at the points of production. State power and private relations are legally related but technically separate. The institutional linkages between points of actual production and the state are relatively distant and loose. Since the state has been mandated historically to employ its power to enforce the rights of privacy and contracts in the preservation of property rules for organizing the economy, legal articulations when not smashed stretch and drag out over long periods of time. If conditions are such that a shorter route to change is not available, then there are no alternatives but to face the long haul. Exactly how long the "long haul" is will be determined by the resilience of the existing system on the one hand, and the capacities of a socialist movement to acquire and use state power on the other.

Another important implication of bifurcation in capitalist societies is that which falls under the rubric of economism. Economic struggles do not clearly translate themselves into political ones, since the economy is not organically intertwined with the state apparatus. Economism, when generalized, defines "solutions" to particular problems in piecemeal terms without relating them to the whole environment or to ultimate and centralizing objectives. It separates political matters from economic ones, and thereby obliterates the ideological meaning of events and issues. Buttressing generalized economism are various institutional mechanisms that are employed to limit the boundaries of class conflict, such as collective bargaining contracts, mediation and arbitration, processing industrial grievances through the unions.[30]

Viewed from the leftist perspective aimed at establishing a socialist society in which public planning and workers' control become dominant in the mode of production, bifurcation requires that socialists devote more — not less — energy to popular ideological work. This is necessary because economic struggles do not readily translate themselves into political ones. The acquisition of political power and its use to change the economic order require internalized ideological coherence among large segments of the electorate. To counteract capitalist ideological hegemony, with its emphasis on "me-tooism," individualism, and privacy, it is necessary to imbue the labor movement and other nonpropertied segments of the population with a self-disciplined and self-defined cooperative spirit and their own sense of power so that they can think and act in the name of the whole community rather than of some particular self-serving game plan. This requires, as Antonio Gramsci suggested, that the "working class, before it [acquires] state power, must establish its claim to be a ruling class in the political, cultural and 'ethical' fields."[31] How to establish this claim before acquiring state power is the purpose of ideological work.

Public versus Private Spheres

The political struggle in democratic capitalist societies between socialists and welfare-liberal advocates of mixed capitalism on the one hand and advocates of "pure" capitalism on the other can be "thought of as a historical effort to counteract [the private tendency to rule] and permit the public, in the sense of 'the people,' to determine what is public,"[32] to increase the extent of public entitlements over the previously defined private ones. Between qualitatively different kinds of societies, what constitutes "public" and "private," of course, changes with the nature of the state and society. In feudalism, religion was by no means a private affair. In primitive society, sex is subject to public scrutiny.[33]

Within the modern capitalist societies themselves, the meaning of public ranges from gentle "jawboning" by the state, aimed at "persuading" private capital to behave in the public interest, to complete public ownership of capital by the state or cooperative bodies. Between these poles are numerous intermediate mechanisms, such as regulatory agencies that can in theory control industries without owning them, and state expenditures that, although channeled through the private sector, can be used to affect the allocation of privately owned resources. These gray areas between the poles are the most difficult to evaluate and offer the major source of confusion for socialists and welfare-liberal pluralists alike. Many of these areas, moreover, are assumed to be, to one degree or another, in the direction of socialism. It is not without reason, one might argue, that business rhetoric is defensive and saturated with a concern about its loss of status and influence, although its actual power appears to be intact.[34] Marxists, in contrast, have at times argued that capitalism was made even stronger because the state has become more rational in relation to it, or that the basic tenets of property relations and the private accumulation of capital remain unchanged,[35] although the mechanisms of the welfare state have in theory encroached upon the rights of capital.

The problem here is defining socialism. To anti-Marxian, procapitalist ideologues, the host of formations (regulatory agencies, government spending, minimum income guarantees) that operate outside the market system are frequently defined as socialistic in direction. In contrast, the present discussion of the capitalist state by Marxists tends to deny that the "welfare" creations of the capitalist state are of that nature. Behind this denial is, among other considerations, either a notion of socialism derived from Marx's actual pronouncements on the subject or one derived from some arbitrarily idealized construction. Socialism cannot be so rigidly defined, or conceived in such arbitrarily utopian terms, as to eliminate all situations as a result of the "purity" of one's definition. Socialism is a process that emerges inside and in reaction to the ebb and flow of the capitalist system. Socialist struggles and "creations," therefore, must have their ups and downs, retreats and advances. But whatever their fluctuations, they must get their definitions from the actual formations within the society, not from totally abstracted ones.

The problem here is to build a movement of sufficient durability to keep the embryonic socialist edifices that are created within capitalist societies from experiencing complete commercial debasement over time. Ultimately this process will be most assured when socialists acquire permanent power enclaves in which they both govern and rule. That is to say, they must acquire administrative control of the supply side of a sector (for instance, the health industry) and sufficient political and social power to prevent such sectors from being manipulated and invaded by private business interests. At the same time, the socialist sector must seek to serve the widest possible public efficiently and humanely. Its moral standards and ethical commitment to serve must be experienced as a superior alternative to that which typically takes place in private enterprises driven by the imperatives of the market.

The cumbersomeness and inefficiency of the modern capitalist state and its network of agencies are due not only to factors of scale, but also to the fact that the state's functioning is debased by the furies of profit-oriented interests. Socialists, therefore, must differentiate welfare-liberal state creations (welfare transfer instruments that generate intra-working-class divisions or indirect regulatory commissions that are manipulated by industries for private ends) from their own effort aimed at building productive public enclaves that equalize the distribution of income and simultaneously meet important needs. This cannot be done in isolation but requires an aroused public consciousness and commitment to the development of various kinds of public institutions aimed at solving particular problems that relate to a large cross section of the population. Medical and health reform in the direction of socialized medicine, for example, should not be geared solely to the bottom fifth of the population. A partial solution in this direction will result in an overused and underfinanced constellation of facilities in ghetto areas, which will be corrupted and therefore become a symbol of public failure. Public enterprising efforts need wide support and must be a solution to the problems confronting the middle layers of the population as well as those at the bottom. Only with wide support can public enterprise hope to acquire sufficient independence and therefore protection from becoming weak counterparts to the most inefficient and badly run private corporations that are dependent upon government contracts and subsidies.

Socialists should conceive their tasks in terms of the creation of public institutions in which the governing and ruling components of making decisions are united to meet general social needs. Only in this way can the public sector, or various parts of it, become more than either an instrument of capital or a receptacle to care for the residual problems of a faltering market system. While the general integrationist trend in advanced capitalism between governing and ruling is taking place, albeit in fits and starts, at the apex of the given system in selective spheres (for instance, the Pentagon and big corporations), the process is far from complete and can be readily exaggerated because of the absence of any popular challenges to the business system's influence in the halls of government. In any event, the needed integration between ruling and governing that socialists envision involves a change in the ownership and control of the means of production. This change involves socializing production from the bottom (democratizing the workplace through workers' control), and nationalizing production (integrating industry decisions into a national plan). These twin processes are not necessarily simultaneous, and they represent one reason that nationalization without socialization may produce bureaucratic disillusionment; or that socialization at the micro level without nationalization may prove to be unstable — i.e., still retain some of the anarchy of production inherent in competitive capitalism.

It must be stressed that the public concern and domain are determined by the balance of power between the political and economic spheres. If the main focus of power is outside the public sphere, it follows that the public domain must be relegated to an inferior role. The acquisition of governing power by representatives of the propertyless, although resisted by various and sundry means among owners of property, does not simultaneously require the elimination of ruling-class power. This is precisely why a labor party via the reformist route is able to acquire political power behind the back of capital and, of course, to prove at the same time ineffective in the forging of a dramatic change in the economy. But this ineffectiveness should not be misinterpreted. It represents labor's *subjective* limitations, not those which are defined by some structuralist notions provided by Marxists who set up a tautological argument to prove that reformist means are not viable.

Conclusion and Implications

The reformist road to transforming capitalism is possible, although not without intense struggle and possible setbacks, precisely because managing the state does not automatically mean usurping those who rule. It allows for the gradual erosion, however uncertain, of the privileges and power associated with the private accumulation of capital; it allows for the development of sources of power and income outside market and property relations. This point suggests that when socialists achieve governing power via the electoral process (a route that does not exclude nonparliamentary forms of struggle at the community, industry, and enterprise levels), their capacity to succeed in transforming capitalism needs tremendous majoritarian support and a highly self-disciplined populace. If these are not present, governing socialists in a bifurcated system, because they lack ruling-class power, can readily prove inadequate to the tasks of overcoming the circumstances that brought them to power. This not infrequently leads to a decline in popular support and an inability to deal effectively with the economic environment. The ebb and flow of the British Labour Party exemplify this process par excellence. It will no doubt have to undergo changes from within before it succeeds in going beyond its accomplishments to date. There is no easy way out of this quagmire, and socialists of all persuasions must learn to cope with the uncertainties of the reformist route. Needless to say, there is little evidence that Leninist alternatives are more likely to serve as effective means of transforming advanced capitalist systems. In any event, to avoid struggling along the reformist path is to surrender doing serious political work in democratic capitalist societies.

The democratic capitalist state cannot be adequately characterized as a state standing above classes responding impartially to the general needs of the society as implicitly assumed by pluralists. Nor is the state like that often assumed by hard-nosed Leninists: an obdurate guardian of the dominant class that can readily dissolve the democratic state when it ceases to be serviceable to the maintenance of the capitalist system. For this reason, it is argued, the state must be smashed and an appropriate preparation must be made for that purpose. In a sense, the business class in a capitalist society is as inadequate at governing as the governing officials are at ruling. This "break" is due to capitalism's fundamental split between those who govern and those who rule. This is why capitalist governments find it extremely difficult, if not impossible, to rescue the society from its economic doldrums, even when the voices of many segments of the nonpropertied classes are heard in the halls of government. The demise of "classical" laissez-faire government was a result of the government's inability to govern in a crisis period. The welfare state—a more extended government—emerged from the Great Depression of the 1930s to take its place. However, the welfare state still appears to be a frail or inadequate instrument for dealing with the present, growing contradictions of the advanced capitalist economy.

During the next crisis there will be an accelerated need to move toward an integration between governing and ruling institutions. The challenge to socialists and the more general Left (however defined) is to move toward the development of national planning, the establishment of democratic work places, and the generation of more income and wealth equality. This must be accomplished without forgoing the maintenance of civil rights and liberties that constitute our legal heritage. The alternative is not a free-market utopia or more of the present brand of mixed capitalism, but an integrated corporate state system that may be concerned with the imposition of order at the expense of social justice and the protection of civil liberties.

One final thought with regard to some practical implications of my general thesis about party, class, and state must be considered. Much of what I have argued rests on the conviction that many past and contemporary American socialists have misconceived or are insufficiently aware of the broader theoretical principles implicit in their ongoing activities. This is problematic because the specifics of any particular set of issues (for example, shall we work within or outside the Democratic Party?) make sense only when there is an explicit understanding of the historic relationship between party and class and the way the state can be used to transform advanced capitalist countries. Since these larger questions have not been resolved or explicitly clarified—let alone realized objectively to some degree in the political arena—much of the dialogue among socialists tends to proceed in circles or fails to clarify basic directions. There are many discussions about tactics and strategies in the absence of a general socialist consciousness of movement. Therefore, the correctness of the various arguments put forth can never be tested or validated in any meaningful way.

The question, for example, of whether socialists should work inside the Democratic Party implicitly suggests at least two propositions: (1) the Democratic Party can be converted to a legitimate vehicle representing something akin to a genuine labor party; (2) the Democratic Party must be joined as a tactic simply because it represents "where the people are." Both would be legitimate concerns for socialists if there were in fact a consequential socialist movement, however small relative to the majority party. But socialists do not have a constituency that defines a movement. Thus, we neither are sought as allies nor possess much influence. In this context, the question of working inside or outside the Democratic Party is irrelevant; it has no political meaning for socialists qua socialists, however gratifying it might be for particular individuals. It might become a vital question under other circumstances. But until that time arrives, we would do better to expend our energies in another direction; that is, in the development of organizations and vehicles that facilitate a broad ideological confrontation with the specific ways in which the system acquires hegemony over American *minds;* with the ways in which the system determines and perpetuates its legitimacy. This process of changing the social perceptions of the American people involves changing our own perceptions about how tactics and strategies as matters of principle are related to our ideas about the capitalist state, one aspect of which justifies the reformist orientation argued in this essay.

Notes

1. Quoted by Nathan Leites, *A Study of Bolshevism* (Glencoe, Ill.: Free Press, 1953), p. 283; and V. I. Lenin, *Selected Works,* vol. 8 (New York: International Publishers, 1943), p. 42.

2. "What Is to Be Done," V. I. Lenin, *Collected Works,* vol. 4, part 2 (New York: International Publishers, 1929), pp. 196, 198.

3. Ibid., p. 200.

4. See James E. Connor, ed., *Lenin on Politics and Revolution: Selected Writings* (New York: Pegasus, 1968), p. 40.

5. In my judgment, Lenin and Marx are divided on this point, corresponding to the matter of making a revolution or the unfolding of the revolutionary process. Whereas Marx tended to think about a successful revolutionary possibility in terms of the maturity of the objective conditions—that is, as being an outcome of the complete unfolding of the historical process—Lenin tended to accent the subjective will to make a revolution, even in the absence of the full-blown objective conditions. Whereas Marx tended to envision the revolutionary party as growing out of a well-formed trade-union movement with long years of experience, Lenin tended to envision the revolutionary party as developing in place of a well-formed, independent trade-union movement. See "Letter from Marx to F. Bolte in New York," in Karl Marx, *Selected Works in One Volume* (New York: International Publishers, 1972), p. 683.

6. V. I. Lenin, Collected Works, vol. 23 (New York: International Publishers, 1929), p. 94.

7. No Leninist ever states his or her attitude in these terms. The attitude emerges in a more subtle form: the belief that all individuals outside the party, however clever and/or correct for the moment, have a limited grasp or understanding. Outsiders have transient positions that must be manipulated or castigated as being dangerous, or, perhaps, positions that

must be adjusted to momentarily until the "real" truth that verifies that party's orientation emerges. In any event, history will vindicate or grace the party's ultimate perspective on capitalism, however adverse prospects for change appear at the moment. It is in this sense that being in a Leninist party, armed with a Marxist-Leninist perspective, has a religious quality. And it is for this reason that discussions between Leninist and non-Leninist socialists frequently are sterile; the discussions are not among assumed equals in which intelligence, reason, and facts mediate inquiries.

8. *Writings and Speeches of Eugene V. Debs* (New York: Hermitage Press, 1948), p. 353.

9. Ibid., p. 354.

10. Ibid., p. 353.

11. Ibid., p. 355.

12. Ibid., p. 355.

13. Ibid., p. 353.

14. *Capital,* vol. 1 (Kerr edition, 1906, reprinted, New York: Random House), p. 823.

15. For a discussion of this interpretation, see Barrington Moore, Jr., *Social Origins of Dictatorship and Democracy* (Boston: Beacon Press, 1967).

16. History has a way of catching up with efforts aimed at bypassing it. By this I mean that the residue of habits derived from the past in the process of making a revolution reemerge in different guises, so that newly created institutions not infrequently display qualities of the old institutions that were destroyed. No group can escape the historic legacy of its own evolution. In spite of this fact, the revolutionary process brings about real and substantive material and social changes. History is not simply a cynical circle, but it does have unintended consequences conducive to the making of cynics.

17. Irving Howe stated the matter of evaluating the role of Marxism in Third World countries in a similar vein. See "What Trotsky Taught," *New York Review of Books,* February 9, 1978, p. 21.

18. The full implications of this position are beyond the scope of this chapter. Nevertheless, they warrant some additional comment. My colleague Frank Warren has persuasively argued that Western socialists cannot ignore or soft-pedal the atrocities that might accompany statecraft building and industrializing under the guise of Marxism-Leninism. It is possible to view the Leninist-type development process in the same way that Marx viewed the early stages of industrial capitalism: as a progressive historical force relative to the preceding period, but one whose inhumanity and hypocrisy needed exposing.

19. "Self-Reliance and the New International Economic Order," *Monthly Review* 29 (July-August 1977):9.

20. See David A. Gold, Clarence Y. H. Lo, and Erik Olin Wright, "Recent Developments in Marxist Theories of the Capitalist State," Part 1, *Monthly Review,* November 1975, pp. 36–51. One should also consult the new Marxist journal, *Kapitalistate.*

21. Fred Block, "Classes and the State," *Socialist Revolution,* no. 3 (May-June 1977), p. 6.

22. Ibid., p. 12.

23. Ibid., p. 12.

24. For a recent effort to correct this failure among Marxian scholars, see Goran Therborn, "The Rule of Capital and the Rise of Democracy," *New Left Review* 103 (May-June 1977):3–41.

25. *Monthly Review* 10 (January 1959):340.

26. Peter T. Manicus, *The Death of the State* (New York: Putnam's, 1974), p. 31.

27. See Ralph Miliband, *The State in Capitalist Society* (New York: Basic Books, 1969), p. 146.

28. With the development of Euro-Communism, this matter appears to be in a state of considerable flux. Yet there are still influential Marxists like Paul Sweezy and Harry Magdoff who articulate strong objections to any movement that theorizes in the reformist direction. See their recent critique of Italian communism, "The New Reformism," *Monthly Review* 28 (June 1976):1–11; and "More on New Reformism," *Monthly Review* 28 (November 1976):5–13.

29. "Critique of Hegel's Philosophy of Rights" (MS); cited by Hal Draper, *Karl Marx's Theory of Revolution,* book 2 (New York: Monthly Review Press, 1977), p. 470.

30. See Bertram Silverman and Murray Yanowitch, eds., *The Worker in "Post-Industrial" Capitalism* (New York: Free Press, 1974), chap. 9.

31. Cited by Douglas F. Dowd, *The Twisted Dream* (Cambridge, Mass.: Winthrop Publishers, 1974), p. 300.

32. Manicus, *The Death of the State,* pp. 7–8. The issue of "external diseconomies" is basically about the definition of what constitutes public rather than private. The bifurcation of the society has led to the need for a bifurcated economics. It is no accident that private market theory is so better developed than the theory of state decision making. This will necessarily change as state economic planning increases in scope and depth.

33. Ibid., p. 5.

34. For an interesting interpretation of an aspect of this problem, see Earl F. Cheit, "The New Place of Business," in Cheit, ed., *The Business Establishment* (New York: John Wiley, 1964), pp. 152–92.

35. For the "stronger-than-ever" view, see Fred Block, "Classes and the State," p. 7. It is un-Marxian on the part of some Marxists to repeat continuously that "capitalism is capitalism." It is one of Marx's central notions that new systems are born within old ones. Just as capitalism was born inside feudalism, just as capitalist relations (and capitalist elements) were formed alongside feudal ones, Marxists should expect and look for forms of socialist relations (primitive socialism if you will) within the womb of mature capitalist societies. Ought not these be identified and discussed? It should be further noted that conservative critics of socialist ideas may be more correct in this sphere than Marxists; the former tend to view almost all the dimensions of the welfare state as socialistic.

5   Unions, Parties, the State, and Liberal Corporatism

PETER LANGE

The chapter that follows is more the skeleton than the corpus of an argument. Starting with some problems posed by Italian developments during the 1970s, it seeks to provide systematically linked hypotheses that would explain these developments in ways useful for comparative analysis. The two central issues addressed are, Under what conditions are unions more or less likely to seek to press their interests through action at the level of the state? and, Under what conditions is state-oriented activity by the unions likely to take a liberal corporatist form? Both issues seem of major importance for the analysis of political-economic development in the last decade. They are also directly relevant to the ongoing research project, funded by the Ford Foundation, on "Trade Union Responses to the Economic Crisis" in five advanced industrial democracies, of which I am a part. As noted, the paper is heavily loaded toward the explication of a set of hypotheses. Further analysis of our own project's data and that of other research currently being conducted will be necessary before these hypotheses can be accepted, revised and refined, or rejected.

Italy had one of the most tumultuous labor-capital relationships in all of Europe during the 1970s. After a long postwar period of labor isolation followed by fitful and only limitedly successful attempts by the labor movement to achieve more systematic recognition, the 1970s were marked by a prominent and often highly conflictual role for the trade-union movement in the Italian political economy.[1] At the same time, and not coincidentally, the Italian postwar political equilibrium based on the permanent exclusion of the Italian Communist Party from possible national governmental participation has broken down. The "Communist question" has moved to the center of the political agenda, and a variety of experiments based on the cooperation of the PCI in the formation of national governments have taken place. Our discussion begins with two observations about developments in this decade of change.

There has been a rather clear and widely agreed-upon evolution of trade-union policy, in which new demands focused on new arenas have been added to the existing ones, generally taking prominence over them. The unions

This essay was published in Italian in *Il Mulino* 28 (November-December 1979). My thanks to Peter Hall, who gave me extensive and extremely useful comments on early drafts of portions of this paper, and to Marino Regini, who, during a six-month stay at the Center for European Studies, provided a wealth of stimulation and ideas. Neither, of course, bears any responsibility for what I have written.

have moved from (1) demands focused on the work place and concerned primarily with wages, hours, the organization of work, work-place institutions of union representation and the power of these institutions to intervene or control on behalf of workers on a number of issues having to do with the conditions of work; to (2) demands focused on the state and concerned with reforms of the system of welfare and social security and with the generalization of union rights; and (3) demands focused on the state and concerned with the formation of what the unions have sometimes called a "new economic policy" involving structural reforms of the economy (reorganization of economic sectors, for example), planning, the direction and control of investment, and the establishment of policies to assure a reduction of regional inequalities and the growth of employment.[2]

The second observation is that there has been a parallelism between this evolution of trade-union policy (especially of the Communist-dominated CGIL) and the policy evolution of the PCI.[3] This parallelism has been most evident, though by no means perfect, with respect to the contents and arenas of policy. With regard to the modes by which policy goals were to be pursued, differences have been more defined. This is a point to which I shall return later.

These two observations raise a question that, while growing out of the Italian experience, seems to involve issues of more general interest. This basic question is, of course, how this parallelism is to be explained. Three hypotheses can be suggested:

1. The parallelism is accidental. The union and party policy evolutions are expressions of autonomous processes of policy formation and of different logics of action. They do not share causes, nor do they represent responses to shared institutional concerns. Aside from the fact that such an explanatory hypothesis wholly lacks parsimony, it does not appear credible in light of the history of relationships between the trade-union movement, and especially the CGIL, and the PCI. I will not seek to explore it further.

2. The union movement has been acting as the "transmission belt" or, more subtly, as a dependent of the party. In this case, the CGIL (as the traditionally Communist-led and most powerful union) would either be taking commands from or simply following, out of necessity, the lead of the PCI and would then, through its superior strength, be imposing these party-generated policy directives on the other unions. On the face of it, this hypothesis has some credibility. The PCI has tended to formulate and encourage certain policies prior to the formulation and advancement of these policies by the unions, and the CGIL has generally taken the lead in the union movement in pressing for the evolution of the policy described. Nonetheless, there are reasons to question the hypothesis: the unions and the PCI have differed significantly on various points of policy; there have been notable, public polemics between even the CGIL and the PCI; the strength that the CISL (the union formerly closely linked to the Christian Democratic Party) has developed in recent years makes the idea of the CGIL's imposing policies on the CISL implausible; and, more generally, the union movement has in the last decade grown too strong and developed

too much internal cohesion to have to accept party commands for policies contrary to or of low priority for the unions' institutional interests or union developments.[4]

3. This then suggests a third hypothesis, the one that I shall expore in the coming pages: the party and the union share a number of institutional interests that lead them to respond to pressures and constraints in the economic, social, and political environment in which they operate in similar ways. In other words, while the unions and party are largely autonomous of one another (in the sense that neither can command or is directly answerable to the other), they share interests that promote the parallelism of policy developments observed in response to changing conditions in their shared environment.[5]

I will not dwell here on the PCI's policy evolution or the reasons for it. I have recently written on this subject, and it will be touched on in the discussion that follows.[6] Instead, what I will undertake is an initial exploration of an hypothesized logic of union behavior that can explain, without the variable of direct party control, the parallels between the policy evolution of the Italian unions and the PCI. I also hope to suggest that this logic may be of more general applicability in seeking to explain union behavior in the advanced capitalist democracies with respect to the extent to which they seek to pursue their institutional interests in the state and, sometimes, through corporatist arrangements.

I begin with a premise: that "the union is an actor in its own right, not only developing its own specific interest, but being capable of carrying out a strategy, that is a succession of inter-temporal decisions in which present action is evaluated in terms of its consequences for future goals."[7] The principal implications of this premise are, first, that the action of the union reflects something more than the vector or demands of its members, and second, that the union does not always and necessarily work to maximize short-term gains but may instead "underexploit" short-term market power in order to pursue longer-term goals. A third implicit aspect of this definition is that, depending on a variety of conditions, the union will be able to engage in such underexploitation without suffering immediate and catastrophic losses of consent. The importance of this definition of the union will emerge as I proceed.[8]

As indicated, the evolution of Italian trade-union policy in the last decade has been marked by an increasing "politicization" of the goals being pursued, in the sense that those goals have increasingly been dependent on actions of the state. Whether in the form of generalization and legal formalization of union rights, or social welfare reforms or investment control and planning, the unions have sought to get the state to intervene to pursue policies that they desired. Pizzorno has pointed out that when unions turn to the state, they engage in an explicit or implicit exchange relationship in which they offer consent in exchange for state policies.[9] The question which is posed is, Under what conditions is the union more or less likely to look to action within the state for the advancement of its interests?

Figure 5.1   Hypothesis of Relationship between Union Resort to
State Action and Union Capacity to Disrupt Economy

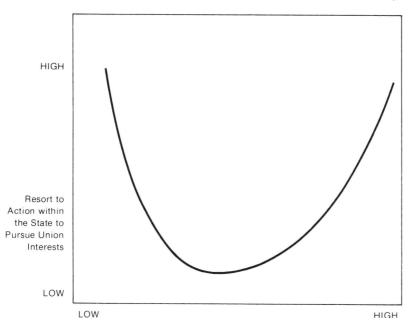

HIGH

Resort to
Action within
the State to
Pursue Union
Interests

LOW

LOW   HIGH

Union Capacity to Disrupt General Economic Performance through Market
Action

As a first approximation, appropriate to Italian circumstances and
possibly of more general utility, I would propose the hypothesis presented
in Figure 5.1 to describe the general relationship between the indicated
variables in industrial capitalist societies of relatively similar levels of
economic developments. The general hypothesis is that the most important
variable in explaining when the union will place more or less emphasis on
state action in the pursuit of its interests is the ability of the union to disrupt
the general economy through wage and hours gains won through market
action. More specifically, I argue that this relationship takes the general
form of a U curve in which the resort to state action becomes more probable
when union disruptive capacity is low or high, less probable when it is
moderate.

Why this may be the case will be examined in a moment. Before doing
so, however, I need briefly to make some specifications about the character
of the relationship being proposed in Figure 5.1. First, with respect to the
vertical axis:

The fact that the union looks to state action tells us nothing about the
goals that the unions hope to advance through such action. These goals can
of course vary widely. At least five categories can be identified:

1. institutional rights — laws, administrative interventions, and the like affecting the ability of the union to organize and to mobilize its support;

2. regulations affecting wages, hours, etc. (such regulations, like those affecting institutional rights, may sometimes be generalizing conditions already won in direct bargaining with employers in some sectors);

3. macroeconomic policy — decisions affecting the specific content of macroeconomic management policies by the state;

4. social security reforms — that whole range of laws and regulations characteristic of the modern state through which the state transfers resources from some social groups to others;

5. structural reforms of the economy — policies explicitly designed to restructure the economy and/or the way the basic decisions affecting the structure of the economy are made (these include things like planning, forms of control on private investment, policies to transfer the assets of private firms to the state or the workers, and *autogestion*).

The fact that the union looks to state action in order to pursue its interests also tells us nothing about the structures through which those interests are pursued. A number of authors have proposed the existence of an analytical continuum between pluralism and liberal or societal corporatism along which such structures might be ranged.[10] Here Regini's dimensions for examining the degree of corporatism are very useful. They lead us to pose the following distinctions:

1. To what extent does the union pursue its goals within the state autonomously, through direct pressure-group politics, rather than through relationships of cooperation with opposing interests and representatives of the state?

2. To what extent are the relationships between the unions and both opposing interests (in particular, representatives of capital) and the state institutionalized rather than being left to the initiative, on a case-by-case basis, of the various parties? (It should be noted that institutionalization usually grants some level of formal parity to labor and capital.)

3. To what extent does the union pursue its interests within the state through bargaining within the executive organs of government, or the bureaucracy of specially constituted boards and commissions, thereby bypassing the quintessential pluralist institutions of Parliament and the political parties and party system rather than accepting the mediation of these institutions?[11]

Introduction of these distinctions with respect to the structures through which the union pursues its interests within the state underlines the point that the recourse to the state by the union does not necessarily imply the development of corporatist structures or even movement in that direction. It is, in fact, of critical importance to explain why and under what conditions liberal corporatism does emerge. This will be discussed below.

Turning now to some specifications with regard to the horizontal axis of Figure 5.1, note that this axis refers to the ability of union wage and hours gains significantly to disrupt the general functioning of the economy — that is, to the "disruptive potential" of the unions. What variables need to be considered in examining the extent to which this ability is present?[12] Five seem of particular importance:

1. The militance of the work force. The tightness of the general labor market or of particularly important (in terms of the functioning of the economy) segments of the labor market would seem the most critical factor affecting militance. Obviously, a wide range of other factors also affect militance and may come into play in any particular instance. Pizzorno and his colleagues have highlighted a particularly interesting one: the formation of new collective identities within the work force.[13]

2. The degree of union penetration or density in the work force, particularly of the major industrial sectors. This variable is of importance because it will have a major impact on the ability of capital to avoid the costs of union action by moving production to nonunionized plants;

3. The ability of capital to use work-place-level responses (including reorganizations of work, technological innovations, layoffs, and speedups) rapidly to reabsorb or reduce the impacts of wage push and other union gains. It is worth noting that this ability will affect as well the efficacy of macroeconomic management techniques (such as recession) as means of restoring pre-wage-push equilibria.

4. The degree of dependence of the national economy on exports from the sectors impacted by union-won wage gains and the extent to which exports from those sectors are dependent on labor cost advantages. Especially in so-called transformation economies, which are heavily dependent on exports from industrial sectors to pay for raw material and energy imports in which export advantages may accrue from relatively low wage structures, the impacts of significant wage gains by unions may be very great.

5. The state of the international economy. Of particular importance in this regard would appear to be the state of international demand for the exports of the impacted sectors (where demand is high and relatively inelastic, disruptions are likely to be lower) and the rate of international inflation and thus the degree to which inflation in the costs of products in the national economy due to wage push are without consequence for the relative costs of those products in the international economy. Also of importance will be the degree to which new, low-cost competitors are entering the international market for goods in sectors impacted by union action.

The specifications so far introduced refer to the relationship hypothesized in Figure 5.1, allowing one to predict the degree to which union movements in different countries are likely to resort to political action at similar stages in their economic development. It is also evident, however, that changes in the role of the state and the structure of the national and international economy over time, in the course of the development of an advanced industrial capitalist political economy, are likely to affect the parameters of the general relationship. Put most boldly, political economic development is likely to lift the bottom of the hypothesized curve, increasing the extent to which unions can be expected to resort to the state no matter what the conjunctural state of the factors listed above. This would seem the case for the following reasons:

1. the growing role of the state in macroeconomic management, which has made anything approximating unalloyed pursuit of a market strategy unsuitable;

2. the growing role of the state in the provision of benefits enjoyed by union members and which these members expect the union to defend, which has made action in the state sphere necessary;

3. the growing role of the state in the establishment of at least some of the rules governing the regulation of industrial conflict and the industrial relations system more generally.

The preceding refer to the changing role of the state. Changes in the character of the domestic and international economy accompanying the development of an advanced industrial economy and the system of such economies also tend to raise the bottom of the curve:

4. the increasing scale, rigidity, and interdependence of sectors within the national economy and thus the growing vulnerability of individual sectors and of the economy more generally to significant wage push in any single or several sectors;

5. the growing interdependence of the economies of the advanced industrial capitalist democracies.

In addition to the five secular changes just listed, there would also appear to be some changes in the 1970s that have even further tended to raise the bottom of the curve, increasing the continual need for unions to resort in part to action within the state. These changes may be secular or they may be a function of a peculiar interaction of factors in the past decade. Nonetheless, they are of importance for our considerations:

6. a seemingly growing ability of unions to develop institutional mechanisms protecting their constituents from the effects of traditional mechanisms of adjustment to cost push and inflation (recessionary policies, layoffs, speedups, and the like);

7. the rise of developing industrial capitalist economies producing goods at considerably lower cost (especially labor cost) competing with the production of sectors of the advanced industrial capitalist economies and thus further aggravating the competitiveness of those sectors in the international market.

Why, having introduced these specifications with regard to the two variables in Figure 5.1, does the hypothesized relationship between them seem a reasonable one? And how does it help us to explain the problem indicated at the outset of this paper?

Let us start with the not unreasonable assumption that, in the best of all (not necessarily possible) worlds, unions would prefer to confine the pursuit of their interests to action within the market without taking any recourse to the state. This would seem the case because action within the market allows for a more direct and unmediated pursuit of institutional interest. Recourse to action within the state—that is, to the use of political means—will necessarily involve the union in that whole set of requirements and constraints associated with democratic politics. In particular, the union will have to pay attention to the impact of its actions on the electoral game and it will also have to search for social and political allies, with all the compromises of interest that necessarily accompany such alliances. Action within the state and through political means necessarily will infringe on the autonomy of the union to pursue its interests, and it is therefore likely to be avoided when possible. Why then does the union turn to action within the state to pursue its interests?

It is first of all clear why at least some level of recourse to action within the state has become increasingly necessary with the development of the advanced industrial capitalist democracies: the interests of the unions, both in terms of their own structures and rights and in terms of the interests of their constituents, have become increasingly intertwined with state policies. Although the extent of governmental intervention in these various areas may differ (less of social welfare is provided through the state in Japan than in most of the other countries, for instance, and the Italian state has been less involved in regulating industrial relations and conflict), there has been a tendency common to all these systems for state intervention to increase. Thus, the unions in these systems cannot pursue their interests as strategic actors without being concerned with the policy outputs of the state and without therefore either directly or indirectly seeking to influence those outputs. This has necessarily made them at least to some extent *political* actors, playing the political game. Whether, and to what extent, they do so directly or instead consign most of the concern for these political matters to mediating structures like political parties will vary from system to system. Nonetheless, even when they rely primarily on mediating structures, they must take an interest in the conditions promoting the strength (political strength) of those structures. Whatever the degree of reliance on direct or indirect means of protecting these interests, to this limited extent the logic of action of unions and of political parties linked to unions begins to overlap.

This point, however, only explains why, to a limited degree, unions have had to take increasing recourse to action within the state and thus adopt some of the logic of action of the political actor. It does not explain the variations in the relationship between power to disrupt economically and action within the state, as illustrated in Figure 5.1.

Why can unions be expected to resort to action in the state as they become weaker? The answer is fairly clear. Unable to advance their interests in the market, unions try to do so through state action. They hope thereby to secure benefits for themselves as institutions (such as regulations affecting rights of unionization or collective bargaining) and for their constituents (such as minimum wage and/or maximum hour legislation and social welfare programs). In doing so, of course, they rely on a quintessentially political resource in exchange for state policies: their role as mediating structures for the vote and, more generally, of consent. It is interesting to note that when the political resources of number (the vote) and of consent are unlikely to elicit responses from the political authorities, the unions tend to try to maintain and build their internal strength and cohesion through another political means, ideology. In this there is a resemblance between unions in this situation and parties that find themselves relatively permanently excluded from the exercise of political power. Italy in the

1950s would appear to provide a good example of this situation. The unions, especially the CGIL, were both weak and unable to secure benefits from the state, in part because the PCI and the Socialist Party were also excluded. The CGIL was, in this situation, very ideological and closely linked to the PCI. This was the period of the "transmission belt." As the decade came to a close, and especially in the 1960s, however, the labor market strength and disruptive capacity of the unions increased. Accompanying this change (a move to the right on the horizontal axis in Diagram 1), there was also a decline in the ideological character of union appeals, greater cooperation between the confederations in labor market action, and more intense use of militancy in the labor market to win gains for the workers (a downward move on the vertical axis).[14]

The preceding relationship is relatively straightforward. The more interesting question is, Why does the resort to action within the state and through politics become more probable as the unions' ability to disrupt the general economy becomes greater? I would offer the following arguments in support of the hypothesis:

When unions make significant wage gains in a context characterized by the conditions specified above — strong worker militance, high degree of union density, sharp constraints on management work-place adjustment mechanisms, high dependence of the national economy on exports advantaged by low wages, an international economy characterized by depressed demand rates of inflation lower than those resulting from the wage gains and by the rise of new, low-cost competitors — a series of external diseconomies can be expected to result that, if their effects are to be managed and controlled in order to do least damage to the interests of the unions, must be dealt with through the state.[15]

The most general of these diseconomies is the endangerment of the prospects for economic growth: the rise in wages, coming in a situation in which these costs cannot easily be avoided by the employer, will create a profits squeeze and thus the potential for a fall in investment and eventually in employment. Thus, in the presence of the conditions specified, the wage gains attained are likely to endanger two other goals of particular importance to the unions and their constituents: growth and employment expansion.[16] Clearly, here is a situation in which the union, as strategic actor, could be expected to act. I will return in a moment to why this action could be expected to be directed toward the state. Before doing so, however, other diseconomies should be noted.

The situation resulting from a wage push in the context described is likely, because of its disruptive effects on the economy at large (stagflation being perhaps the most important in recent years), to create threats both to the system of social welfare and to some of the ways the state has helped union organization. These threats can arise from at least three different kinds of processes. First, the social security system, with its onerous burden for the state budget and, particularly in Italy, for firms, may become a target for those hoping to create new economic margins for investment either through reductions in individual tax burdens or through reduction of the competition between the state and the private sector for capital held in the banking system. Second, the social alliances or coalition supporting the social security system and/or state guarantees of union rights may be upset as the disruptive effects of the new economic situation undermine the equilibria which were part and parcel of these coalitions, and resentments develop between different segments of the previous coalition. Third, the effects already noted may upset the political alliances of the unions by threatening the electoral bases and strength of the parties to which the unions are most clearly linked and, possibly, by creating significant tensions between the unions and their political party allies.

In light of these considerations, it is clear that resort to a primarily market strategy in the kinds of conditions described does not work to the unions' benefit: wage gains not only appear to be "functionless"[17] as they are eaten up by inflation, but they also endanger a series of other interests of the union. Furthermore, once the process described has been set in motion by significant wage gains, the potentially deleterious political effects push the union to accentuate its already existent interest in the political in an effort to ward off attacks on existing state policies that are to its benefit.

The simplest union policy, and one that would not represent a major increase in the union's propensity to resort to the state, would be wage restraint.[18] In theory it should resolve the growth problem as well as ease the tensions and strains, and this without any significant increase in state action. If, as is likely, the union would be unable to sell its constituents on the idea that the market, *by itself*, would restore the old equilibria and provide a surge to growth sufficient to make wage restraint palatable, some state action might be required to oversee the process and provide certain guarantees, and the union could be expected to act within the state to seek to assure the best formulation and implementation of such action. Pizzorno and Regalia and associates have also pointed out that bargaining with the state over state policy is one way that union leadership can recentralize power in the union after a wave of decentralized militance.[19] Such recentralization also restores a greater capacity for strategic behavior. Nonetheless, the overall increase in the level of state, as contrasted to market, action would not look like that suggested in my hypothesis.

However, as Pizzorno, Lehmbruch, and others have argued theoretically, and as most of the empirical evidence seems to confirm, a policy of wage restraint in exchange for growth prospects, even when guaranteed by the state, is not a viable strategy for the union to pursue over an extended period of time.[20] I will not dwell on the reasons for this here. It can simply be said that there appears to be a tendency for the union to seek repeatedly to enlarge the scope of the issues to be bargained over in exchange for "good" wage behavior and that this enlarged scope of issues increasingly requires the production of new political quid pro quo actions.[21] The process seems in some ways analogous to a "ratchet" in which stability is acquired at any particular level of exchange for a period of time but then either the stabilization itself (reducing the willingness of workers to accept the union's underexploitation of their market power) or an explicit or implicit attempt by the union to up the stakes through the threat of renewed wage militance leads to the search for a new bargain incorporating new issues.[22]

Whatever the process, this enlarging scope means that in a situation in which the basic economic disruptive capacity of the union remains high, there will be a tendency for the union to pursue more and more of its interests within the state sphere.

At this point, I can return to the initial question of whether there is a logic of union action that might explain the parallelism of union and party policy observed in Italy. In advanced industrial capitalist democracies, unions already share some political interests with the political parties that most closely seek to represent the unions and the union constituencies. When union market action can significantly disrupt the entire economic process, the overlap of union and party interests is dramatically increased, as the union finds itself in need of pursuing more and more of its interests within the state and thus sharing more and more the logic of action and the strategic concerns of the party. Of course, the extent of overlap can be expected to vary significantly from case to case. Among other things, the degree to which the union and party see the pursuit of their interests as dependent on their mutual strength will have an important effect. So too will the degree to which the union leadership is able to control the wage militance of the rank and file. Thus, to cite but one example, the PCI and the CGIL (and, to a lesser extent, the other Italian union confederations) seem more aware of their dependence on their mutual strength, and the Italian unions appear to have been more able increasingly to exert central control, than has been true in Britain.[23] These two cases are, of course, particularly interesting because the underlying ability of the unions to disrupt overall economic performance through wage gains appears as similar as in any two European countries. Despite variations from system to system, however, the general relationship hypothesized seems plausible.

If this is the case, it also provides us with an explanation for our Italian observations. Changes in Italian conditions in the 1970s sharply increased the disruptive capacity of unions (a rightward move on the horizontal axis in Figure 5.1). Militance increased, work-place prerogatives of capital were significantly reduced, and Italy's ability to maintain its international economic position while absorbing the major wage gains of 1969 was sharply constrained. The only factor not fitting the pattern was the marked growth of the "hidden economy" and of the use of "black labor,"—that is, the development economic activity not covered by the union even as the level of unionization of the official work force grew.[24] Nonetheless, in this general situation one would expect the unions, because of the pursuit of their own interests, to seek increasingly to focus their action on the state and within state institutions while becoming less willing to rely primarily on obtaining real wage gains (an upward move on the vertical axis in Figure 5.1). The policy evolution described at the outset of this essay fits this expectation. This increasing focus of action within the state, however, also could be expected to lead to the development of the kinds of mutuality of interests and of logic of action between the unions and the party most closely linked to the union that would promote parallelism of union and party policy without any notion of a "transmission belt."

None of the processes so far described need of necessity lead to the development of a liberal corporatist system or even to the appearance of features of such a system. There is nothing about the tendency for unions increasingly to have recourse to action within the state that necessarily would lead them to seek cooperative, institutionalized relationships with the organizations of capital mediated by the state in order to regulate distributional conflict, thereby bypassing the traditional institutions of pluralist democracy. The unions could well choose to stick to pluralist modes of interest intermediation, especially bilateral relationships with state institutions, in hopes of thereby maximizing their political gains at the expense of capital. As already noted, the "ratchet effects" appear to accompany the appearance of union bargains with the state under the conditions described. As these effects expand the scope of the issues covered in these implicit or explicit bargains, it appears that the trade-offs increasingly become ones of union restraint in the market in exchange for increases in union power with respect to the making of state policy and eventually with respect to matters affecting the prerogatives of capital. In the Italian case, the shift to economic structural reforms is emblematic of such a development for other systems.

Thus, there seem to be good reasons that unions, if it were possible, would seek to avoid corporatist arrangements that tend to grant something approximating formal parity status, both economic and political, to the associations of labor and capital. In the absence of constraints, labor could try to push its functional power and the political power derived from it (as well as from the vote) to the limits through the pluralist institutions plus special bilateral arrangements, perhaps even setting as its goal a gradual socialist transformation of the political economy.

The argument that growing recourse to the state by the unions can take pan-syndicalist rather than liberal corporatist forms is borne out by the Italian experience in the early 1970s. At that time, the unions gave increasing emphasis to the reformist component of their strategy (seeking state reforms in housing and health policy). They sought to promote reforms through the use of mass mobilization and the threat of it in order to get the most out of direct bilateral bargaining in which the union leadership engaged with the government, and they refused to participate in trilateral arrangements that would have included industry representatives.[25] The Italian Communist Party was strongly and outspokenly opposed to the unions' participation in direct bargaining with the government, although it favored policy goals similar to those of the unions. Here was a perfect example of union rejection of proposed liberal corporatist arrangements in favor of modes of pressing their interests that would not require cooperation with the associations of capital; and of party opposition to procedures that would bypass the deliberative and real decisional powers of Parliament and depriving the PCI of a possible mediating role.

The unions' effort, however, proved a failure; they were unable to win from the state the kinds of policy outcomes that they desired. The Christian Democractic Party–dominated government was unable or unwilling to carry its own Parliamentary constituency for the policies (already rather weak in the unions' eyes) that had been agreed to with the unions. A watered-down housing reform did finally pass, but only because the PCI abstained. Thus, pan-syndicalist approaches were judged ineffective. Furthermore, Regini has shown that there was some movement toward the establishment of liberal corporatist arrangements in this decade, but that this movement was halting and limited. Some features, such as increasing cooperation between the associations of labor and capital and the unions' increased participation in state organs implementing state policy have appeared, but along the other dimensions of liberal corporatism movement has been less evident. The PCI, without to my knowledge explicitly criticizing these developments, has made clear its hostility to liberal corporatism more generally.

These observations on the Italian experience once again raise several interesting questions of possibly more general interest. What are the factors that constrain unions' temptation (when their capacity to disrupt the economy is high) to stick to pluralist modes and/or to follow a pan-syndicalist strategy in pursuit of their interests and, in contrast, to move in a liberal corporatist direction? What are the factors that make full participation of unions in liberal corporatism difficult, which might lead them to take a very restrained and cautious approach to such arrangements? Finally, what is the particular role of the political parties of labor, those most closely tied to the union movement, in promoting or discouraging the full development of liberal corporatism?

What are the constraints on unions' temptation to stick with pluralism or to pursue a pan-syndicalist strategy and which, instead, push toward liberal corporatism?

The most important would seem to be the basic power of capital to resist. There is here an important distinction to make between labor and capital. In the advanced industrial capitalist democracies labor has the ability to undertake conditional withdrawals (the strike) from its normal economic functions. The same holds true for capital. It too can conditionally withdraw, not so much by the old means of the lockout, but through self-restraint on investment. For labor, and even for capital although in a longer time frame and with important differences from sector to sector, these modes of action are of limited utility, for even with the cushions available to both sides against the short-run damages to their own interests imposed by utilization of these modes of action, the costs come to outstrip the benefits. While such conditional mechanisms largely exhaust the repertoire of labor, however, this is not the case for capital. It also has another, less conditional and conditioned option — that of exit from the economy or from the sector.[26]

The importance of the potential national and international mobility of capital is great and seems to me to have been underestimated in the literature on the development of corporatist tendencies in the advanced industrial capitalist societies. The ability to exit, even if sometimes at considerable cost, gives capital very large and wide-ranging leverage and therefore represents a major constraint on unions and on their strategic behavior. The leverage is great because it means that capital can, autonomously, deliver enormous blows to the growth prospects of the economy. Its scope is very large because it means that capital can invoke the entire range of economic, social, and political conditions that affect its propensity to remain in (and invest) or to exit from the national economy in seeking to maintain its prerogatives and power. Under these conditions, the interests of unions as strategic actors concerned with the longer-term prospects of the economy lead them to seek to provide to capital sufficient incentives (or perhaps to avoid creating sufficient disincentives) to remain rather than to exit. The threshold at which significant amounts of capital will exit in any system will, of course, vary over time and from country to country, and thus the constraint that capital exit represents on union action will also vary. Nonetheless, at some point exit will almost always be a real possibility for significant amounts of capital, and the unions will have to seek to prevent it with their function of offering greater stability, regularity, and predictability to a situation in which major economic disruption is always possible. This may be effective, while at the same time offering to the unions means for pursuing some of their own interests. In this sense, liberal corporatism appears to be a kind of institutional minimax solution for labor (and for capital and the state).[27]

The constraints pushing labor toward liberal corporatist modes, however, are not solely related to those derived from the direct economic power and choices of capital. They are more directly political as well. We have already noted that, under conditions in which labor's ability significantly to disrupt the economy is high, and especially after a round of such disruption has occurred, there are important reasons for labor to direct its attention toward the state: the economic disruption threatens to undermine the coalitions (social and political) that support a series of state policies in which the union has an interest.

The structural power of capital accentuates these reasons and creates incentives for the union to find ways to come to agreements with capital about how these state policies should be managed. Here again, the "ratchet effect" comes into play for, as noted, it leads to an expansion of the issues covered by the bargains into which labor enters in exchange for market restraint. This expanding scope of issues is likely to include many of the state policies that are of direct interest to the union but that may become the focus of capital's attempts to build counter-coalitions and to restore its economic margins. Pluralist or purely bilateral pursuit by labor of its interests is threatened by failure as capital's resistance increases. After all, capital too can play the pluralist game and may be able, under the conditions of great economic uncertainty, to build winning coalitions. This will not, of course, solve the problem, for if the union fails to gain the quid pro quo from the state in exchange for its market restraint, it is likely either to promote a new round of wage pressure or simply to lose control of its rank and file. In either case, this would create the potential for further aggravation of an economic situation unfavorable to the union's interests. Thus, there is a strong political incentive for unions to seek arrangements with capital that allow for a mutual adjustment of interest — that is, for liberal corporatist arrangements that can elicit the cooperation of the state.

It is worth noting that we are here in the presence of a delicate, high-stakes game of "chicken" being played out between the associations of capital and labor. Both sides must maintain the image (and the reality) of their general ability to control those actors whose cooperation is essential to any bargains reached between them. At the same time, however, if either side seems no longer capable of undertaking those actions (wage push and strike, investment restraint and exit) which represent the structural incentive to bargain in the first place, then there will be no reason for the other side to enter into those liberal corporatist arrangements. This situation, therefore, is one in which neither side can appear either too compliant or out of control. It is the continual possibility of controlled exit from the liberal corporatist arrangements that makes those arrangements functional to both sides.

There is a third constraint on the union's ability to pursue a purely pluralist or bilateral mode of mediation of its interests within the state: the threat that such a course of action will undermine the legitimacy of the political system as a whole. This constraint will, of course, vary widely from country to country: the legitimacy of the democratic institutions is far greater in some countries than in others. Nonetheless, to a greater or lesser extent in various systems, the severe economic disruptions that the unions' market action can inflict may give rise to calls, supported by potentially large coalitions, to alter the basic democratic rules.[28] Such alterations, which would undoubtedly come at labor's expense, threaten an absolutely fundamental interest of the unions. Thus, they are once again constrained to seek to assure that capital, and the major political parties representing its interests, not become a pole for the coagulation of such delegitimation forces. This then provides another incentive for the union to enter into liberal corporatist arrangements, which offer at least the hope of avoiding such an outcome by drawing capital's associations into arrangements permitting a mutual adjustment of interests.[29]

Having indicated the reasons that the union may be drawn toward liberal corporatist modes of mediation of those interests that it pursues through the state, it would be useful now to indicate the instabilities of liberal corporatist arrangements — the reasons they may have a tendency to break down. Because this subject has been extensively covered in the burgeoning literature on liberal corporatism, I will simply list some of them with citations where appropriate. Liberal corporatist arrangements seem subject to breakdown and decay for some combination of the following reasons:

1. a weakening of the original conditions that made it difficult for the traditional response mechanisms of the economy to wage push to operate;

2. loss of control of the union rank and file by the leadership[30] or the inability of the organizations of capital to achieve discipline from employers and/or to prevent employers' exit from the sector or the economy;

3. the rise of leadership within either the union or the associations of capital, which challenges the appropriateness of the liberal corporatist ar-

rangements and mobilizes the support of the rank and file;[31]

4. an employment of the ratchet (perhaps in order to maintain control of the rank and file or to ward off competitive leadership) beyond the tolerance of capital's associations;

5. a decision by the association of capital to force a confrontation with the unions, risking the costs of major economic disruption in order to create a more favorable medium and long-term economic and especially political climate;[32]

6. the electoral and/or organizational mobilization of groups on the margins or left out of the liberal corporatist bargains, which often tend to pay the costs of such bargains.[33]

It does seem, in fact, that liberal corporatist arrangements often redistribute costs away from organized labor and capital and onto social forces that are not organized and that have great difficulty in becoming organized. A great deal of the battle for social and political alliances that accompanies the processes that we have described revolves around these forces, and whether they will support the state policies of interest to labor or perhaps even the basic legitimacy of the political institutions. It is, in part, to try to maintain or develop alliances with these forces that the union must turn to action in the state (seeking to assure policies that can also win the consent of some of these forces or at least prevent their counter-mobilization). Further, the desire to provide capital with incentives that will keep it from trying to win the allegiance of these forces around policies detrimental to the union's interests may be a motivation for the union's entry into liberal corporatist arrangements. It is also clear, however, that precisely these arrangements have the possibility of promoting counter-mobilization by these forces.

These, then, seem to be some of the primary reasons that, despite the incentives toward the development of liberal corporatist arrangement that I have noted, such arrangements may prove decidedly unstable. A far more extensive discussion of these sources of breakdown and decay is, of course, necessary. Instead of undertaking it here, however, I want briefly to address two other issues.

I noted above that, alongside the failed pan-syndicalist efforts in the 1970s, the Italian unions have come to participate, albeit in a very partial manner, in some liberal corporatist arrangements. On the basis of this analysis of the factors discouraging pluralist or pan-syndicalist modes of action and encouraging liberal corporatist ones, this is not surprising. There were signs of a propensity to capital exit; the unions became increasingly aware of the possibility of the development of social and political coalitions that might undermine some of their interests with regard to state policy and of the need to take a direct hand in the reform and implementation of diverse aspects of the system of social security; and the unions were acutely aware, in light of the risk in terrorism both on the right and on the left and of the spread of signs of severe social disorder in the South, that the legitimacy of the democratic regime might be tenuous.[34] The fact that the unions' primary political party representative was the PCI only made some of these matters worse. The long-term exclusion of the Communists from government meant that the bureaucracy was wholly colonized by bureaucrats loyal to the Christian Democratic Party and disinclined to implement the kinds of social security reforms that the unions preferred. The legitimacy problems of the PCI only augmented those already created by the unstable economic situation as the PCI becomes a more likely government participant.

All of these factors push toward the expectation of the development of full liberal corporatist arrangements. Yet, as Regini demonstrates, this has not occurred, except in a very limited manner.[35] Why, in the specific Italian circumstance, should this be the case?

There seems to be a number of reasons, many of them related to the model which I have laid out. Among other things:

1. Capital has, in fact, over time been able to develop mechanisms to avoid some of the costs of wage push (the nonunionized sector, the use of "black labor," etc.) These phenomena were already present prior to the 1970s but seem to have spread significantly in recent years.[36] Their spread reduces the incentives of both the unions and the associations of capital to enter into liberal corporatist arrangements and, in fact, may eventually lead to a sufficient decline in the disruptive capacity of market action by the unions to lead them once again to resort to a militant market strategy.

2. The problem of marginal groups has been particularly acute in Italy due especially to the historical inequalities of development between North and South. Furthermore, even large sectors of those employed in nonmarginal labor owe their jobs to the irrationalities and clientelism that have been so much a part of postwar development.[37] If Regini is correct that very high labor stability is one likely outcome of liberal corporatist arrangements, then this represents a brake on the development of such arrangements.[38]

Other reasons for the slow and fitful development of liberal corporatist modes of interest intermediation in Italy could be cited. Regini has pointed to a number of them.[39] In the space remaining, however, I want to point to one in particular, the role of the political party.[40]

What should be the stance of the political parties of the working class, those which see in the union movement their prime referent and principal source of electoral and structural support to the development of liberal corporatist arrangements? A general rule can be formulated, but it must be specified, particularly in terms of the variable of the party's probability of governance.

As a general rule, parties should be skeptical about the appropriateness of liberal corporatist arrangements because such arrangements shift power away from the parties and the party and parliamentary system. It is, in fact, the essence of the notion of liberal corporatism that it is based on forms of direct adjustment of functional interests within the state between the associations of labor and capital, bypassing the parties. Yet we know that some parties, the Swedish Social Democratic Party for instance, have promoted liberal corporatism, while others, including the PCI, have opposed it.

Why is this so? It seems to me that the answer, in its first approximation, can best be examined by looking at limiting cases: parties that have expectations of remaining in government for a long time and parties that, at least in electoral terms, do not seem to have prospects of governing in the near future.

For a labor party of long-term governance, the advantages of liberal corporatist arrangements are fairly obvious (on the Swedish case see Korpi and Martin).[41] First, they provide a means for major economic disruptions that might seriously erode their winning coalition. Second, because these parties are in control of the state, they can seek to use state policy to assure that the prospective losers of the corporatist arrangements are taken care of to the degree necessary to maintain their support or at least allegiance to their regime. In general, then, such arrangements appear to be for such parties an effective mechanism for the mobilization of consent. Furthermore, in regimes governed for lengthy periods by labor parties, even the danger of a bypass of the party and parliamentary system seems less great. This is due to the fact that the party becomes itself intertwined with the state. It is not just an organ of mediation between society and the government and bureaucracy but is itself implanted in these. Thus, since liberal corporatist arrangements are linked to the executive and administrative organs, the party's functions would seem in no way damaged and may even be augmented. This seems to have been the case in Sweden.

The incentives for the unions to accept liberal corporatist arrangements when there is long-term labor party governance also seem clear. The unions, can, in fact, count on the basic sensitivity of the state and its policies to their interests.[42] Furthermore, Korpi has argued that long-term labor governance tends to inhibit the militance of capital.[43] Third, since the benefits are high and, over time, fairly evident, the rank and file are likely to be more willing to sacrifice the immediate costs in wage terms that such arrangements may imply. Finally, the level of benefits that accrue in terms of the unions' interests will make less desirable a return to a more militant market strategy with its potential costs for the electoral and social coalition that assures the long-term governance of the labor party.

All this should not suggest that there will not be tensions between the unions and the parties, that their interests will not conflict. The greater support from the union rank and file does not mean that the "ratchet" may not come into play, particularly if there is no redistribution between the shares of national income going to labor and capital over long periods of time. In addition, situations may arise in which the economic condition requires economic restraint by unionized labor (to restore the conditions for investment), which necessitates political trade-offs that go beyond the party's sense of its own interests. Such a situation is particularly likely in cases, such as those suggested by Schmitter,[44] in which the organizational density of the society is very high, making the political risks of redistributions of costs (be they economic or in terms of power) likewise very high. It may indeed be the case that one output of long-term governance by a labor party is such organizational density.

For a labor party of long-term opposition, liberal corporatist arrangements would seem much less desirable. The economic and political motivation to establish such arrangements will be greatest, as has been shown, when the disruptive capacity for the union's market militance is greatest. This is also when, however, the ability of the labor party to act as the critical mechanism of mediation between the unions, on the one hand, and the state, other parties and the associations of capital, on the other hand, is also greatest. And this mediational capacity can be a major means by which the labor party can seek to break out of its oppositional status both by using its "reasonableness" and the possibility that it can better "control" the unions to build electoral support and by making arguments for the need to include it in the national government even in the absence of changes in electoral support.

This does not, of course, mean that the labor party does not want the union to reorient its demands and militance from the market to the state. It can, in fact, be expected to encourage such a reorientation, for a focus on state outputs increases the mediational importance of the party.[45] Furthermore, such a reorientation may be necessary in order to avoid some of the deleterious consequences in terms of the social and political alliances supporting the union and the party previously examined. This is another reason that there may be a convergence of party and union policy positions. None of this, however, implies party support for liberal corporatism.

Does this mean that the long-term opposition party can be expected to completely oppose the development of liberal corporatist arrangements? The answer would seem to be no, for, as we have seen, these arrangements may be indispensable to the maintenance of the overall political and social support of the unions and their party, to the indispensable co-optation of capital, and, in certain cases, to the protection of the legitimacy of the regime (a case that may be particularly likely when the party of labor has been isolated for a long time on ideological grounds). Nevertheless, the degree of interest of the party will be strictly limited, and the party is likely to represent a brake on the development of liberal corporatist arrangement, at least until it is itself firmly ensconced in government.

The absence of party support for liberal corporatism is also likely to limit the enthusiasm of the union. First, under conditions in which its social and political alliances are already threatened by its market militance, it is unlikely to confront the party over these institutional issues. Second, and perhaps more fundamentally, under conditions in which its party is excluded from power, the union cannot expect fully institutionalized liberal corporatism to work to its benefit. The uncertainty of only partial establishment of liberal corporatism, the sense that the union might easily exit from such arrangements, represents a source of strength while not entirely eliminating the benefits that accrue from some degree of cooperation with capital.[46] Third, in the absence of the labor party in government, the ability of the union to convince the rank and file that market restraint will be compensated by commensurate political quid pro quo is limited. Finally, since the union too has an interest in the participation of the labor party in government, it too can play an implicit or explicit role in seeking to promote such an outcome by on the one hand indicating its potential cooperativeness while on the other hand maintaining its freedom of action to the greatest extent possible.

This discussion has begun to suggest how the role of political parties enters into the analysis of the likely development of liberal corporatist arrangements. The introduction of this political-party factor, in addition to the others already cited, allows us to explain why, despite the tremendous upheaval in the Italian economy that the unions have been able (in combination with other factors) to generate in recent years, liberal corporatism has appeared only in the weakest of forms.

In place of a conclusion to the arguments of this chapter, I want to pose several questions. First, is the unions' recent level of emphasis on action within the state likely to continue in the coming period or can we expect the unions to promote a revival of market militance? Second, if state action remains of primary importance, will there be further movement toward liberal corporatism or will the current, very limited form continue? As this analysis has suggested, full answers to these questions would require the examination of the likely developments with respect to a number of variables. It is interesting to note, however, that what role the PCI comes to play in the system could have a very large bearing on the answer. If the Communists join a government, it would seem likely that, despite protests and difficulties, further movement toward liberal corporatism might occur. If, instead, the PCI returns or is returned to the opposition, thus reducing the prospect for the unions that they can gain major quid pro quo for restraint, even a small reduction in the probability that wage gains would promote major economic disruptions might be accompanied by a new wave of militance initiated either by the leadership or by the rank and file. If these are realistic hypotheses about the consequences of the future status of the PCI (hypotheses clearly linked to this analysis), we are once again encouraged to explore more fully the relationship between liberal corporatism and political parties, the party system, and the partisan coloration of the state.

Notes

1. Douglas A. Hibbs, Jr., has shown that even during the unions' period of complete isolation, as well as in the 1960s, Italian strike activity was, by comparative standards, quite high. What stands out about the "hot autumn" and much of the 1970s is the number of hours lost to strikes, the changing balance of the types of issues for which strikes occur, and the dramatically altered institutional position of the unions in the work place and in their relations with employers. See Hibbs, "On the Political Economy of Long Run Trends in Strike Activity," *British Journal of Political Science* 8 (April 1978):173–75.

2. Ida Regalia, Marino Regini, and Emilio Regneri, "Labor Conflicts and Industrial Relations in Italy," in Colin Crouch and Alessandro Pizzorno, eds., *The Resurgence of Class Conflict in Western Europe since 1968,* vol. 1. (London: Macmillan, 1978).

3. Peter Lange, "Crisis and Consent, Change and Compromise: Dilemmas of Italian Communism in the 1970's," in Peter Lange and Sidney Tarrow, eds., *Italy in Transition: Conflict and Consensus* (London: Frank Cass, 1979); also published as a special issue of *West European Politics* (Fall 1979).

4. Regalia et al., "Labor Conflicts."

5. This hypothesis allows for the possibility that, for historical and other reasons, union and party leaders may have similar ideological inclinations. The operative variables, however, are considered to be structural ones affecting the institutional interests of the union.

6. Lange, "Crisis and Consent."

7. Alessandro Pizzorno, "Political Exchange and Collective Identity in Industrial

Conflict," in Crouch and Pizzorono, eds., *Resurgence of Class Conflict,* vol. 2, p. 281.

8. Ibid., pp. 277–85.

9. Ibid., pp. 283–84.

10. Marino Regini, "I Rapporti fra sindacati e Stato nella formazione della politica economica in Italia: Verso un sistema neo-corporativo?" Center for European Studies, Harvard University, 1978, mimeo. To be published in Gerhard Lehmbruch and Philippe Schmitter, eds., *Corporatist Policy Formation in Comparative Perspective,* forthcoming.

11. I am omitting Regini's dimension of the scope of the sectors of public intervention brought within the framework of union-industrial association bargaining. Regini argues that these are of necessity rather limited and fractured. As will be indicated later, I am not certain that this need necessarily be the case. Regini's discussion in the paper cited above (pp. 5–12) is particularly enlightening not only for the dimensions of liberal or neocorporatism he points to, but also because of his insistence on the fact that the movement from pluralism to neocorporatism should be understood to be along a multidimensional continuum.

12. This variable is different from simple union strength as that term is usually specified, for its use here involves a relativity between the strength of the unions and features of the political economic context in which the unions operate, between the strength of the unions and what might be called the "vulnerability" of the economy to union gains. As we specify this dimension, furthermore, we place a good deal of importance on the place of the national economy in the international economy. The importance of the latter for the vulnerability of the national economy and especially for an understanding of the ability of labor to disrupt the economy is often neglected.

13. Pizzorno, "Political Exchange."

14. Alessandro Pizzorno, "I sindacati nel sistema politico italiano: aspetti storici," *Rivista trimestrale di diritto politico* 21 (1971), pp. 1510–59.

15. The concept of external diseconomies is being developed by Peter Hall of the Center of European Studies and Government Department, Harvard University, in connection with his dissertation on British economic policymaking. I am indebted to him for letting me use it here.

16. Gerhard Lehmbruch, "Corporatism, Labour and Public Policy," paper delivered at Ninth World Congress of Sociology, Uppsala, August 1978.

17. Ibid. Lehmbruch here is quoting the West German Council of Economic Advisors.

18. Ibid.

19. Pizzorno, "Political Exchange"; Regalia et al., "Labor Conflicts."

20. Pizzorno, "Political Exchange"; Lehmbruch, "Corporatism, Labour and Public Policy."

21. Lehmbruch, "Corporatism, Labour and Public Policy."

22. Pizzorno, "Political Exchange"; here Pizzorno makes a similar point.

23. This is also a contrast in which ideological factors and the history of union-party relationships might play a role. Our argument, however, would suggest that these factors have tended to receive too much attention and that a large part of the variance is to be explained by the structural factors outlined here.

24. For some of these points, see Regalia et al., "Labor Conflicts."

25. Ibid.

26. The increase in recent years in the number of conglomerates, multinational firms, and the like supports the "exit" possibilities of capital. So too does the shift in production to subcontractors and the secondary sector. It should be argued, in fact, that these represent responses of capital to the growth in the ability of the unions to inflict damage.

27. The problem of capital exit is obviously also a major concern of the state and may be one of the reasons it promotes corporatist arrangements when the potential for economic disruption is particularly high or has already been demonstrated. A state concerned with this problem but anxious to limit the blackmail power inherent in the possibility of capital exit would pursue policies designed to raise the threshold of significant capital exit.

28. One can think not only of Italy in the 1970s but also of Conservative Party discussions of the fact that the strength and behavior of British unions were contrary to British democratic traditions and might require significant legal changes.

29. Schmitter has made an argument that liberal corporatist arrangements (he calls them societal corporatist, in part because of his concern with the inputs side of corporatism [see

Lehmbruch, "Corporatism, Labour and Public Policy"]) can make a significant contribution to the "governability" problems of the advanced industrial capitalist democracies. His point fits well with the preceding arguments, for it suggests that unions, in opting for liberal corporatist arrangements, are in fact contributing to the management of problems of governance for which they might well be blamed. Were these problems to fester, they might contribute to the decay of the social and political alliances of the unions, which we have discussed. See Philippe Schmitter, "Interest Intermediation and Regime Governability in Contemporary Western Europe," University of Chicago, 1978, mimeo. A revised draft is to be published in Suzanne Berger, ed., *Organizing Interests in Western Europe* (New York: Cambridge University Press, 1981).

30. Pizzorno points out that this can be caused by both growing discontent of the traditional rank and file of the union and the emergence of what he calls new "collective indentities" that are less willing to accept the interpretation of interest utilized by the union leadership. In both cases there is a dispersion to the periphery of the power previously largely centralized in the union leadership. See Pizzorno, "Political Exchange"; Regini, "I Rapporti"; Lehmbruch, "Corporatism, Labour and Public Policy."

31. Charles Sabel, "The Internal Politics of Trade Unions," MIT, 1978, mimeo. To be published in Berger, *Organizing Interests.*

32. This could be the counterpart of the ratchet used by the union. The associations of capital, making short-run decision to grant union demands with respect to an expanding scope of issues, may eventually find that their prerogatives are threatened to the point where confrontation is preferable to further cooperation.

33. I am concentrating here on labor and the unions, but it is to be noted that similar problems can arise within capital. Liberal corporatist arrangements, for instance, can shift costs onto the weaker firms in a sector or in the economy as a whole, and these may become the source of counter-mobilizations. In this regard see T. J. Pempel, "The International Arena and Domestic Associability: Corporation as a Defense Mechsnism," paper delivered at the annual meeting of the American Political Science Association, Washington, September 1979.

34. Regalia et al., "Labor Conflicts."

35. Regini, "I Rapporti."

36. Giorgio Fua, *Occupazione e capacità produttive: la realtà italiana* (Bologna: Il Mulino, 1976).

37. Paolo Sylos Labini, *Saggio sulle classi sociali* (Rome: Laterza, 1975).

38. Regini, "I Rapporti," pp. 31–32.

39. Ibid.

40. The role of political parties has been one of the most neglected issues in the corporatism debate. This is a void that should be filled, for there is increasing evidence that the status of the parties of labor in the political system is of major importance to union policy. In this connection, see Schmitter, "Interest Intermediation"; Pizzorno, "Political Exchange"; and Walter Korpi, *The Working Class in Welfare Capitalism: Work, Unions and Politics in Sweden* (London: Routledge and Kegan Paul, 1978).

41. Korpi, *The Working Class*; also Andrew Martin, "The Configuration of Power in the Political Arena and the Labor Market"; Harvard University, Conference on Government and Industry in Western Europe, 1971, mimeo.; also Martin, "Labor Movement, Parties and Inflation: Contrasting Responses in Britain and Sweden," *Polity* 7 (1975).

42. Douglas A. Hibbs, Jr., "Political Parties and Macroeconomic Policy," *American Political Science Review* 71 (1977):1467–68. Also Martin, "Labor Movement."

43. Korpi, *The Working Class.*

44. Schmitter, "Interest Intermediation."

45. Lange, "Crisis and Consent."

46. Regini, "I Rapporti."

6 The Modernizing Role of the Working-Class Parties in Southern Europe

FRANCO FERRAROTTI

Roughly two years after the word was first invented and launched by E. Berlinguer, the debate on Euro-Communism finds itself caught in a most awkward position. On the one hand, it is too narrow-gauged and confined to limited issues of domestic political topography, rubbing elbows with invidious and understandably resentful socialists and diffident Christian Democrats. On the other, it develops on a highly doctrinaire level where major theoretical questions are invoked as basic criteria to determine the degree of bona fide allegiance to democracy on the part of the supposed "neoconverts" and to the democratic rules of the game. Moreover, there are some specialists in Marxist philology, such as Ernest Mandel,[1] who maintain that the real issue cannot be apprehended without reconsidering the post–Bolshevik Revolution years and that Euro-Communism is nothing but the "bitter fruit" of Stalinism and of its theory of socialism in one country.

Once the debate is accepted along these lines, one is likely to forget or to lose sight of some obvious facts. First, Euro-Communism does not derive from a clear-cut theoretical platform but rather from practical political expediency. Second, despite its name it does not concern the whole of Europe but only Southern Europe. Third, within Southern Europe it concerns directly and most immediately Spain and Italy, while the French situation shows peculiar social and political characteristics, and Portugal seems to be far enough removed to be only tangentially involved. In essence, Euro-Communism is a typically Mediterranean phenomenon.

To explore and understand this phenomenon, I submit that a different angle or vantage point from which the issue should be tackled might in the end prove more productive.

In the first place, while political expediency at the domestic parliamentary level and theoretical (ideological) platforms do play a role, it seems important to bear in mind the general (international) military context, traditions—that is, historical roots—and geographic setting with its special strategic corollaries.

There might be a quick return to some sort of Cold War but, at least for the time being, one should not overlook the simple fact that Euro-Communism, more than the unconscious "fruit of Stalinism," as Mandel would have it, is the product of détente. The general consequences of détente are well known. As has been aptly pointed out:

The age of détente has made possible some shifting of attention away from the struggle with the Soviet Union. . . . Change has taken place in three ways. First, military power is no longer the almost exclusive factor in defining the hierarchy of nations; it has been joined by an underlying constituent — economic power — that again has become important in its own right. Second, with relative success in managing military relations between East and West, the most central unmet threats to "security" for most nations are now in the economic realm, with the locus of challenge no longer the Soviet Union. And third, the "peace" from economic conflict, chaos, or deep uncertainty.[2]

This statement is sufficiently accurate as far as the relationship of the United States with the rest of the world is concerned. It fails, however, to take into account and to explain one of the most remarkable consequences of détente: the request for at least a relative autonomy from the Soviet Union on the part of the most powerful Western European Communist parties. Usually, the "roots" of Euro-Communism are seen in the secret Khrushchev report of 1956 at the Twentieth Congress of the Communist (Bolshevik) Party of the Soviet Union with the merciless disclosure of Stalin's crimes. This might be regarded as a necessary but not sufficient condition. In fact, it was détente that enacted the essential conditions for the flourishing, especially in Italy, Spain and, to a lesser degree, in France, of Euro-Communism.

The Cold War had frozen all the implicit needs for an autonomous "national road to socialism." Both the Soviet Union and the United States would conceive their "security" in narrow military terms that would allow almost no margin for independent decision to their allies. In this context Western Communist parties, if not a *longa manus* or a fifth column in the proper sense, would out of necessity act as a propaganda sounding board, more or less closely bound to the changing attitude of the hegemonic state and of its leading political elite. As a result of détente, the situation presents itself as profoundly changed in Europe and on a world scale. This change is quite visible but the full realization of it is not easy. Political stereotypes and ideological habits die hard.

The attitude of policymakers, especially among United States politicians and official political analysts, seems to lag behind actual political reality. There is here a widening gap that could in the long run prove fatal to United States–Europe relationships. As a result of this gap, at the present time one senses in Western Europe a growing awareness and concern vis-à-vis United States policy. This policy is perceived as rigid or at least not sufficiently flexible. Confronted with the major changes in political attitude and general political outlook of various Western European Communist parties, one has the feeling that American foreign policy tends to view United States relations with European nations, especially in the Mediterranean area, primarily in a Soviet context rather than in their own specific terms, be these deemed positive or negative from a United States national interest point of view.

Thus, it is no wonder that Europe, especially Mediterranean Europe, is confirmed in its nature and feels itself to be instrumentally exploited, rather than sharing in a partnership, for a political — a diplomatic and military — game, the rules of which escape its control and even its knowledge.

For this reason, a purely ideological analysis does not seem satisfactory. For instance, the idea of asking the Spanish or the Italian Communists for a certificate of allegiance to democracy as if they had to pass some sort of scholastic admission test strikes one as both naive and counterproductive. Neither statements nor purely verbal reassurances but facts — that is, specific and practical positions actually taken — provide the decisive criteria for understanding and evaluating a political organized force. Moreover, whenever a political force has reached the dimensions of a huge mass party, it is increasingly difficult on the part of its leaders to practice, with a moderate amount of success, a "doublethink" policy. Only in a small clandestine revolutionary party organized along military lines, in which total secrecy and absolute obedience were accepted as normal conditions by all members, could a double standard succeed.

Similar shortcomings characterize the purely ideological debate that has been underlying for the past two years, but more particularly during the last few months, the development of Euro-Communism. In Italy, the PSI socialists have unearthed for the occasion the venerable classic Pierre Joseph Proudhon in order to embarrass the Communists, who supposedly are still devoted followers of Lenin.[3] According to these socialists, Proudhon was right in denouncing the archaic nature of Communism and all the evils of monolithic centralized state structure (in particular, systematic destruction of any individual thinking, and therefore of any freedom of thought; the abolition of any local or cooperative, community-based, power; police inquisition; bureaucratic centralized dictatorship, and so on).

What is interesting to observe is that Proudhon is pitted against Lenin as if they were contemporaries, despite the fact that the two socialist leaders are at least fifty years apart. Furthermore, some aspects of Proudhon's thinking are snatched away from the whole body of his thought. His libertarian polemical stand against the central power of the state is emphasized, but his dreaming about a patriarchal craft-based and essentially conservative society that does not anticipate anything about present-day technology is not even mentioned. Thus, while the quoted text might be correct, the overall context is clearly ignored.

It has been easy for the Italian Communists to reply that Lenin is more often quoted than carefully read and that historical circumstances should be taken into consideration if one is to understand fully, and not only at the level of their verbal expression, complex ideological and political stands. Marxists, obsessed with the idea of preserving the purity of Marx's teaching against Lenin's Jacobin corruption, as the socialists in Italy would like to be, end up ironically in the trap of an anti-Marxist approach. More specifically, what the secretary of the PSI condemns at present in Lenin's model is claimed by the PCI to have been denounced and discarded by P. Togliatti in 1943, at the time of the "Salerno turn," and later in 1945, when he launched the idea of the "partito nuovo."

Santiago Carrillo, for the PCE, has faced the question of the modern state rather squarely and in more explicit terms than the PCI. In his book

Eurocommunism and the State, Carrillo recalls the conception of the state put forward by Marx and Engels. It is curious that he would not notice any difference between Marx and Engels, on the one hand, and Lenin, on the other. The notion of the "vanishing state," which is essential for the reasoning of Marx and Engels, does not fit within the framework of Lenin's *State and Revolution.* Yet the convergent point among Marx, Engels, and Lenin is given by the concept of the state as "the general business committee for the interests of high level bourgeoisie."

According to Santiago Carrillo, this concept is no longer tenable. New developments have taken place that cannot be explained or simply understood in their specific terms on the basis of that concept. Carrillo gives credit to Gramsci and Althusser for their attempts to bring the Marxist theory of the state up to date through the introduction of the special category of "ideological apparatus." Through this apparatus the dominant groups and the economically ruling class are supposed to influence citizens' awareness and value orientation without having to resort to purely coercive violence. In this connection, one should mention religious bodies and organizations such as established churches and denominations of various kinds; the educational system; the prevailing type of family socialization; the legal and political institutions; mass media and information agencies; and so on.

In the opinion of Carrillo, however, these additional refinements, valuable as they are, are not sufficient. "There is still another dimension," he writes, "capitalist state is taking up more and more, insofar as it represents the dominant economic groups, the control of the economic development; as a result of this situation, those economic activities which escape the direct intervention of the state tended to become less and less significant." For Santiago Carrillo, the very development of technology is responsible for the crisis of private enterprise. In this respect, Carrillo, as well as the other Euro-Communist leaders, feels that the existing state structures can be used for a socialist purpose. It is no longer a question of destroying the state, as was the case with the traditional socialist doctrine, but rather of reorienting it to a new set of goals. It is obvious that the major difficulty in this connection that Euro-Communists will face is an entrenched, hypertrophic and inefficient state bureaucracy, which is a typical characteristic of Southern European countries.

In this respect what might be in the end a retarding factor for Euro-Communism is actually Europe itself. The rift between the PCI and PCE, on the one hand, and the PCF on the other, is serious. French Communists, not unlike some sectors of the left-wing Labour Party in England, are in general quite hostile to the revamping of a united European program. Amazingly, French Communists are talking and acting like right-wing "poujadists," trying to capitalize on the Gaullist heritage that Valery Giscard d'Estaing is attempting with difficulty to retain in his quest for self-identity through differentiating from his predecessors.

For the Spanish and Italian Communists, on the contrary, a united Europe is an ideal exit, a way out of their domestic contradictions. The only reservation concerns the kind of Europe that will finally emerge. There is a certain amount of apprehension for what is vaguely termed "Europe of big monopoly capital." But this does not seem to go beyond a lipservice tribute to the socialist tradition, and, at least for the time being, it has not materialized in a definite socialist policy for a united Europe. It seems that the real difficulty lies in the fact that, through the building process of a united Western Europe, both Southern and Northern Europe come together, and Southern Europe is bound to take the role of a subordinate partner.

This leads to the core of my contention. It is difficult, if not impossible, to understand the relevance of PCI and PCE in their respective countries without taking into consideration the fact that these two parties are de facto engaged in a process of modernization — that is, of rationalization — that is bound to bring to completion the "industrial revolution" that the national bourgeoisie of both countries has left unfinished. If one considers Spain and Italy, one is likely to detect that, despite many fundamental differences, the two countries show a basic convergence, linked with the fact that they had neither a religious reformation, as did Germany, nor a political revolution, as did France. Spain and Italy are premodern countries, marked by distinctive traits that to this day set them apart from the rest of Europe: (1) Catholic families; (2) a political system dominated by a clientele paternalism that thwarts the "rule of law" and accounts for the malfunctioning of democratic institutions with, as a consequence, a widespread "Mafia," turned from a local phenomenon into a problem of national development, and huge pockets of parasitism both in the private and in the public sectors of the economy; (3) lack of entrepreneurship; (4) a still prevailing conception and perception of power as a personal prerogative.

Under these conditions, the modernizing function of working-class parties, in the sense that they tend to cut across entrenched vested interests of a parasitic nature, especially in the public-administration sphere and in state industry, becomes clear.

The case is fairly evident for Spain, which has only recently emerged from a forty-year-long political dictatorship and economic isolation. But it is also true for Italy. As has been aptly pointed out, Italy entered the 1960s with a long backlog of much-needed reform, which had been postponed during the Fascist regime, the hungry forties, and the stringent fifties. As a result, the Italy of the 1970s is still plagued by structural problems that date from the 1920s. In this sense, it is correct to assert that the objective, social, and economic bases of Fascism have not yet been removed. Among these problems one could mention (1) the tax system, which can be termed "Bourbonic" and "electronic" at the same time; (2) the educational system, which is at present almost totally devoid of any selection standard; and, (3) most important as a negative factor, a chaotic public administration, characterized by thousands of official boards, agencies, and commissions that seem to exist without any visible purpose and certainly without any proper supervision.

What is most striking, however, is the obvious inability of the government to exercise power. Based on a system of fragile multiparty coalitions, the executive in Italy seems to be vitally interested only in its own existence rather than in deciding and in implementing a definite policy. Political life has therefore been turned into entertainment; its function is purely theatrical. It is desperate and futile at the same time. Politicians are rapidly becoming irrelevant. It is a fact that interest groups, militants, and all sorts of protestors no longer express themselves in the traditional political channels but rather in strikes, street demonstrations, and occasionally violence.

Especially in Italy, the Communist Party has already had a chance to prove its value as a modernizing and rationalizing factor in the administration of important city governments where it has, since the elections of June 20, 1976, a clear electoral majority. For two years, major Italian cities such as Turin, Rome, and Naples have been governed by a Communist municipal "giunta," with a Communist mayor. What are the results? (The case of Bologna has special characteristics, and it is still doubtful whether it is a showpiece or a fraud.)

These results are, by and large, disappointing. Communist-run administrations have been effective in blocking urban land speculation — and this is no small achievement, especially in a city such as Rome, which, for almost a hundred years, had been subject to massive "wild urban development" by all the major property-owning groups, ranging from the Vatican to the old aristocratic families. What is missing is the ability to draft and implement a positive plan for action. Caught between the need for local extensive reforms, and the central — that is, national — appeasement attitude with the Christian Democrats, which underlies the strategy for the so-called historical compromise, Communist administrations do not seem to be able to become politically effective in the positive sense.

Moreover, one senses the political and psychological difficulty in which the former opposition militant finds himself, once in power at the local level. Here we encounter the problem of the "organic intellectual," in Gramsci's sense — that is, of the intellectual who is supposed to be not only a specialist but also a political leader. The "organic intellectual," once turned into an administrative official of the city government, soon discovers the "facts of life." Ideology can be in this connection of little help. The present-day Communist intellectual, whom the party has destined to some official job, is experiencing the theoretical and existential contradictions of a revolutionary political organization that has administrative duties without having at the same time central — that is, decisive — political power.

However, the "administrative intellectual" of the PCI is the rationalizing instrument of the Italian political system. He is the medium through which the PCI connects itself with the social substance of the country. Fieldwork has already been conducted on this subject, but more extensive research seems to be necessary.[4]

Within the category of "administrative intellectual" will be found varying concentrations of state and public functions in general. At one extreme is found the individual whose administrative duties are subordinated to professional-technical service, and for whom membership of the category of "administrative intellectual" derives immediately from the recent electoral success of the PCI and subsequent opportunities of articulating a social strategy on a broad front of state and "semistate" institutions. At the other extreme is the "public figure" who operates solely within the parameters of his political functions and skills and, in the long term, makes of these his professional objectives.

In all cases, however, the characteristics of the administrative intellectual (as distinct from the Weberian bureaucrat) are his political commitment, and his function in the division of labor as public administrator. This additional latter function involves a measure of *control* of the social division of labor and of its effective employment, and the coordination of production by means of the state structure — as opposed simply to the function of providing technical advice or consultations, or in the case of the bureaucrat, "neutral-rational mediation." The novel features of the administrative intellectual can be expressed summarily in the contrast between the doctor with a specialization in public health, who happens to be a Communist, and the same figure in a regional administration of the Left, where he functions as a particular kind of intellectual *because* he is a Communist.

The new specialists (technocrats and technicians, publicists, mass educators, and workers in the cultural industry and in the state and commercial-industrial bureaucracy) in turn had both differences and common understanding with the mass of intellectual labor, which found itself variously unqualified, ("in formation," that is), unemployed, and de- or unqualified by technological developments. However, in contrast with these types, the new intellectual of the 1970s is undoubtedly and preeminently political. He is a specialist, his position salient: above all, he is a creation of the PCI, though he is to be found in other parties of the left.

This new intellectual is not that of Bon and Burnier — a technician — nor is he, as described by Lelli, defined by technique and division of labor; he is a specialist. He may be subdivided into two diverse types. The first is the Party intellectual, whose function is that of consultation and advice concerning policy; he is not a figurehead, as were the older humanist-literary intellectuals. These economists, urbanists, jurists, and political analysts are to be distinguished from the administrative intellectual, who is often an elected official. His function is that of the active pursuit and even invention of the local Party program, under the general direction of the PCI concerning the fulfillment of his responsibility, which, being bureaucratically defined and often electorally reinforced, already establishes a distance between administrative intellectual and Party apparatus.

On these intellectuals, to an extent unthinkable for the "show-window" intellectuals of the 1950s and 1960s, rests the case for the PCI's organic links with the subaltern classes, the elements of reformism in the Italian road to socialism, its "long march through the institutions."

The first of these types no more than reflects the success of the Party as on the threshold of government. Their recruitment acknowledges the eclipse, or at least the overtaking, of the literary generalist intellectual by new tasks and problems. Where the humanist and generalist had within the Party the task of establishing relations with other intellectuals and those publicly impressed by their prestige, the new Party specialist undertakes a practical analysis of problems denied to earlier intellectuals — less for reasons of lack of confidence in their advice than a basic lack of refined skills. If the basis of the new skills is diverse and eclectic, it could be more easily assimilated to the philosophical position of the PCI than was the Crocean idealism of their predecessors, especially now that the demise of a cultural policy directed toward intellectuals (rather than the population at large) has not been compensated for by a scientific policy.

The other new type, that of administrative intellectual, as *sindaco, assessore, consigliere communale,* president or member of a communal or regional commission, or director of a public institution, owes his position not only to his specialized skills but to his social prestige and the confidence of the Party (and, reciprocally, his loyalty to it— and not his philosophy). This intellectual occupies a key and increasingly influential position in Italian society. He differs both from the new specialist-consultant and from the older militant propagandist: he does not (at least as yet) displace the political intellectual in the direction of the Party but is nonetheless a political figure. The point that such new administrative intellectuals are peculiarly related to the *compromesso storico* is almost a truism when applied to the political function and representative character of these intellectuals: the local giuntas, the local emphasis on decentralization (and hence on popular, interclassist participation on a residential basis), and the necessity of working within a restrictive and antiquated juridical structure all contribute to the necessity of accepting the limitations as well as the promise of political power confined both by popular consensus and state structures.

The literature about intellectuals, written predominantly by literary humanist intellectuals between 1961 and 1967, offers an insight into the crisis—falsely believed to be terminal—of a section of the intellectual community. The scientific-technical or bureaucratic intellectuals were largely silent in boom and decline, despite the growth of these sectors. Only in the 1970s has their corporatism become salient. Second, the attempt by literary intellectuals to become organic ideologues of the proletariat, despite the prior position of the PCI, and even to become its leaders depite their own relation as mediated by the PCI vis-à-vis the working-class movement, presents only a partial picture. They included much that was important but excluded not only the problem of the class character and interests of intellectuals—especially those more closely engaged in material production—but the phenomenon of the absorption and integration of intellectuals into state and political structures.

Thus, the technical intellectual did not act as a proletarian in the political sense, through impulses experienced as a result of his position in the division of labor. It was not so much that the literary intellectual was challenged or dethroned by the technical; rather, in terms of hegemony within the category of intellectual, the literary and technical were both replaced by the new *political* intellectual. The political intellectual finally disposes of the myth of the potentially wholly autonomous intellectual (the literary utopian myth) and of the wholly subordinate one (that of the technical apocalypse). The political intellectual is organically part of society. His existence, however, does not demystify intellectual specialization, as was hoped in the 1960s—at once recognition of the devaluation and of the universalization of intellect. The new political function instrumentalizes intellect and intellectual: it attempts self-valuation of intellect, not merely the realization of capitalist valuation of intellect, and provides a new function for specialist intellectuals in a generalized social role.

What, then, is the relation of these new intellectuals (new, also, in relation to the new intellectuals of the 1960s) to the old ideologues? What is the significance of their organic links primarily with the PCI, and not with the working class nor the scientific-technical apparatus of neocapitalism? The new "state servants" — in the service of Party and people — are peculiarly representatives of intellectuals as a social category and not merely in terms of their aspiration to win stability and continuity from the PCI as guarantor of the social value of their expertise and activity as agents of planned social change. The literary intellectual was co-opted from a precapitalist ideological function. Superficially, the technical intellectual was created for a nonideological function in the spheres of production and circulation. Both, in other words, were not easily assimilable to a movement that criticized the very basis of their self-definition, and of the convergence of interests and conditions.

The traditional *critical* intellectual believed that it was from culture (and not from politics itself) that criticism of politics is derived. For him, the crisis of humanism makes resolution of the problematic of politics impossible. His choices lie between conformity and suicide: self-transcendence involves self-extinction as a separate intellectual grounded in universalistic humanism. If he does not choose suicide, he betrays "culture and the critical spirit"; conformism is thus a crueller form of suicide, which arrives at the same end. That the choices are ideological derivatives of the "autonomy" permitted by bourgeois society only increases the critical intellectual's sense of anguish.

The PCI had seen the spirit of compromise embodied in the cultural autonomy of the *politica culturale* evaporate in the political crisis of 1956: only the letter of the *politica culturale* remained to be cancelled in 1966. The new compromise, of a "conformist eclecticism," did little to resolve the crisis of literary intellectuals, which was essentially a crisis of bourgeois cosmology — but it did offer a pleasing respite from thoughts of suicide. If the PCI did not produce the Gramscian organic intellectual or the Gramscian function for intellectuals in the Party, articulating all its levels, it offered organization of the militancy and aspirations of intellectual labor power.

The PCI, however, came to share with the sociologist a belief that "intellectual labor power" had become a formless definition. Having prided itself on the major intellectuals in its leadership, the PCI in the 1970s broadened the Gramscian notion of the function of intellectuals in society to cover "intellectual labor," employed and unemployed, and the middle, modest intellectuals — especially those in the service of the state. Many such elements of intellectual labor power clearly do not have the Gramscian "function" of intellectuals. The term "intellectual" does, however, remain useful.

First, ideological elaboration remains a function of intellectuals, and ideology is peculiarly the terrain of intellectuals' self-identification. The elaboration of ideology is for intellectuals the *internal* field of pseudo–class struggle, the basis for alliances between groups of intellectuals and the ground from which they make alliances with elements of the *ceti medi* and other classes. This level of articulation, then, provides objective referents that may overcome subjective allegiances by individual intellectuals.

Second, the technical aspect of division of labor is still the responsibility of intellectuals, who determine its hierarchical aspects by and large in favor of intellectual labor. In Italy, however, this favoring of intellectual labor is contradicted by the oversupply and dysfunctional production of "intellectuals" for debased or nonexistent intellectual labor. Thus, from a corporative as well as an ideological point of view, it has become the function of specialist intellectuals to destroy the very value of their own labor in general, and hence devalue their own function.

Third, this internal division between qualified and dequalified labor power notwithstanding, the process of formation of intellectual labor power perpetuates the intellectual as a specialist in its production as still relatively privileged in the division of labor.

Though the "crisis" of humanist intellectuals owes much to images of past or utopian models of universalistic intellectuality, it also derives from the crisis of performing intellectual functions in the present. The "independent" intellectual, however, is increasingly frequently transformed into a technical specialist, a lesser and subordinate figure, in the arts as well as in production, bureaucracy, or the professions. As the dominant class sinks more deeply into crisis, intellectuals have tried to detach themselves and claim in a concrete sense the "independence" that bourgeois society has conferred on them only in an ideological sense. The supportive intellectual can no longer survive the decay of his dominant class. Historically, we observe intellectuals developing their own group ideologies. Mannheim's is the classic case, but we might also cite Berger and Luckmann's notion of the intellectual as designer of alternative cosmologies to which he leads the masses in an attempt to concretize his fantasy. Gouldner has also presented the intellectual as master of language for purposes of revolution or mediation. Such formulas are designed by intellectuals to resist absorption into the *ceti medi* (where, of course, in Kautsky's thesis, they already belong), or to retain a position of privilege and leadership sanctioned by an imaginative world-view which gives them a value higher than that conceded by civil society.

This ideological refuge can, however, be only temporary. The Italian intellectual of the 1960s changed his social function by becoming an employee of the cultural industry. He tried to exploit the "space" of the review to avoid absorption into the industry. However, between 1963 and 1967, the literary-political intellectual continued to approach politics through the medium of literature. Literary intellectuals still considered themselves spokesmen for all intellectuals, and intellect in general.

However, in the division of labor, it is not intellect but intellectual specialization that defines its social function. The argument that neocapitalism tends both toward universal intellectualization of labor and toward its proletarianization is important above all as half-truth. It is also a movement *against* manual labor (paradoxically, thus strengthening the economistic position of manual labor), and also *against* traditional intellectuality. Of course, the eclipse of individual and subjective creativity is only one form of intellectual subordination. However, the victory of intellectual over manual labor is pyrrhic, since its own proletarianization marks its subordinacy, not the superiority of its level of consciousness.

There is much sociological utility in Gramsci's conception of intellectual function. However, it should be noted that the political-ideological function must be broken down into many different subfunctions in the maintenance of hegemony and challenge to hegemony. Of course, for Gramsci, intellectual as specialist in culture was equivalent to *political* intellectual. In the PCI, however, there are two types of intellectual not conceived by Gramsci — the intellectual who is a leader of the Party, a generalist, and the specialist intellectual who is not a Gramscian "specialist in the politics of the Party" but rather a "specialist in neo-capitalism in the service of the Party." It must remain an open question whether these specialists, like their bourgeois predecessors, can be transformed into organic intellectuals of the proletariat — a "suicide" with respect to privileges conferred by bourgeois society. The PCI has followed the crises of various strata of intellectuals, always distinguishing between the utility of the specialization of the "strong" intellectuals and the mass character of the modest, middle, or inferior intellectual laborer.

To the humanist intellectual, the crisis of the capitalist mode of production is presented as destroying the belief that intellect is the seat of reason. Intellect may be privileged or devalued in neocapitalism, but it ceases to enjoy the ideological values invested in it, and so deeply enjoyed by traditional literary intellectuals. Of course, it might be argued that the "crisis" of the literary intellectual is his raison d'être, a guarantee against extinction. Italian literary intellectuals, however, have had little wish to live dangerously as expositors of crisis. Nevertheless, neocapitalism transformed the literary intellectual and his desire for cultural autonomy even within the framework of the political left. Even in defeat, some literary intellectuals insisted that bourgeois society (that is, their autonomy) was inconsistent with capitalist development — that one could choose bourgeois ideology without capitalism.

The PCI has not been in a position to resist this transformation of intellectual labor; in that sense, it must take the divisions of civil society as given. It can offer a refuge for the disillusioned literary intellectual but cannot re-create his autonomy. It can utilize the specialization of the technical intellectual for social ends, but cannot make him a "political leader."

The only compensation the PCI can hope for is in the political arena — that is to say, in its access to national political power not only as a member of a variegated, and therefore powerless, majority — which it has already achieved — but as a full member of a national government with ministerial responsibilities. To this end, the PCI, as well as the PCE, is ready to pay an electoral price. To think that this would be regarded as a symptom of crisis is both naive and misleading. Robin Blackburn has recently argued that because of electoral losses in France and Spain, but also in Italy (see Castellammare, Trento, and Trieste), Euro-Communism is in crisis:

If the Eurocommunist parties now suffer a crisis of perspectives — as they do — it is one of their own making, and it arises from the discrepancy between their real strength and their inability to find a political strategy which taps it. The Eurocommunist strategy has so far been *negative* — an incomplete rejection of Stalinist models — and *derivative* — an unconvincing attempt to mimic Eurosocialism. A positive and original strategy would require a novel combination of the best communist traditions (of anti-Stalinist Marxism) and of the themes of social revolt which have emerged, or reemerged, since the sixties (workers' control, women's liberation, the ecological movement, the contestation of bureaucracy, hierarchy and cultural manipulation).[5]

Blackburn's reasoning gives rise to mixed feelings. The PCE and PCI in particular are doing some of the very things he advocates, but anybody who has even a superficial acquaintance with the PSI, for instance, knows that any comparison with the PSI does not hold. The Center-Left government's experience has proven *ad abundantiam* that much of PSI leadership is no longer concerned with socialist issues. Thus, far from being in crisis, the historical function of Euro-Communism in Mediterranean Europe — that is, the function of modernizing rationalization in order to pave the way for an advanced socialist society — has hardly begun.

In this light, one could perhaps understand present-day Italian and Spanish terrorism as a desperate attempt to stop a political process in full swing.[6] The PCI especially, approaching government area and direct ministerial responsibilities, upsets vast economic and political interests that cut across the political spectrum: from certain groups in the state bourgeoisie, pro-Fascist and right-wing Christian Democrats, down to wealthy landowners and right-wing, conservative Social Democrats.

On the other hand, the present economic depression and political crisis are an objective help to terrorism. The crisis is structural and hits especially the young who have not yet entered the labor market. They are likely to resent union protection of the workers already at work. Social emargination and an increasing feeling of political exclusion are becoming important aspects of Italian social life. One notices a concomitant loss of representativeness on the part of democratic representative institutions, particularly of the Parliament. Under these conditions, it is no wonder that Euro-Communism emerges as a fundamental pillar of the existing order and as a major factor for its renewal.

Notes

1. E. Mandel, *From Stalinism to Eurocommunism* (Thetford, Norfolk: Lowe & Brydone, 1978); original ed., *Critique de l'Eurocommunisme* (Paris: François Maspero, 1978).

2. See R. Hunter, "The Setting," in VVAA, Detente and the Atlantic Nations (Chicago, 1976), p. 3.

3. See the essay by B. Craxi, secretary of the PSI, "The Socialist Gospel," *L'Expresso.*

4. During a two-year period, in cooperation with my assistants at the University of Rome, and in particular with M. Michelti and J. Fraser, I conducted in-depth interviews with Communist intellectuals who are currently engaged in municipal administrative affairs.

5. R. Blackburn, "Eurocommunism in Crisis?" *New Society* (May 18, 1978), pp. 359–261; italics in original.

6. With reference to the political meaning of present-day terrorism, see my book, *Alle radici della violenza (At the Roots of Violence*; Milan: Rizzoli).

7 French Socialist Foreign Policy: Atlantic Relations, Defense, and European Unity

NANCY I. LIEBER

If we consider Eurosocialism to be the recent tendency of Western European Left socialists to challenge the postwar model of social democracy on the one hand, while continuing to shun all forms of Leninism on the other, we can consider the French *Parti Socialiste* (PS) as perhaps the foremost example of that movement.* While the new Eurosocialists, or democratic socialists, are found in the left wings of most European social democratic, labor, or socialist parties, they predominate in the French PS. For unlike the British Labour Party and the German Social Democratic Party, for example, the status of French socialism has changed markedly since the old SFIO of Guy Mollet gave way in 1971 to the new PS of François Mitterrand. This *Parti Socialiste* has experienced an evolution not only of its ideology, strategy, party organization, and leadership, but, as this chapter will show, of its foreign policy as well.

In terms of ideology, the new French Socialists have been at the forefront of a trend in Europe to define a viable alternative to the two principal existing models of socialism — those of Western European social democracy and Soviet bureaucratic collectivism. That third, or democratic socialist, model they call *socialisme autogestionnaire* — a decentralized, self-governing, self-managing socialism.

The problem with existing social democratic policies, say the French Socialists, is that they are inherently limited to managing the capitalist system in a more humane way. The resulting welfare state and managed-economy systems have undeniably improved the lot of millions of people through a certain measure of income redistribution and social benefits, but these same social democratic arrangements have fostered the growth of a governmental bureaucracy increasingly perceived as too large and centralized, and therefore unresponsive and uncontrollable. On the other hand, the Soviet model is rejected by the French Socialists because not only does it place all economic and social decision making in the hands of huge centralized bureaucracies, but, by denying a democratic political process, it totally eliminates the possibility of the people's controlling or changing that

*I would like to thank the Columbia University Research Institute on International Change for partial funding of a summer 1977 research trip to Paris that allowed me to revise and expand this paper through interviews with foreign-policy makers in the *Parti Socialiste*. An earlier version of this paper was delivered at the March 1977 meeting of the International Studies Association in St. Louis, Missouri.

economic system, let alone exercising fundamental political and human rights.

In contrast, the French Socialist model is based on policies that are designed to extend the democratic principle to the economic, as well as political and social, spheres of life. These policies include eventual collective ownership of the nation's productive, distributive, and financial facilities (whether via national, regional, municipal, or cooperative ownership), enhanced workers' control and management at the place of work (democratic assemblies to determine certain policies and personnel procedures), and the institution of democratic economic planning (voting procedures for the formulation of overall economic and social priorities). The elements of this self-managing socialism are not necessarily new to socialist ideology. Workers' control, decentralization, direct democracy, utopia — these all lay at the core of nineteenth-century syndicalism, anarchism, and cooperativism. But these original socialist components were submerged in the twentieth century by the state-oriented socialisms of social democracy and Communism. It was not until after World War II that many socialists became increasingly aware of the failures of both these models to fulfill the original socialist vision. Influenced by the European New Left's popularization of concepts from the recently discovered early works of Karl Marx — concepts dealing with alienation, democracy, and bureaucracy — and by the events of May 1968 in France, which centered around the suspicion of concentrated hierarchical authority, the new PS of 1971 moved quickly to define and adopt this synthesis of old and new socialist theory and practice known as *socialisme autogestionnaire*. It remains a unique contribution on the part of the French Socialists to democratic socialist ideology.

In terms of strategy, the contrast between the old SFIO and the new PS is particularly striking. Throughout the Fourth Republic, the SFIO had espoused the familiar social democratic strategy of anti-Communism. By 1963, influenced by both international and domestic factors, the SFIO began to consider the possibility of working *with* the PCF in opposition to the Gaullist phenomenon in the new Fifth Republic. Putting aside previous centrist strategies, the SFIO nevertheless was not able to move beyond electoral cooperation with the PCF (and onto, for instance, the level of common governmental commitment) as long as it (the SFIO) continued to insist on prior philosophical and ideological agreement.

The new Socialists of 1971, however, based their strategy on an old Left slogan, "Let us retain what unites us, and throw out what divides us." That is, they hoped to solidify unity between the PS and the PCF at the electoral and programmatic (but not the philosophical or organizational) levels by writing a detailed common governmental program that would serve as a minimal and transitional five-year legislative contract. If the more far-reaching differences between Socialists and Communists could ever be transcended, reasoned the Socialists, this would occur only through the Left's attainment of majority status in French society and politics. Thus, as *autogestion* became the party's ideology, "union of the Left" became its strategy.

But if a socialist France was the ultimate goal, a stronger Socialist Party organization was the immediate goal. From 1920 to World War II, the SFIO had constituted the majority part on the left, but in the postwar period the situation was reversed, and it was the Communist Party that predominated. Throughout the 1950s and 1960s, the social democratic SFIO continued to experience an overall decline in structure, membership, votes, elected officials, spirit, and vision. A low point was reached in the 1969 presidential election, when the Socialist candidate, Gaston Defferre, received a paltry 5 percent of the vote compared to the Communist candidate's 20 percent. Thus, in adopting new directions with *autogestion* and union of the Left, the new PS sought not only to strengthen the united Left's position in French politics in general, but in the process to restore the Socialists to the position of leadership on the French Left. If they were successful, this achievement would allow them to become the senior partner in any coalition of the Left. Paradoxically, this same achievement would also weaken the incentives for the Communist Party to cooperate.

By early 1978 (when this chapter was written), the PS had succeeded in that aim, with the polls consistently giving the PS around 30 percent to the Communists' 20 percent. Indeed, the PS had come to replace the Gaullist party as the largest vote-getter in French politics. In other areas of party life the PS had also been reinforced. Its membership had more than doubled since 1971 (to 160,000); it had achieved organizational implantation on a nationwide scale (compared to the SFIO's overconcentration in three large *départements*); its press had become thriving and diverse; it had achieved greater working-class support with the establishment of over 1,000 workplace sections and through its affinity with the CFDT trade-union confederation; its sociological base had been enlarged to draw proportionately from most social classes in France; it had integrated the Catholic Left in a way the resolutely secularist SFIO had been unable to do; it had completed the gradual absorption of diverse groups on the non-Communist Left, particularly much of the PSU and former clubs; it had consolidated its multiple factions into two major ones—the Mitterrand majority (76 percent of the delegates' votes at the previous Congress) and the CERES minority (*Centre d'étude, de recherche, et d'éducation socialistes*—24 percent of the congressional vote); and its political image had been greatly enhanced by the leadership role of François Mitterrand, considered by friend and foe alike as a rare and consummate politician. All these signs pointed to a thriving and renewed party, and accounted for a most important political fact: for the first time in two decades, the French Socialists represented a serious governmental alternative.[1]

Along with the ideological, strategic, and organizational transformation of the French Socialist Party, foreign-policy attitudes (though not so much actual policies) have likewise changed. And as the Socialists' credibility as a governing force has grown, France's traditional European and American allies have found increased salience in the Socialists' positions regarding national security and European unity questions in particular. The purpose of this chapter, then, is to outline and analyze the changes in foreign policy between the old SFIO and the new PS as they pertain to (1) political and military aspects of the Atlantic Alliance, (2) defense questions involving nuclear weapons and the armed forces, and (3) political and economic aspects of European unity.

National Security

The traditional purpose of a nation's foreign policy is to ensure first and foremost the security of its people and territory, optimally by achieving a situation of international peace and harmony, minimally by ensuring adequate measures of military defense. The aspiration of the PS for a French Socialist government is to seek a new era of international peace through active participation in multilateral disarmament conferences, while at the same time maintaining a strong national defense. In Europe, specifically, the PS's optimal policy calls for negotiations leading to the freezing of military expenditures in the Atlantic and Warsaw pacts, the freezing of arms and the creation of denuclearized zones in Central Europe, mutual and balanced force reductions in Europe, and a system of collective security based on bilateral nonaggression pacts between all countries in the two blocs. The Socialists' aim, in the very long term, is the simultaneous dissolution of both the Atlantic Alliance and the Warsaw Pact.[2]

THE ATLANTIC ALLIANCE

Until such time as those long-term goals are accomplished, however, it is the policy of the French Socialists to maintain France's existing commitments to the Atlantic Alliance. While this represents a continuation of prior SFIO policy, the new PS's begrudging acceptance of the Atlantic Alliance contrasts with the former SFIO's enthusiastic Atlanticism. What explains this reluctance and why has the PS nevertheless opted to remain in the Atlantic Alliance?

The Socialists' major reservations concern the nature and purpose of the Atlantic Alliance as it has evolved since its inception in 1949. Originally conceived as a means to deter Soviet expansion into Western Europe (through its military arm, NATO), the Atlantic Alliance has in the view of the Socialists taken on another purpose — maintenance of the political and economic status quo in Western Europe. While the Socialists do not equate American influence in Europe with the degree of influence the Soviets have over their Eastern European bloc partners, they nevertheless fear U.S. intervention into French domestic politics, particularly in the event that they achieve governmental power in coalition with the French Communists.

Disquieting signs of U.S. hostility to a Left victory had become manifest by 1975. In November, in conversation with Mitterrand, Kissinger referred to the Atlantic Alliance quite specifically as an "anti-communist alliance."[3] Several months later, emissaries from the American Embassy in Paris called on several Socialist leaders with the message that the United States would not tolerate a Left government in France that included Communist ministers.[4] At a June 1976 meeting of the heads of leading Atlantic nations in Puerto Rico, a confidential agreement was made to deny financial aid to an Italian government that included Communist ministers — implying similar treatment in the French case. In addition, the Socialists did not rule out other forms of U.S. interference; for example, a chilling of diplomatic relations, CIA aid and support to the Right opposition groups, and continued or intensified economic and monetary pressure. To the nagging question of "Alliance militaire ou alliance politique?"[5] the Socialists respond that the Alliance must remain strictly a military one. As Charles Hernu, a leading PS defense expert, has put it:

The ideological base of the Atlantic Alliance is not capitalism and its multinationals, but the respect and defense of freedom, of democracy, of political pluralism. To refuse a democratic alternation of power in France is to deny the pluralist spirit of the Alliance.[6]

The Socialists' second major reservation with regard to the Atlantic Alliance concerns its very will and ability to protect the Europeans from Soviet attack. The PS Program of 1972 referred to the "nonnegligible risks" of membership in the Alliance and the "inconveniences" of the bloc system. U.S. withdrawal from Vietnam, talk of removal of some U.S. troops from Europe, general questioning in the United States about its role as "world policeman" — all these led the Socialists to question the automaticity of American aid in case of direct Soviet attack. In addition, the Socialists feared that Europe could become the victim of a preventive attack in the event of a direct superpower confrontation, that it would become "a privileged battlefield at the whim of either Soviet or American strategy."[7] What good, some Socialists asked, is an alliance that offers dependence without security?

Yet, despite these persistent reservations and criticisms, which contrast so vividly with the former SFIO Atlanticism, the PS position on alliances has not changed since the 1971 PS Congress (and subsequent reaffirmations of policy found in the 1972 party program, the Common Program of 1972, the abortive updating of that Common Program in September 1977, and the party's January 1978 special convention on defense policy). France, say the Socialists, should remain temporarily in the Atlantic Alliance, while resolutely rejecting a return to NATO's integrated military command.[8] As Mitterrand explains it:

France belongs to the Western world, to the Atlantic world. It is a participant in an alliance, the Atlantic Alliance. And the problem for France is to determine whether it is good to separate itself from this security system. When I answer this question, I'll say yes, *provided we have another system.*[9]

The Mitterrand majority, then, simply does not consider "another system" to be both imminent and viable. The simultaneous dissolution of the superpower blocs is an ultimate and far-off goal; a uniquely European defense system, while ideal, is not considered to be presently possible.[10] The best the Socialists can hope for, therefore, is to increase France's "autonomy of decision" within the existing system of alliances.

The CERES minority faction of the party, however, *does* envisage "another system" of national security, and that system is one of national independence. The CERES argues that, since France's existing allies (particularly the United States, but even the United Kingdom and West Germany) will be tempted politically, economically, even militarily to threaten a socialist experiment in France, a French Left government can survive only by withdrawing France from the Atlantic Alliance and relying on a system of total self-defense. In rejecting the notion of mutual collective security, the CERES position implies that a socialist France would not concern itself with the security of the rest of Europe. If Germany were invaded by the Soviet Union, for example, a socialist France would not come to its aid but would simply see to it that the invasion did not continue onto French territory.[11] To its critics, the CERES argues that its position of military nonalignment does not reflect so much on extreme nationalism as on the absolute priority of the protection of socialism in France. But if the CERES rejects the American nuclear umbrella afforded by participation in the Atlantic Alliance, how does it propose to ensure France's "total self-defense"? Its answer is to dramatically upgrade the deterrent capability of France's nuclear weapons, the FNS (*force nucléaire stratégique*).

NUCLEAR WEAPONS

Officially, the French Socialists have been opposed to the development and use of nuclear weapons throughout the Fifth Republic. Protesting from the time of the first nuclear tests in February 1960, they stood for the "interdiction" of the *force de frappe* (or unilateral nuclear disarmament) in Mitterrand's 1965 presidential campaign, the "interruption" of *force de frappe* construction in their 1972 program, and the "renunciation" of the strategic nuclear force, "immediate halt" to the production of the *force de frappe,* and reconversion of nuclear military industry into peaceful atomic industry in the Common Program of 1972. Yet, five years later, the antinuclear majority in the party had eroded. At a January 1978 special convention, the PS officially endorsed by a three-to-one margin the position that a French Left government would maintain the French nuclear deterrent.

That with time the question of nuclear weapons might require reexamination was evident to some in the PS several years before it became an open issue. While most militants' attitudes toward nuclear weapons continued to be determined by the vague antimilitarist and pacifist traditions of socialism, many of the party's defense experts (such as Charles Hernu and those on the *Commission de Défense Nationale*) had held a pronuclear stand ever since the party's founding in 1971. Thus one of the crucial concessions wrung from the Communists in the 1972 Common Program concerned the stated refusal of a future Left government to destroy the existing nuclear stockpiles — coupled, of course, with both parties' agreement to halt further production of the *force de frappe.* In his 1974 presidential campaign, Mitterrand was quite explicit about the need to reevaluate the party's nuclear position in the light of new developments.

There is no question of our destroying existing stockpiles in a unilateral bonfire. That is not how I conceive of foreign policy and national defense.[12]

Soon our atomic force will be an irreversible reality; we cannot drown it as we would new-born puppies.[13]

Philosophically, politically . . . I am against the development of national nuclear forces. But here you are asking me that question in 1974, and I am a realistic politician, and I must assume responsibilities for France. Over the last fifteen years, the *force de frappe* has become a reality, it exists.[14]

From a decision not to destroy the now mature *force de frappe,* the PS experts did not find it difficult to pass to the position of endorsing its use.

Thus, at an important November 1976 *Comité Directeur* meeting devoted to the question of defense, the three top defense experts — Robert Pontillon, Charles Hernu, and Jean-Pierre Chevènement — displayed remarkable unanimity in their endorsement of nuclear weapons. Their (and other experts') arguments ran as follows.[15] First, pacifism and antimilitarism could not be considered serious and responsible positions for a French Left assuming power for the first time in a full-fledged nuclear age. More specifically, initial charges that France, with a derisory *bombinette,* would be dwarfed by the superpowers were no longer valid. France was now a middle nuclear power, with a deterrence force already in its third generation and consisting of five nuclear-missile-launching submarines, eighteen land-based intermediate range ballistic missiles, and scores of strategic nuclear bombers. In addition, advanced technology had allowed a miniaturization of tactical nuclear weapons, thereby somewhat decreasing the difference between them and classical artillery. This meant that they could be used in ways more limited than the well-remembered Hiroshima and Nagasaki options (although, all together, the explosive power of the FNS equals 28,000 times the force of the Hiroshima bomb). Furthermore, the nuclear option could conceivably result in lower military expenditures than those needed for a modernized conventional army. Finally, it was pointed out that the original, much-criticized atmospheric nuclear tests (which caused radioactive fallout) could now be done underground, and that the earlier fear of contributing to nuclear proliferation was no longer relevant, since proliferation had occurred despite Socialist opposition.

Although these party experts agreed on the need to reverse the PS's official opposition to nuclear weapons, their conceptions of how the FNS fit into an overall national security policy differed crucially. It has been shown that the CERES leadership's strongly pronuclear position was a necessary corollary to its notion of "national independence" and withdrawal from membership in the Atlantic Alliance. As de Gaulle could pull out of the NATO integrated military command only after the *force de frappe* was credible, the CERES could seriously postulate a French Left pullout of the Atlantic Alliance only if the French nuclear force were expanded and achieved maximum deterrent capability. In addition, the CERES went so far as to retrieve a discarded Gaullist notion — that of a *tous azimuts* defense. *Tous azimuts,* literally "all points of the compass," meant that defense capabilities should not be geared to any anticipated or predesignated enemy (such as the Soviet Union) but should be ready to defend from any direction. Thus, in several ways, the CERES had outdistanced the Gaullists in the "Gaullist" nature of its national security policy.

In contrast to the CERES position, most of the defense experts in the Mitterrand majority (with the notable exception of Hernu) were unenthusiastic in their support of nuclear weapons. Most expressed a visceral revulsion against the nuclear option, but were reluctantly willing to bow to irreversible realities. Nevertheless, they stressed, the FNS made sense only within the context of France's adherence to the Atlantic Alliance. The FNS, in its present state, simply could not provide adequate, effective defense and therefore national security. To achieve a truly independent national defense capability would require an increase (based on the CERES's own figures) in the national military budget from 3 percent of the GNP to 5 percent.[16] The resultant 67 percent increase in defense spending would never be supported or tolerated by the Left's major constituencies. Furthermore, even if those increased funds allowed the FNS to become independent (through the development of France's own system of guidance, radar and satellites) the doctrine of *tous azimuts* remained absurd. The party experts' calculations were that the FNS could destroy some 14 percent of the industrial capacity and 15 percent of the population of the Soviet Union (which, after all, remained the potential enemy). Except for the submarine-launched missiles, these same weapons turned in the opposite direction would be able to reach perhaps to the mid-Atlantic, but no further. And, granted they could reach the U.K., there was no point, as Mitterrand put it, in aiming French missiles at France's own allies.

Why then maintain the FNS? The Mitterrand majority acknowledged a deterrent factor, but not the explicitly military one of the CERES. Rather, the FNS was seen as a possible bargaining card, a negotiating force for independence from the United States in particular. Crudely put, these Socialists reasoned that if the U.S. government did not allow the French to determine their own government and society (for instance, to vote for and support a socialist France), that Socialist government should be in a position to threaten a pullout from the Atlantic Alliance and to threaten rapid development of its nuclear force from a minimal into a maximum state of readiness. As Hernu put it:

The possession of nuclear weapons by a Socialist government as it comes into power would offer it a capacity of diplomatic deterrence. . . . It is a political as well as a military tool, and alone bestows, if not true independence, at least relative autonomy, which is something the left has discovered it will need when it comes to power.[17]

Until the spring of 1977, the nuclear debate had been carried out in the PS primarily at the level of expert commissions and leadership councils, and the changing consensus therein seemed to point to official ratification of a pronuclear stand at the party's June Congress. But in May the nuclear debate suddenly came into the open, as the PCF reversed its previous antinuclear position. The Communist leadership not only accepted the existing FNS but endorsed its further expansion as the sine qua non of national independence and French neutrality. The PS defense experts reacted in varying ways to the PCF's new nuclear policy. The most pronuclear experts anticipated that it would strengthen their case within the PS. The Common Program updating (in preparation for the 1978 legislative elections) was about to get under way, and a Socialist-Communist consensus on defense policy would be imperative. Other experts were disturbed not so much by the PCF policy reversal itself as by the fact that the various conditions placed on the FNS by the Communists seemed designed to undercut its credibility.[18] At the same time, the PCF announcement proved to be a catalyst to the antinuclear sentiment of many PS rank and filers, who suddenly became aware of the impending shift in official nuclear policy.[19]

Given the open divisions within the PS and the union of the Left, Mitterrand decided to postpone any nuclear decision by the party until a special convention could be held sometime before the elections. But in between June and that convention of January 1978, events moved rapidly to suspend the Common Program updating, the union of the Left, and, therefore, the hopes for a French Left government. By the end of July, the Common Program negotiators had unanimously resolved the nuclear-policy question by calling for a nationwide referendum. One week later PCF leader Georges Marchais contradicted his own negotiators by vehemently denouncing that idea (which had been proposed by Mitterrand). In the off-again, on-again September negotiations, the parties again reached agreement on the nuclear question, but all went for nought as the Communist leadership, in effect, put an end to any possibility of the French Left's approaching the March elections on the basis of a Common Program.

When the Socialist delegates met in early January 1978 to ratify their nuclear-defense position, technically they were no longer bound by the Common Program nor limited by PCF reactions. Nevertheless, they passed a motion (endorsed by 73 percent of those voting) aimed at alienating as few as possible both within the PS and in the Left in general. Specifically, the motion reiterated that the long-term (rhetorical) objective of a Left government would remain the renunciation of the FNS; that a Left government would work for general disarmament through the convening of and participation in world conferences to that end; that in the meantime, a Left government would maintain the FNS in working condition; and that any final decision would rest with the French people. A key amendment calling for partial unilateral disarmament (everything, in effect, except the five nuclear submarines) was defeated by a two-to-one vote. While rejecting the overly Atlanticist orientation of the party's antinuclear wing, the delegates similarly rejected a CERES amendment that sought to emphasize the goal of complete national military independence. Underlying the convention proceedings was Mitterrand's message that a Left government should remain "a loyal but not an integrated ally"[20] within the Atlantic Alliance, that a course of unilateral disarmament would be irresponsible, a course of further expansion of France's nuclear-defense capability unnecessary. Above all, the synthesis motion as adopted contained enough ambiguity to allow Mitterrand the free hand he insisted on in national security policy in the event that the Socialists achieved governmental power.

THE NEW ARMY

Unlike the debate over alliance participation and nuclear weapons, little disagreement has met the recent and innovative proposals put forth by party experts regarding the armed forces—proposals designed to create a "new army."

As questions of security, defense, and alliances traditionally had evoked disinterest or negative responses from French socialist militants, so too did the question of the army go long overlooked. From the Socialists' viewpoint, the army represented one more repressive instrument in the hands of the ruling bourgeoisie, and as such could not be considered an instrument of democracy. Rather, the army, the military, and the state in general could be transformed only after a decisive rupture with the status quo. Socialist militants, therefore, preferred to spend time and energy preparing for that political, social, and economic rupture which would lead France down the road to socialism.

By 1973, however, domestic and international events had moved domestic military affairs into the forefront of PS policy concerns. What happened in 1973–74? First, there was a growing malaise within the French army. Senior and junior officers and conscripts questioned what their role and mission might be in the age of heavy reliance on the nuclear deterrent. The army experienced difficulties in recruiting officers and specialists, and keeping them in career service. Then in the spring of 1973, demonstrations centering on changes in military service deferments took on a larger and decidedly antimilitary character. Public controversy surrounding the military was further fueled when the French government resumed nuclear tests in the Pacific in the summer of that year. By the fall of 1974, conscript discontent would spill over into street demonstrations, an event that raised a new issue—soldiers' rights to unionize within the army.

But the greatest jolt to Socialist complacency regarding the military was the Chilean coup in September 1973. With their own newly cemented strategy of union of the Left, the French Socialists naturally had been intrigued with the situation in Chile; Mitterrand had traveled there to discuss with Allende the latter's experiment in coming to power democratically in a coalition with the Communists. The September coup in Chile rudely reminded the French Socialists of the fact that in a progressive, democratic society the army does not automatically become a neutral instrument, that it can hijack the state on its "transition road to socialism."

Yet six months later events in Portugal gave the Socialists another lesson. It was the Portuguese army that finally ended that country's half-century of dictatorship. More to the point, unlike Third World and Arab "leftist" military regimes, the Portuguese army proceeded a year later to turn constitutional authority back to the civilians, thereby permitting the election of a Socialist government. Clearly, a nation's army could be friend or foe of the Left. Yet in 1974, with the increasing possibility of a leftist electoral victory in France, the Socialists' lack of any real and positive military policy placed them in a vulnerable position.

The initiative for formulating a new military policy came not from the antimilitary pacifist wings of the party but from those who upheld another tradition — one that went back to Jean Jaurès and his advocacy of a republican army, a "new army." The Jauresian viewpoint held that indifference or hostility to military and defense problems in no way served the interests of socialism. The solution, rather, was to achieve a profound transformation of the existing military establishment that would reintegrate it and reconcile it with the interests of the entire nation. Almost by self-selection, the modern Jauresian currents early on had dominated the PS's large and official *Commission de Défense Nationale*. In April 1974, proponents of this approach moved to set up the unofficial *Convention de l'Armée Nouvelle*.[21] Its purpose was to bring PS experts and militants together with socialist sympathizers in the armed forces in order to discuss freely problems of the military, establish important communication contacts, and, of course, increase party inroads into a previously ignored constituency. The first *Convention Nationale pour l'Armée Nouvelle* met in March 1975. Its reports and voting, while unofficial, gave much impetus to the growing consensus on the part of party experts that a Socialist defense policy should rest on "nuclear deterrence plus popular mobilization"; that together these constituted a uniquely socialist *force de dissuasion généralisée*.

What is meant by an army of "popular mobilization"? At a minimum, an army that is open and democratic and reflects the will of the majority. First and foremost it means a conscript army, not a professional or voluntary army. In the Socialists' view, a professional army will end up as a right-wing military corps, tied to the dominant ideology and all too concerned with defending against the "internal adversary" — that is, the Left. Nineteenth-century French military history tends to illustrate this charge well (for example, the police states of the two Napoleons, or the crushing of the Paris Commune). On the other hand, an army of obligatory conscription for all would be more likely to perceive its charge as limited to defending the nation from external military threats, not from legitimate domestic political change.

Besides continuation of universal service, the army should be further democratized, say the French Socialists, by reforming the material and moral terms and conditions of service. Instead of a full one-year service, which may account for the great sense of boredom and "lost time" expressed by conscripts, many French Socialists propose a six-month period of more intense military instruction; this initial service period would be followed by four years of brief retraining periods in the reserves.[22] Altogether, at any one time, the nation could count on a permanent body of 1.5 million trained combatants — double the number now in actual service.[23] In addition, conscripts would be assigned to units as close to their homes as possible. Then too, some experts acknowledge that a truly "socialist army" would entail the drafting of women, but this is by no means official policy.

Along with changing the terms of service, the Socialists advocate increasing soldiers' pay, upgrading the living standards of the barracks, and in general "liberalizing" the individual soldier's rights while in military service.

These new rights would include the right to form representative organizations or consultative commissions (to perform, in effect, an ombudsman role), the right to maintain pluralist life-styles (an end to military haircuts, for example) and to exercise freedoms outside of instruction hours (including political and intellectual activities in the barracks), and full recognition by the military of the rights of conscientious objectors. To sum up, the French Socialists say a soldier should have all the rights of civilians; he should be considered (as Charles Hernu entitled his book) a "soldat-citoyen."

To some Socialists (notably those in the CERES), however, the term "popular mobilization" means considerably more than reforming the conscript's daily life and democratizing the army structures. What these Socialists envisage is a vast network of citizens' militias, in the style of the present Swiss, Yugoslav, and Israeli armies. They point to the World War II Resistance Movement (in which Socialists and Communists, men and women, played leading roles) as a vivid example of true popular mobilization to defend a nation's independence. The CERES minority's concept of a more autonomous French defense is thus one of a maximum FNS and voluntary support and intervention forces for external defense, combined with the forces of popular mobilization to thwart internal threats to a socialist France.

European Construction

As the old SFIO embraced the Atlantic Alliance, it likewise embraced the notion of a United Europe. A united capitalist Europe today perhaps, but the dream envisaged a united socialist Europe tomorrow. The French Socialists of today no longer believe that evolution likely, and have adopted therefore a policy as expressed by Mitterrand: "Europe shall be Socialist or it simply shall not be."[24]

Originally the new PS had retained the SFIO policy of favoring the "progressive delegation of sovereignty on the part of member states" to a European organization, as stated in the 1972 PS program. Months later, however, PS negotiators were forced to drop temporarily their supranational proposals in order to permit the signing of the Common Program with the Communists. The compromise agreed on stipulated that a Left government in France would participate in the construction of Europe while maintaining liberty of action to implement its domestic common program. This "compromise" position then became official PS policy at a special conference on Europe held at Bagnolet in December of 1973. Thus the PS has gradually abandoned any notion of supranational powers. Why have the French Socialists pulled away from their earlier strong commitment to an emerging European community?

Basically, and in varying degrees, the French Socialists see the European Community as an integral part of the international capitalist system, which is itself dominated by American monetary and economic power via the multinationals. The EC is, therefore, the economic arm of American domination in Europe, just as the Atlantic Alliance is seen as its political-military arm. Whereas Soviet imperialism is geographically confined to Eastern Europe, American imperialism is a reality in Europe; whereas the Soviets present a hypothetical and future danger of Finlandization, the American presence in Europe brings a real and actual danger of Canadization.[25] Within the former SFIO this American connection was not contested because the party's intent was not primarily one of rupture with the capitalist status quo. The new French Socialists, however, mean to move beyond social democratic management of a predominantly capitalist society to a new socialist economy, based on major nationalizations, democratic planning and control, and *autogestion* (workers' self-management). This experiment could possibly find itself challenged, constrained, even doomed, by its EC and Atlantic surroundings. The Socialists' wariness toward the present EC, therefore, is twofold: on a more theoretical level, they do not wish to strengthen a capitalist (albeit reformed) Europe; on a practical level, they do not wish to risk sabotage of the creation of socialism in France.

An illustration of the party's unwillingness to endorse a "liberal Europe" was reflected in its stand on the February 1976 Tindemans Report. Leo Tindemans, the Belgian Prime Minister, had been charged by the 1974 Paris Summit to analyze and report on the status of European Union. In unanimously rejecting the document, the Socialists charged that it merely reflected Tindemans' personal preferences for an "advanced liberal society." The omissions in his report were almost as revealing as the propositions put forth, noted the Socialists. That is, nothing was said about the prevailing economic crisis, inflation, or unemployment; nothing about American hegemony and the grip of the multinationals; nothing about the role of trade unions or workers in a European construct. Five of the proposals in the report were categorized by the Socialists as either dangerous or contrary to PS or Common Program policy. They included an emphasis on "Atlantic allegiance"; policing by the Nine (the Atlantic powers) of crises in Europe and the Mediterranean basin; continuation of the monetary "snake" and accompanying austerity economics for the Nine; the proposed extension of EC institutional powers; and abandonment of the unanimity rule.[26]

In the view of the PS, adoption by the EC of the Tindemans Report would have limited the freedom of action of a future Left government. In any case, the Report met considerable opposition from various governments among the Nine, and its recommendations were largely ignored. But beyond this, the question of to what extent continued EC participation in general would constrain the French Left's domestic course of action remains a divisive one within the PS.

The skeptical, often anti-Europe, wing of the party is made up of the CERES and a contingent of the Mitterrand majority led by Pierre Joxe and Nicole Questiaux (who formerly headed the PS Policy Commission on Europe). This coalition argues as follows: after several decades of serious attempts at European unity, nation-states remain a profound reality. Therefore, the best way to make progress with European construction and the regeneration of the workers' movement in Europe is via the creation of a *"pôle socialiste autogestionnaire"* in France.[27] These Socialists are keenly aware that, in instigating radical domestic reforms, a Left government would meet with hostile reactions on the part of international monetary institutions and the U.S. government. Other members of the EC, particularly the U.K. and West Germany, might also be pressured to take measures to inhibit those economic and social reforms. But, reason these Socialists, France is not Chile or Portugal—her economy is considerably stronger and more self-sufficient. And, given the economic interdependence of the European nations within the European Community, officials in Brussels, as well as governmental leaders in Bonn and London, would probably decide to grant economic and financial aid to a radical and temporarily beleaguered France, rather than risk the health of the entire European economy.

The Mitterrand majority rejects this "socialism in one country" approach. A socialist France, they say, could not endure long in a hostile international environment without resorting to a posture of closure, of economic, monetary and trade protectionism, which would ultimately lead to self-destructive autarky. On the contrary, a socialist France can only survive *within* the larger context of a democratic and socialist Europe. What then, according to the Mitterrand wing, is the proper course of action for the party? To transform progressively the European entity by achieving immediate improvements in the common lot of European workers (antiinflationary measures, upward harmonization of social legislation, workers' control over work conditions, reduction of the work week) and by "opening" the EC to permit labor's interests to prevail over those of capital, to permit "the massive entry of workers into [the EC's] institutions."[28] Thus the need for strict control of multinational activities and foreign investments, common industrial and economic planning via the creation of a European public sector, increased trade-union representation in the European Steel Community and increased powers for that body, and direct elections to the European Parliament.

The recent issue of direct elections to the European Parliament provides an excellent example of the differing strategies within the PS regarding European construction. At first glance, it might be surprising to find opposition to that most democratic proposal, a proposal envisaged in the original Treaty of Rome (which the Socialists have always accepted), and reaffirmed in the March 1972 PS Program, the Common Program, and the Bagnolet Motion of 1973. Yet the CERES wing vociferously opposed ratification of the proposal for several reasons. First, the CERES charged that, like Pompidou's 1972 referendum on U.K. admittance to the EC, this proposal constituted a device to split the Left, to force its divisions out into the open. For while it was true that the Left had previously agreed on direct elections to the European Parliament, the French Communist Party this time had come out *against* the proposal. Georges Marchais had gone so far as to call the proposal "a crime against France, against her people"[29] Any issue that created a wedge in the union of the Left was harmful; therefore, argued the CERES wing, it was not in the interest of the PS to endorse direct elections.

There was a second—and more rational—reason for CERES opposition. The 1973 Bagnolet Motion had endorsed efforts at European construction *provided* they would neither bring antisocial policies, nor limit the freedom of action of a Left government, nor forestall or compromise the arrival of a Socialist Europe.[30] While the CERES wing was not saying that direct elections would necessarily work against these conditions, it felt that the party should use the issue to hold out for more progress in social policy reform, for instance. That is, the quid pro quo for Socialist endorsement of direct elections should be EC action going far beyond the scope of the Tindemans Report. As it was, Mitterrand was getting no concessions in return for his acceptance of direct elections — an acceptance he shared with the radicals, centrists, and Giscard's Independent Republicans!

Mitterrand and the majority responded by pointing out that democratization of EC institutions was precisely the way the *forces populaires* could make their weight, their interests, their demands felt, just as the purpose of the Left's domestic Common Program was to democratize French society in order to permit working-class hegemony and therefore begin the transition road to socialism. In the end, Mitterrand's wing triumphed. In February 1976, the *Comité Directeur* voted 97 to 34 in favor of direct elections to the European Parliament.

Conclusion

It is important to note that on the major foreign-policy issues examined here, the official PS position — qualified membership in the Atlantic Alliance, qualified maintenance of the FNS, qualified endorsement of European construction — represents more of a continuation than a break with French foreign policy in the Fifth Republic. It is equally important to realize that the practical reasons and philosophical assumptions behind the Socialists' positions, however, differ from those of the Right, whether Gaullist or Giscardian. The latter, basically content with the domestic socioeconomic status quo, tend to find foreign-policy motivation in such intangibles as the pursuit of grandeur and an enhanced international standing for the French nation. Conversely, the Socialists' priorities lie with peaceful albeit radical economic and social change. They hesitate, therefore, to combine that domestic course of action with drastic breaks with France's international commitments, especially when those commitments do not necessarily inhibit domestic change.

It is precisely on the point of international constraints, however, that opinions differ, not only within the PS (between the Mitterrand majority and the CERES) but between the PS and the PCF. The CERES and PCF, whose foreign-policy positions tend to coincide, have moved well beyond the original Gaullist notion of national independence. Their positions are more reminiscent of the short-lived postwar aim (of Communists and independent Left socialists) of a "neutral France." While more suspicious Socialists see such a posture as logical for the PCF, they bitterly criticize the CERES for what they consider to be a naive, outmoded, retrograde neutralist position.[31] Neutralism, the Mitterrand majority argues, means a weakened defense system and a weakened economic system, and would lead France into true Finlandization. Sweden's neutrality may be permitted by her peripheral position in Europe; Switzerland's by her difficult terrain. But France lies at the center of Europe. As Mitterrand explains:

First, let's look at where France is found. Am I going to challenge a geographical and historical description? It is useless; France belongs to Western Europe by geography and by the web of history; she must remain loyal to it.[32]

But that by no means implies unquestioning loyalty. As we have seen, the French Socialists are committed to continuing France's existing foreign policies only because they are considered less offensive than any of the alternatives. It follows, then, that the Socialists' approach is "to accept the physical body in order to transform its essence."[33] That is, to maintain a critical presence within what are recognized to be the flawed frameworks of the Atlantic and European communities and to work from within to shape policies that will allow dialectical change, meaning transcendence of the politico-military status quo in Europe.

Thus Mitterrand's foreign policy should be viewed in the light of his earlier "gamble" regarding domestic politics. In that situation, Mitterrand anticipated that, by committing the new PS to an electoral and programmatic union with the larger PCF, not only could the Left in time become a majority force in French politics, but the Socialist Party in the process would replace the PCF as the dominant partner of that coalition. Similarly, in the Socialists' efforts to change the very nature and content of the Atlantic Alliance and European Community, Mitterrand anticipates that a new solidarity will emerge between the more traditional social democrats of Northern Europe (including the Scandinavians) and the emerging democratic socialists of Southern Europe, that new solidarity and strength to be known as Eurosocialism.[34] Eurosocialism, to the French Socialists, means the creation of an independent and democratic socialist Europe, a European entity uniquely combining the notion of a decentralized, self-managing economic democracy, with the humane achievements of Western European social democracy, in strict adherence to the traditions of Western political democracy.

That goal of moving "beyond social democracy" is in itself an ambitious one, but the French Socialists go further and see Eurosocialism as offering real potential for international change: contagion into and therefore movement within Eastern Europe. Even beyond that, continues the Socialist argument, the resulting challenge to Soviet domination in Eastern Europe would not leave unaffected the Soviet government's relationship to its own people. Similarly, vis-à-vis the United States, the French Socialists say that a third-force Europe would directly challenge American economic domination, which in turn could have significant domestic implications for the U.S. government and economy. Thus Mitterrand's specific European policy is inextricably bound to, is indeed the condition for, the ultimate goal of his national-security policy—the end of postwar superpower domination of Europe and the simultaneous dissolution of both the Atlantic and Soviet blocs.

This essay concludes on a note of irony. Because of international and domestic changes over the past decade, the Western European Left no longer reflects the simple social democrat versus Stalinist split of the last half-century. Instead, as the recently emerging "Euro-Communist" parties attempt to distance themselves from their prior Soviet connection, they have placed great emphasis on individual *national* roads to socialism. In contrast, the newly felt Eurosocialist movement seeks to reverse the nationalist framework and ethos of its post–World War I social democratic heritage and to reassert the specifically international character of the nineteenth-century socialist movement. Paradoxically, then, changes within the Western European Left in the 1970s seem to be cementing the demise of the former Communist International at the same time that they are rejuvenating the original organization of democratic socialist solidarity, the Socialist International.

Notes

1. See my "Politics of the French Left: A Review Essay," *American Political Science Review* 69 (1975):1406–19 and "Ideology and Tactics of the French Socialist Party," *Government and Opposition* 12 (Autumn 1977):455–73.

2. See section IV, chap. 8 of the Common Program of 1972.

3. Reprinted in *Le Monde,* March 16, 1976.

4. A similar theme pervaded General Haig's remarks to a February conference on defense in Munich. Charles Hernu, a participant, gives an account in *La Nouvelle Revue Socialiste,* no. 20, 1976, pp. 51–53.

5. See article of same name by Jacques Huntzinger, *Le Monde,* May 2, 1976.

6. Charles Hernu, *La Nouvelle Revue Socialiste,* No. 20, 1976, pp. 51–53.

7. From the *Commission de Défense Nationale* Report of 1977, reprinted in *Faire,* February 1977, p. 39.

8. While France may remain outside the NATO integrated command, the existence of the Ailleret/Lemnitzer Accords of 1967 allows a coordinated military effort between France and NATO in the event, for example, of a Soviet attack across the Czech-German border. However, these prearranged defense plans are *not* binding on a French government. It has not yet been established whether a Left government would honor the Accords. It probably would.

9. Mitterrand press conference, April 12, 1974. Italics added.

10. Ironically, the French government is presently bound to the 1948 Treaty of Brussels, to which the six (France, Federal Republic of Germany, Italy, Benelux) plus Britain adhere. This Western European Union defense provision, however, is without an integrated military command, and—mainly because of the "German problem"—the French Socialists rule out such integration for the present.

11. When asked by the author if he thought the CERES would advocate a Left government's coming to *anyone's* aid, one CERES spokesman replied, "Perhaps a National Liberation Movement."

12. Interview with Mitterrand, *Paris Match,* May 1974, cited in Charles Hernu, *Soldat-Citoyen,* p. 246.

13. Cited by Jacques Huntzinger, "Le Parti Socialiste et la défense nationale," *Projet,* April 1976, p. 455.

14. Ibid.

15. See the resulting 1977 Report of the *Commission de Défense Nationale,* and further pro-nuclear arguments in articles by Jacques Huntzinger, *Nouvel Observateur,* November 15, 1976, p. 44; Gilles Martinet, *Nouvel Observateur,* November 22, 1976, and again in *Faire,* February 1977.

16. *Reperes,* April 1977, p. 36.

17. Hernu, *Soldat-Citoyen,* p. 197, and as cited in Pierre Dabezies, "Défense Ambiguë," *Projet,* April 1976, p. 430.

18. For instance, the PCF advocated that the FNS defense option replace France's

membership in the Atlantic Alliance; that the decision to use the nuclear weapons be made collegially by four or five key government people; that the FNS be based on an "anticity" strategy, be declared of a purely defensive nature, and be based on the policy of *tous azimuts*.

19. Many antinuclear militants felt the nuclear debate had been carried out in a way that was not conducive to an open and democratic party decision. As one of them put it regarding the (advisory) *Commission de Défense Nationale:* "We sometimes had the impression that instead of creating a socialist pressure group in the midst of the army, we ended up creating a military pressure group in the midst of the PS." *Faire,* July-August, 1977, p. 7.

20. *Le Monde,* January 10, 1978. See this and issue of January 8–9, 1978, for details of convention.

21. Instigated by Charles Hernu, Robert Pontillon, Jean-Pierre Chevènement, General Jean Bécam (Air Force), and Albert Dureau (Navy).

22. The proposed six-month service period is opposed, however, by the party's professional military experts, who consider that short a period of military training almost worthless.

23. Presently, one-third of eligible recruits are exempt from service. The Socialists would tighten up exemptions.

24. *L'Unité,* January 21, 1976.

25. *Frontière,* November 1973, pp. 54 and 58.

26. The Tindemans Report was published as a January 1976 supplement to the *Bulletin of the European Communities.* The Socialist case is stated by Jean-Pierre Cot in his January 29, 1976, press conference and again in *Faire,* May 1976, pp. 10–11.

27. *Reperes,* April 1977, p. 8.

28. Bagnolet Motion, December 1973.

29. On France Inter Radio, cited in *Le Monde,* January 28, 1976.

30. See the full argument in *Reperes,* February 1976, pp. 29–41.

31. Some even go so far as to characterize the CERES as "communo-gaullist national socialist"!

32. May 2, 1974, press conference, cited in Huntzinger, "La Politique étrangère du Parti Socialiste," *Politique Étrangère* 2 (1975):183.

33. Robert Pontillon, citing Mitterrand, in *La Nouvelle Revue Socialiste,* no. 23, 1977, p. 13.

34. To explore the idea of a uniquely Southern European socialist grouping, Mitterrand assembled socialist party chiefs from Italy, Spain, Portugal, and Belgium at a May 1975 meeting in his country home in Latche. The group then held a Paris conference on January 24–25, 1976, with observers from the distinctly northern European Finnish, Swedish, Dutch, Swiss, and Luxembourg socialist parties. This meeting followed by a few days the Socialist International preparatory meeting at Helsingör, Denmark, at which Schmidt's "social democratic liberalism" was criticized by the "Southern European democratic socialists." In the end, geographical considerations were recognized as secondary to ideological ones, and all parties were actively present at the November 1976 Socialist International Congress in Geneva. See the PS publication, "Conférence des Partis Socialistes d'Europe du Sud," 1976.

A Note on Sources

Primary sources on PS foreign policy include:

1972 PS Program *Changer la vie* (Flammarion, 1972).

1972 PS-PCF *Programme commun de gouvernement* (Flammarion, 1973, or Editions Sociales, 1972).

1974 PS Assises du socialisme *Pour le socialisme* (Editions Stock, 1974).

1975 PS "Quinze thèses sur l'autogestion," pamphlet supplement to *Le Poing et la rose,* no. 45, November 15, 1975.

1978 PS Program "Propositions socialistes pour l'actualisation du programme commun de gouvernement de la gauche."

Motions from 1971, 1973, 1975, 1977 PS Congresses and special conventions on European Policy (Bagnolet, December 1973) and Nuclear Defense (Paris, January 1978).

In addition, see *Pour une reflexion ouverte sur la sécurité et la paix,* a collection of unofficial documents of the *Commission de Défense Nationale* and the *Conventions pour l'Armée Nouvelle,* put out by the latter, 1977.

See also the following specific issues of these party-related journals:

La Nouvelle Revue Socialiste, nos. 6 (1974), 20 (1976), and 23 (1977).
Faire, nos. 4 (1976), 8 (1976), 16 (1977), 18 (1977), and 25 (1977).
Reperes, nos. 28 (1975), 29 (1976), 33 (1976), and 42 (1977).

Also

Jacques Huntzinger, "La Politique étrangère du Parti Socialiste," *Politique Etrangère* 2 (1975): 177-99.
_____. "Le PS et la défense," *Projet,* April 1976, pp. 450-58.
Jean-Pierre Chevènement and Pierre Messmer, *Le Service militaire,* Balland, 1977.
Charles Hernu, *Soldat-citoyen: essai sur la défense et la sécurité de la France,* Flammarion, 1975.

8 The Ideological Development of the Swedish Social Democrats

JOHN D. STEPHENS

During the 1970s, the Swedish labor movement, the Social Democratic Party, and the Swedish Confederation of Trade Unions (LO) moved from the welfare-statist issues that had concerned them since the Social Democrats' accession to power in 1932 back to the classical issue of socialism — democratic ownership and control of industry — which had concerned them at the initial stages of their development. In this essay, I will argue that the movement from socialism to welfare statism and back to socialism was the result of two developments in the structure of Swedish civil society: changes in the class structure and changes in the distribution of power.

Socialist and Welfare-Statist Ideology Defined

Tingsten defines "ideology" as a collection of political concepts that are developed into a systematic whole and are meant to give a definite and general directive for action. To spell out the essential elements of an ideology in a little more detail, they should include a goal, some valued and possible image of a future state of affairs; an analysis of the deficiencies of the present state of society; and some strategy of how the present order can be changed in order to resemble the desired order. In this definition strategy is broadly conceived to include such basic choices as reform versus revolution as well as broader policy considerations such as nationalization of industry or development of worker-controlled enterprises.[1]

A socialist ideology is one that is aimed at social ownership and democratic control of production. In the early period, the Swedish Social Democrats believed that (democratic) socialization of production would result in a classless society. While this may be definitionally true according to some Marxist definitions of class, it is not true if one defines social class in Weberian terms, since inequalities in other market capacities, such as skill or education, may still differentiate people in market societies. In the ideal type of the competitive market, income distribution is determined by the supply and demand for various market capacities (labor power, skills, and capital). By a welfare-statist ideology is meant one that is aimed at the equalization of market-determined income by any means other than the socialization of property. This includes collective action in bargaining as

This chapter was presented as a paper at the World Congress of Sociology, Uppsala, 1978.

well as redistribution through taxation and the provision of public goods and services. "Economism" is a more pejorative term for this type of ideology. Efforts to promote social mobility will also be considered welfare-statist.

The central argument here is that the policy focus of Swedish social democracy changes from socialist to welfare-statist and back to socialist. The ultimate goal of the movement, a classless society, has never changed. This can be seen not only from examining the party programs and other party publications but also from the writings, particularly the memoirs, of all the party's important leaders and ideologists, such as Branting, Hansson, Wigforss, and Erlander. Furthermore, the changes in the party's analysis of the deficiencies of the present social order (that is, the causes of social inequality) should not be exaggerated. It is true that the welfare-statist phase is associated with increased emphasis in the analysis on the stratifying influence of skills and education and greater devotion to the theoretical reasons for the class asymmetry in acquisition of skills and education. But this has not been deemphasized in the recent return to more socialist policies. And even the most conservative party program, the 1960 program, which marked both the end and the pinnacle of the Social Democrats' welfare-statist phase, emphasized the role of private property as the most important cause of inequality in the distribution of income and control relations in society. It should be clear by now that the terms "socialist ideology" and "welfare-statist ideology" are used only as convenient summarizing terms to characterize the shifts in the focus of the reform work of the Swedish labor movement.

To 1917: Reformist Marxism

During the 1870s Sweden entered a period of rapid industrialization. Vigorous labor organizing began in the next decade. German socialist ideas found their way to Sweden via Denmark, and socialist agitation also began in earnest in this decade. Though Lasallian influences can be found in many early tracts, Marxist ideas were quickly adopted by most of the important leaders once they were introduced in Sweden. The Social Democratic Workers' Party was founded in 1889 and two years later adopted a thoroughly Marxist program, a revised version of the German Erfurt Program, as its first party program. The ideology that dominated the party in this early period can most accurately be characterized as reformist Marxist. Though the Swedes stood slightly to the right of the German party in the Socialist International, the ideological viewpoint best articulated by Karl Kautsky is not far from that of the more sophisticated Swedish leaders.[2] The party's goal was the achievement of a classless society. Following the Marxist analysis of capitalism, the sole deficiency of the prevailing social order was believed to be private ownership of the means of production. The Marxian orthodoxy on the process of transition to socialism was also followed. The material base for socialism, the elimination of scarcity and the socialization of labor, would be developed by the processes of concentration and centralization of capital, which were inherent in capitlist production itself. Capital centralization and the mechanization of skilled labor would result in a huge proletariat faced by a small bourgeois class. This polarization of classes would provide fertile ground for the development of labor organization, which would be further spurred on by periodic crises of capitalism. Though predominantly Marxist in this early phase, the Social Democratic leadership never contained a very big revolutionary component. The strategy was always to build up a mass-based movement aimed at winning universal suffrage and then, by using the vote, to win control of the state to transform capitalist society. The practical political work of the Social Democrats in this period was largely focused on the introduction of universal suffrage and cabinet responsibility to parliament. This goal was achieved in 1918 when the Social Democrats and the Liberals forced the king and the Conservatives to capitulate in the wake of the defeat of Germany.

The only significant revisions of the Social Democrats' ideology in this period were changes in the analysis of the development of the class structure. It seemed apparent that the tendency toward centralization of property did not hold for the countryside. Thus the program was revised to reflect this change. Private small holding was deemed to be compatible with socialism. This change and the subsequent changes in the analysis of the class structure made to accommodate the reality of the growth of propertyless nonmanual workers (that is, the absence of the predicted class polarization) do not in themselves represent a departure from a commitment to socialist ideology as long as the centrality of private ownership is retained. These developments in the class structure do, however, have consequences for party strategy and policy.

Ideological Crisis in the Twenties

Once democracy had been established, the basis for the Social Democratic–Liberal coalition dissolved, and the Social Democrats subsequently formed a minority government. This government then set about to concretize the Social Democrats' plan to transform society in a socialist direction. Two parliamentary commissions were appointed: one on industrial democracy, the other on socialization. This brought the issue of socialization to the center of political debate. The bourgeois parties mounted a major offensive on the issue. The socialist bloc (Social Democrats and Left socialists or Communists) suffered a setback in the election. While there is some doubt as to whether their position on socialization caused this defeat, it seems clear that the Social Democrats' position created little enthusiasm in the electorate.[3] The advent of democracy had not brought the victory for socialism that the early Social Democratic leaders expected. In no election in the twenties did the socialist bloc's share of the vote exceed 46 percent. Furthermore, when the Social Democrats took a step toward more radical policies, as in the 1928 election, they suffered a setback. The voice of the people had been heard, and it did not support socialism. This not only confounded the party leadership's expectations; it also led to a reassessment of the party's program.

Sweden had been plagued by unemployment all through the twenties. Several Social Democratic minority governments had tried to deal with the problem but found no solution. Fortunately the party was blessed by having among its ranks one of international social democracy's most brilliant theoreticians and practical thinkers, Ernst Wigforss. Wigforss had been studying the problem of unemployment, and, through a combination of insights derived from his reading of Keynes's early work and his own Marxist orientation, he developed an underconsumption theory of unemployment. He successfully argued the case for a reflationary program in the party executive. The Social Democrats proposed this program in the Riksdag in 1930, six years before Keynes published his *General Theory*. The reflationary program and expansion of the public sector formed the cornerstone of the Social Democrats' 1932 election program, which propelled them to power. At the same time, the party leadership made a fairly definite commitment to suppress the issue of socialization. It was thus that the transition from a socialist ideology to a welfare-statist ideology was effected.

Causes of the Ideological Transformation

Virtually every author who has addressed himself to the subject agrees that the Social Democrats went through important ideological changes after 1920, but there is very little agreement on what caused the change or even on what elements of the ideology actually changed. Three main points of view arise in the discussion: Tingsten's, Lewin's, and Lindhagen's.[4]

Tingsten begins with a presentation of a Marxist perspective that is actually the rather determinist version of Marxism developed by Engels and later by Kautsky. The development from capitalism to socialism is seen as an *inevitable* event caused by the polarization of classes, the recurrent crises of capitalism, and the socialization of the forces of production within the capitalist relations of production. Tingsten then traces the departures from this Marxism up to 1920, linking them to the failure of social developments to proceed as predicted and the strategical need of the party to appeal to other groups than the industrial working class. After 1920, the party progressively dropped social ownership of production from any consideration in its action program. Its action program and its policy came to be completely determined by practical questions and tactical considerations. The party became social reformist instead of socialist. The Liberals, on the other hand, had moved from classical liberalism to social liberalism, also a social reformist position; thus an end to ideological differences had been effected. The reasons Tingsten gives for the change in the Social Democrats' position focus on the deficiencies of Marxism. First, the determinist view not only gave no guide to action but even was contradictory to any voluntary action; thus it had to be given up. Second, Marx was wrong about social developments and thus no majority existed for socialization, so the Social Democrats had to give up that policy in order to move into a majority position.

Lewin also begins with the premise that the Social Democrats' ideological crisis was caused by the fact that their deterministic version of Marxism gave them no guide for day-to-day political action and policymaking. However, Lewin did not conclude that as a result of dropping Marxism or even a socialization policy, the Social Democrats became unideological or that there were no differences between the parties. Through careful study of the editorializing, speeches, parliamentary debates, and political decisions of the Swedish political parties, he came to the conclusion that there were differences between the Social Democrats and the Liberals in the "collection of political concepts" and that they did result in similar differences in policy suggestions. The difference between them lay in the differences between the socialist idea of freedom and the liberal idea of freedom. The socialist idea of freedom went beyond the liberal idea in that it included freedom from economic hindrances in the individual's pursuit of a satisfying life.

Lindhagen agrees with Tingsten that the Social Democrats gave up their Marxist heritage and became social reformists but disagrees on the causes of this development. Because of the depression and the threat of fascism, the Social Democrats in the thirties and forties were forced to carry out a policy that was not socialist, though the top leadership, Per Albin Hansson, Ernst Wigforss, Rickard Sandler, Gustav Möller, and others, remained Marxists in their convictions. However, the younger generation of Social Democrats developed a nonsocialist ideology in a polemic with the Communists. The fatal development was that this social reformist ideology became a justification of the policy carried out by the leadership and vice versa. Practical politics began to rule without reference to considerations of socialist theory.

There is some truth in all of these explanations, but none of them identifies the single most important factor in the ideological transformation of Swedish social democracy. Lewin and Tingsten are correct that the deterministic version of Marxism gave them no guide to day-to-day action. Of course, neither would any other theory at that level of generality. The need for action only led to the dropping of the more deterministic elements of their ideology in much the same way in which they had revised their analysis of the class structure earlier. But why did this program not involve socialization? Tingsten argues that the electorate was against socialism, in part because the social base of socialism, the industrial working class, was a minority of the population. While it is true that developments in the class structure put the Social Democrats in a much more difficult situation than the early Marxists imagined would be the case, it is not true that support for socialism must be limited to industrial workers. All propertyless employees, manual and nonmanual, urban and rural, have an objective interest in socialism. Thus over 70 percent of the Swedish electorate had an objective interest in socialism in 1920 when the socialist bloc received 39 percent of the vote. Obviously the objective interest in socialism was not being translated into subjective support for it. In fact, it is likely that many of the Social Democrats' own supporters were not socialists—did not favor socialization of the principal means of production. They were non- (not anti-) socialists. At least, we would argue, there was a sizable minority who were not socialists. There can be no conclusive proof of this one way or the other. But the following evidence points in this direction. First, some of the party leadership at the time held this opinion. In 1918, Arthur Engberg wrote, "The socialist view of society has not penetrated the forces we have had up to now . . . the party . . . is four-fifths hostile to the socialist view of life."[5] Second, survey data from the post–World War II era show that the older cohorts of Social Democrats, which were mobilized between 1880 and 1930, are much more conservative than the younger Social Democratic voters. Comparison of survey data from the late forties and the late sixties confirms that this is a change through time and not an aging phenomenon.[6]

Capitalist democracies are historically unique societies in their combination of two characteristics. They are based on the belief among the masses that they (the masses) are sovereign.[7] And the masses do, in fact, elect the incumbents in the state apparatus. Thus, domination in capitalist democracies rests on the subjective consent of the masses to a much greater degree than in traditional authoritarian or socialist authoritarian societies, which lack one or both of these characteristics. Consequently, the cornerstone of bourgeois domination is the control of "public opinion" through control of the media and all other institutions, both public and private, as well as through the sheer weight of tradition. Antonio Gramsci can be credited with the most original and important contribution to the analysis of domination in capitalist democracies in his theorizing of this phenomenon, which he called hegemony.[8] To challenge the hegemony of the bourgeoisie, the socialist movement must develop its own hegemonic presence in society through union and party organization. Though some of the socialist movement's methods of opinion-influencing, such as the establishment of a Socialist press, will mirror bourgeois methods it must rely primarily on building up a network of personal contacts through the extension of formal organizations. By far the most important form of organization is labor organization. Trade unions represent people in the heart of the capitalist mode of production—that is, in their role as individuals dependent on the sale of their labor power. Trade unions perform the double function in negating the pure type of capitalism by ending competition between workers and by confronting capital. And finally, since trade unions represent people in their economic role, they have a financial base that is unparalleled in any other form of popular organization.

In linking hegemony to labor organization, we also link it to Marx's theory of the transition to socialism. Labor organization is the active, conscious side of the transition. Through organization working people begin to transform society in a socialist direction. This transformation begins when the first workers organize: a purely capitalist society no longer exists. Not only do they put an end to competition among themselves and confront capital collectively on the market, they are also able to influence political development. For instance, Marx attributes the passage of the ten-hour bill to working-class political action. This example demonstrates that, for Marx, power is derived from property ownership alone only in the pure type of capitalism—that is, before workers begin to organize. In any transitional form of capitalism, organization will also be a source of power. As

Table 8.1 Percentage of the Labor Force Organized in Sweden

	LO	TCO	SACO/SR
1900	2		
1910	4a		
1920	11		
1930	19	1b	
1940	32	4	
1945	37	7	1c
1950	41	9	1
1960	46	12	2
1965	46	12	3
1970	49	21	3
1975	56	28	5

LO: Landsorganisationen (Swedish Federation of Trade Unions) primarily manual workers; TCO: Tjanstemannens Centralorganisation (Central Organization of Salaried Employees); SACO: Sveriges Akademikers Centralorganisation (The Swedish Confederation of Professional Associations); SR: Statstjanstemannens Riksforbund (National Federation of Civil Servants); a LO lost a general strike in 1909, which resulted in the loss of half of its membership. Consequently the 1910 figure is not reflective of the general trend; b 1931. TCO was reformed in 1944 through a combination of SACO and old TCO. The figures for 1931 and 1940 refer to both organizations; c 1947.

the level of organization increases, the distribution of power in civil society changes. The policy output of the state changes as a result. Given his projections for the development of class structure, Marx certainly expected a rapid transition to occur at some point even in cases where he expected a parliamentary reformist change, as in Holland, the United States, and Britain. In my conception, the change can occur much more gradually, as it has in the Swedish case (see Table 8.1). Gramsci's concept of hegemony allows one to link the changing distribution of power in civil society to the policy output of the state. The buildup of labor organization and the consequent increase in the hegemony of the socialist movement in civil society changes the degree of class consciousness or, in the terms of mainstream sociology, the modal opinion in society. In a democratic society this will have an effect on the policy output of the state.

To return to the Swedish case, the main reason for the transformation of Social Democratic ideology in the late twenties was the weakness of socialist hegemony. With only 20 percent of the labor force organized, the movement's ability to influence opinion was not sufficiently great to reach enough people on radical questions like socialization of property, which is always the first line of defense for bourgeois forces since it is the base of their power. The average voter could not be reached with a socialist program, so the Social Democrats had to modify their program.[9]

The Welfare-Statist Period: 1932–57

Though the socialist bloc won 50 percent of the vote in 1932, it did not reach a parliamentary majority, because the Left socialists and Communists were underrepresented in the lower house and because the upper house represented an older electoral opinion. To pass their program, the Social Democrats made a deal with the Farmers' Party in which they traded price support for farm products for support for their reflationary policies and welfare-statist program. This alliance dominated Swedish politics until 1957, although there was a formal coalition between the two parties only in 1936–39 and 1953–57. Because of their setback in the election of 1948 after a brief and moderate trend toward radicalization of the party's action program, the Social Democrats immediately began to make overtures to the farmers. The policy output of this period can be seen as reflecting the common interests of workers and small farmers. These groups are united by their status as low-income earners and the low educational opportunities for their offspring, but divided by ownership of property. So Social Democratic policy was aimed at redistribution and expansion of higher education, not at socialization of property. The configuration of the class structure thus necessitated an alliance that reinforced the movement of Social Democratic policy from socialism to welfare statism.

It should not be surprising that changes in the class structure in the postwar period were a prime cause of the breakup of the Social Democratic/Farmer coalition. The decline in the farming population and expansion of the ranks of nonmanual employees stimulated the Farmers' Party to attempt to change its image as well as its name (now "Center Party") in order to appeal to urban nonmanuals. The Social Democrats also perceived that their social base, primarily the industrial working class, was eroding,[10] and as a consequence they wanted to reorient their program to attract nonmanual employees. The pension issue gave the Center Party a chance to go its own way, and the coalition broke up in 1957.

Before moving to the last stage of the development of the Swedish Social Democrats' ideology, a few comments on the end of ideology debate are in order here, since the view that the Social Democrats were not different from the Liberals applies to this period more than to any other. Tingsten and Lindhagen both claim that the Social Democrats became a social reformist party not very different from the Liberals.[11] This is a misreading of history. In fact there were substantial differences in the policies of the two parties in this period. And these policy differences did reflect the "collection of political concepts" the parties held. The Social Democrats continued to have a very different analysis of the sources of social injustice than the Liberals. Their analysis was a class analysis that still emphasized the central role of private ownership of property though adding the stratifying influence of education and skills. The Social Democrats' political strategy was also based on this class analysis. In the political debate, they always emphasized the class interest underlying political positions. And the party remained formally committed to the goal of a classless society (though one can question whether the leadership believed that goal to be achievable). Furthermore, within the constraints of the alliance with the farmers, the party's policy was guided by this class analysis.

Lewin, then, is correct that the Social Democrats never became unideological. However, his analysis is misleading on two accounts. First, it was not differences in their "ideas of freedom" that separated the Liberals and the Social Democrats. Rather, it was their analysis of unfreedom, injustice, or inequality that separated them. Second, Lewin exaggerates the continuity in Social Democratic policy. The repression of the issue of socialization was a significant change. Granted that socialism never completely disappeared from the day-to-day policy concerns of the Social Democrats: they always promoted the socialization of control rights of capital. For instance, such decision-making powers as plant location, investment policy, and employment policy were partially or wholly shifted to the state. But the dominant focus of reform was welfare-statist, not socialist. And given the centrality of property ownership in the analysis of the Social Democrats, this focus is not without inconsistencies.[12]

Toward a Wage-Earner Coalition

The strategic aim of Social Democratic policy after 1957 was to broaden the party's base by increasing its support among nonmanual employees. On the whole, the initial effect of this strategy was expressed in a deradicalization of the Social Democrats' program in that it involved a deemphasis on redistribution. In the pension issue that dominated the political debate of the late fifties, the Social Democrats proposed an earnings-related pension. The radical element of the proposal was not the redistributive effects (which were not great) but rather the development of a huge pension fund, which came to dominate the entire credit market. The tax policies of the early sixties also reflect the deemphasis on redistribution. The reforms of this period were financed through the introduction of regressive taxes, such as the national value-added tax.

In the special party congress in 1967 the Social Democratic Party began a process of ideological renewal that culminated in putting the issue of socialization back into the center of the labor movement's program in the mid-seventies. The first big step in this direction was the "enterprise democracy" or employee participation issue, which dominated the Swedish debate from 1971, when the LO proposed massive increases in employee control in the workplace, to 1976, when the last of a series of laws which by and large followed the LO's proposal was passed. These laws all socialized control rights of property without actually transferring the legal title.

The second and current phase of development entails nothing less than the placement of socialism on the immediate political agenda. In 1975, an LO study group proposed the introduction of "wage-earner funds," a form of collective ownership that would gradually come to dominate the entire Swedish economy. The proposal was adopted by the 1976 LO congress. After some vacillation on the issue in the 1976 campaign, the Social Democrats have come down solidly in favor of the concept. In February 1978, an LO–Social Democratic study group presented a revised version of the original LO proposal, which was to be the labor movement's common position on the issue. The proposal is complex, but its main feature is clear enough. Through a profits tax and a tax on the wage bill, a number of wage-earner capital and credit funds would be built up. The voting power of the stock in the capital funds would be shared by the employees in the firm in question and in the county where the firm is located. Because the ownership is to be collective and the shares cannot be sold, the development of the capital funds would insure that ownership of all firms with more than 500 employees would gradually be transferred to the employees. The average time it would take for the employees to reach a majority is calculated to be about 35 years.[13]

The basis for this reorientation of the Swedish labor movement's program was the changes in the class structure already discussed and the changes in the distribution of power in civil society. The labor movement's program came to focus on what unites blue- and white-collar workers: their status as propertyless employees. The growth of nonmanual employees in the work force necessitated some sort of appeal to this group by the Social Democrats. But what made it possible to reach them with such a radical program was the organization of white-collar workers (see Table 8.1). This broke the social and political hegemony of capital over nonmanual employees and caused a decisive change in the distribution of power in civil society. The importance of this change is reflected in the key position of the TCO, the central white-collar union, in Swedish politics. When LO and TCO line up strongly on the same side of an issue, even the two Left bourgeois parties, the Center and the Liberals, cannot afford to oppose them, since a majority of their voters come from trade-union households. This was the case in the enterprise democracy legislation. And the strategy of the LO and the Social Democrats on wage-earner funds is to get the TCO on their side, thereby neutralizing any opposition from the bourgeois Left.

Comparative Implications

This analysis of Sweden has implications for the development of the welfare state and the possibilities of transition to socialism elsewhere in the developed capitalist world. In general, state policy should reflect the degree of labor organization and hegemony in a given society. And, in fact, the size of the nonmilitary public sector is highly correlated (.72) with incumbency of leftist parties in western capitalist societies, and left incumbency in turn is highly correlated with the strength of organized labor in those societies (.81).[14] Thus, it would appear that the pace of welfare-state development is governed by the political and organizational power of labor in society. By extension of this argument, one would expect that the potential for socialist transformation would be greatest in the highly developed welfare states with strong labor movements, such as Norway and Austria, in addition to Sweden.

There is an alternative, and in large part directly contradictory, interpretation to these findings. A number of authors have pointed out that these three societies, along with the Netherlands, Denmark, Finland and Belgium, are characterized by "corporatist" policymaking patterns.[15] In Schmitter's classic formulation, these societies come close to the ideal type of a system of interest representation "in which the constituent units are organized into a limited number of singular, compulsory, non-competitive, hierarchically ordered and functionally differentiated categories . . . licensed . . . by the state and granted a deliberate representational monopoly . . . in exchange for certain controls on selection of their leaders and articulation of demands and supports."[16] All seven of the societies mentioned in this and the previous paragraph are, indeed, characterized by the presence of very centralized labor and employer federations, and most of them by centralized federations of farmers, small businessmen, and other economic interest groups. The implication of the literature on corporatism, particularly that written from a Left perspective, is that the "controls on . . . articulation of demands" are controls on labor, not capital. More specifically, corporatism is seen as a method of controlling labor by incorporating it into the system. Labor is granted representation in the system and influence over economistic (welfare-statist) issues such as wages, hours, public-sector spending, and taxes in return for limiting its demands to such issues and for abstaining from any disruption of the system of production, such as strikes. Cross-national comparisons give some credence to this argument: strike rates are indeed quite low in the societies in question, and the labor movements in all these countries except Belgium have accepted de facto or de jure policies of wage restraint for extended periods in the postwar era.[17] In the "corporatism" analysis, the absorption of labor into the system in these societies indicates that possibilities of socialist transformation are very small, and countries where the labor movement has taken a more radical and oppositional posture and where labor militancy (as measured by strike rates) is very high, such as France and Italy, offer much greater possibilities for a socialist transformation.

Both arguments appear to have their merits, yet they also appear directly contradictory in their conclusions. Let us look more closely at the development of the "corporatist" pattern of policymaking to assess the relative merits of the two points of view.[18] The key event in the development of corporatism is the establishment of centralized nationwide bargaining between capital and labor. This sets the scene for the entrance of the government as the third party in centralized nationwide negotiations over wages, hours, investment, taxes, public spending — in short, the whole range of economic and social policy. In the Swedish case, the development of corporatist policymaking begins with the signing of the Saltsjöbaden peace agreement between labor and capital in 1938 and culminates with the institution of nationwide bargaining in the early postwar period. Thus it develops only after the Social Democrats are in power and organized labor is quite strong. Cross-national comparisons show that this pattern is absolutely invariable. Bargaining centralization never develops until at least 44 percent of all nonagricultural employees are organized *and* the Social Democrats have entered the government either alone or as stable coalition partners with a centrist party. Thus, centralized bargaining seems to grow out of conditions of strong working-class political and economic power. Employers became willing to enter into centralized bargaining only when it becomes obvious that the labor movement is too strong to be defeated and that compromise is necessary. The labor movement, for its part, is willing to accept such corporatist policies as wage restraint only when it feels assured that it can get something in return, such as expansion of redistributive public expenditure and price controls. Only when parties of the labor movement itself are in power does it feel so assured.

This corporatist pattern of policymaking is a compromise between capital and labor, a "historic compromise" not unlike the one now proposed by the PCI, as Korpi points out.[19] And the compromise has not been without its costs to labor. In return for public-sector redistribution, low levels of unemployment, and government control of some of the externalities of capitalist development such as pollution, the labor movement has accepted some wage restraint and largely ceded the control of technological developments, the investment process, and the planning of work (at least as of the mid-sixties). But contrary to the leftist critics of social democracy, the alternative to the corporatist pattern is distinctly worse from the working-class point of view. Not only does the working class do no better in terms of control relations; it does decidedly worse in terms of income distribution. The public sector effects little or no redistribution in countries such as France compared to the massive redistribution achieved in Norway or Sweden. The vaunted militancy of the French working class is actually a product of its political impotence. As Korpi and Shalev show, labor movements only resort to the strike weapon when they cannot achieve their goals through the political process.[20] This is why such otherwise different labor movements as the American and French share the characteristic of having a very high strike rate; both have been largely excluded from the exercise of political power in the postwar period. Thus, the alternative to "corporatism" is not "pluralism," as Schmitter's essay seems to indicate; it is the class rule of the capitalist class. Corporatism represents a deadlock in the class struggle in which the working class is sufficiently strong to force substantial concessions from capital, but not strong enough to take control of the accumulation process itself.

Furthermore, this analysis of Sweden indicates that the buildup of organization and labor hegemony achieved in the development of the welfare state sets the scene for a transcendence of the compromise and a redirection of the program of the labor movement toward socialist goals. A cross-national analysis by Stephens and Stephens confirms that gains in workers' control in the work place in various European countries, since the issue became prominent in the mid-sixties, are directly and strongly related to the political power of the Left.[21] Again, this indicates that the Left critics of social democracy are wrong when they portray it as a movement hopelessly reduced to an economistic program. In fact, this analysis indicates that the possibilities for a socialist transition are much greater in a country like Sweden than in France. The strength of the labor movement and socialist hegemony is the key to the possibilities of putting socialism successfully on the immediate agenda. The marginal voter must be integrated into labor-movement institutions to insure a solid base of support for anticapitalist policies. For instance, from this point of view, the poor showing of the French Socialists in the March 1978 election is not hard to explain. With only 15 percent of the labor force organized, the hegemonic presence of the French Left does not reach outside of the core of the working class — industrial workers in medium and large enterprises. The Socialist support was very shallow on the margin, which helps to explain the big drop between the last polls and the first round of voting.

Notes

1. This follows Ulf Himmelstrand, "Depoliticization and Political Involvement," in Erik Allardt and Stein Rokkan, eds., *Mass Politics* (New York: Free Press, 1970).

2. Hjalmar Branting, the Social Democrats' leaders, was known to have quoted Bernstein favorably, but he certainly would have sided with Kautsky on the role of class struggle, Bernstein's most serious "revision" of Marxism. See John Stephens, *The Transition from Capitalism to Socialism* (London: Macmillan, 1979).

3. John Stephens, "The Consequences of Social Structural Change for the Development of Socialism in Sweden." Unpublished Ph.D. dissertation, Yale University, 1976.

4. See Herbert Tingsten, *The Swedish Social Democrats* (Totowa, N.J.: Bedminster, 1973); Jan Lindhagen, *Socialdemokratins Program: I Rörelsens Tid 1890-1930* (Karlskrona: Tiden, 1972); Lindhagen, *Socialdemokratins Program: Bolsjevikstriden* (Karlskrona: Tiden, 1974); Leif Lewin, *Planhushållningsdebatten* (Stockholm: Almquist and Wiksell, 1967). For a debate on the relative merits of the last two positions, see Von Sydow and Lindhagen, in *Tiden*, no. 4 (1975). One could add a fourth position, the radical Left critique. This view is virtually the same in every country. Its essential element is that the Social Democratic leadership "sold out" the revolutionary working class. Since my disagreement with this position should be obvious, it will not be discussed here.

5. Quoted in Tingsten, *Swedish Social Democrats*.

6. Stephens, "Consequences of Social Structural Change."

7. Perry Anderson, "Antinomies of Antonio Gramsci," *New Left Review* 100 (1977), pp. 5-78.

8. Antonio Gramsci, *Selections from the Prison Notebooks* (New York: International Publishers, 1971), especially pp. 210-77. Anderson presented a view close to mine in 1965, though he later changed his position. See Perry Anderson, "Problems of Socialist Strategy," in Perry Anderson and Robin Blackburn, eds., *Toward Socialism* (London: Fontana, 1965), and Anderson, "Antinomies."

9. Thus there is a certain amount of truth to the Downsian model of democracy. The model does ignore the phenomenon of "mobilizing" elections, which Korpi argues is of great importance in the Swedish case. See Walter Korpi, *The Working Class in Welfare Capitalism* (London: Routledge and Kegan Paul, 1978).

10. This perception was inaccurate, at least as of 1960. See Stephens, "Consequences of Social Structural Change."

11. In the light of this evaluation, their strong partisanship (Tingsten: Liberal; Lindhagen: Social Democrat) is somewhat strange.

12. We found these inconsistencies as late as 1973 in our interviews with Social Democratic Party and trade-union leaders. The speed with which the collective ownership plans advanced in 1976-78 were embraced suggests that they were aware of these difficulties.

13. LO-SAP, *Löntagarfonder och Kapitalbildning* (Stockholm: Tiden, 1978).

14. Stephens, *The Transition*, chap. 4.

15. Philippe Schmitter, "Still the Century of Corporatism," in Frederick B. Pike and Thomas Stritch, eds., *The New Corporatism* (Notre Dame: University of Notre Dame Press, 1974). Also Harold Wilensky, "The New Corporatism, Centralization, and the Welfare State," Sage Professional Papers 06-020 (Beverly Hills, Cal.: Sage Publications, 1976).

16. Schmitter, "Still the Century," pp. 93-94.

17. Walter Korpi and Michael Shalev, "Strikes, Power and Politics in the Western Nations, 1900-1976," *Political Power and Social Theory* 1 (1979).

18. The following section leans heavily on the arguments in my previous work (Stephens, *The Transition*, pp. 120-25).

19. Korpi, *The Working Class*.

20. Korpi and Shalev, "Strikes, Power and Politics."

21. Evelyn H. Stephens and John D. Stephens, "The Labor Movement, Political Power, and Workers' Participation in Western Europe," *Political Power and Social Theory* 3 (1981), forthcoming.

9 Sweden: Paradise in Trouble

ULF HIMMELSTRAND

For over 40 years, ever since Marquis Childs wrote a best-selling book, Sweden has been known as the land of the Middle Way, which was slowly but consistently moving from a backward state toward its present position as the most developed of all welfare societies. Praised by progressive liberals at least outside Sweden itself, its gradually achieved social reforms have been discussed contemptuously by dogmatic revolutionaries who profess to be true Marxists. However "pure" this Marxist criticism may be, armed as it is with the powerful if not flawless analytic tools of historical materialism, the "purer" fact remains that these critics simply bungle the whole story.

Even when critics have got the facts straight about this land of the Middle Way, their image of Sweden has been incomplete and superficial. In place of understanding, we have stale "profundities" about Sweden's being a country that is stagnating morally and culturally—affluence corroded by boredom and drift, and by loss of incentive for work and innovation—so "profound" that once again President Eisenhower's statistical nonsense about suicide is becoming fashionable. The conservative opposition, in the nature of things, always leveled these accusations. With the defeat of the Social Democratic Labor Party in the Swedish general elections of 1976, they could not be so easily dismissed. The election results rocked progressive confidence that Sweden was on the right road to utopia.

Marxists, whether supporters, critics, or merely observers, have been less concerned with moral and cultural decay and the loss of incentives than with the amazing stability of capitalism in a country that for more than 40 years was ruled by a mass labor party. In Sweden, to this day, 94 percent of the means of production in manufacturing are privately owned. Private gross investment (housing excluded) is 57 percent, and private investment in machinery 78 percent. Swedish exports, which constitute nearly a third of the GNP and hence are a crucial factor in the welfare of the country, derive almost completely from private enterprise.

From what I hold to be a more genuine Marxist standpoint, it would seem possible, however, to argue that Swedish social democracy, by helping capitalism develop and mature, in fact (if not in a conscious and deliberate manner) has brought Swedish society closer to a socialist transformation. Socialism is supposed to spring from the internal contradictions, problems, and crises generated within the capitalist order precisely where it is most highly developed. If Marx's prediction about the "bursting asunder" of capitalist social relations of production should be borne out in any highly industrialized nation, Sweden is a natural candidate. Admittedly this "dialectical" interpretation is rather unusual among

149

Marxists commenting on contemporary Sweden. Nevertheless, it deserves closer scrutiny. Even those who reject deterministic prognostications about the social transformations of capitalist societies as propounded by orthodox Marxists might possibly find, in this interpretation of the socialist potential of late capitalism, a basis for a theoretically and empirically meaningful analysis of the Swedish situation.

I do not for a minute accept ideological propositions about the inevitability of socialism as a result of the mobilization of the working class in response to the decay of capitalism. But, after many years of research and political experience, I do believe that Sweden is far from being a stagnant society. It is indeed a country at a crossroad, with an enormous potential for qualitative and structural change, beyond the slowly incremental, and moving in the direction of socialist innovation within the framework of democracy.

Problems of Late Capitalism

Problems abound in Sweden today, but they are the problems of late capitalism, not of democratic socialism. As seen from the "commanding heights" of a capitalist economic policy, several problems are obvious: the loss of incentive, if you wish, since the whole capitalism-cum-welfare system is approaching its limit of growth in consumer demand as well as in fiscal measures; the absence of innovative impulse and farsighted investments, which lead to dwindling competitiveness and diminish the profitability of industrial production. Or as seen in the perspective of the man in the street: the acceleration of the work tempo; an improved but still quite inadequate work environment; poor job satisfaction with spillovers into impoverished and depersonalized use of leisure time; air, water, and traffic pollution; rapidly rising prices for food and services; threats of unemployment and the terror inspired in whole communities dominated by single, crisis-struck, dying industries.

Such lists of problems could be established for any advanced capitalist country. Sweden may exhibit some of them to a lesser extent than some other highly developed capitalist countries, but that is not crucial. The crucial fact is that Sweden, in spite of its extensive efforts to tackle most of these problems, is still unable to achieve real success in solving them — except, perhaps, in a few areas such as water pollution. It is the gap between aspiration and performance that generates a disappointment perhaps more intense in Sweden than in other societies, even though the latter exhibit the same problems of late capitalism to a greater extent.

Since Sweden is probably one of the most politicized countries in the world, these problems are the object of intense political debate. Comparative sociological surveys — most notably by the Finnish sociologist Erik Allardt and the British sociologist Richard Scase — support the conclusion that the Swedish citizenry, beneficiaries of a high level of social welfare, remain more aware than most others of the continuing problems of inequity, justice, and class contradiction. It would therefore seem that the stage is now set for political action to solve these problems and so change society. But it is not that simple.

Problem-Solving in Business and Government

For several decades, the Swedish business community collaborated reasonably well with the Social Democratic government. Until it lost power in the 1976 election, that government was the driving force behind our ambitious but largely piecemeal social-welfare and monetary policies, while the basic problem-generating structures were left very much intact. This social policy imposed certain costs on private enterprise, but also earned it substantial benefits. During the long postwar period of economic growth, private enterprise could depend on a predictable labor market, favorable credit conditions, and an expanding domestic market. The purchasing power of the public grew while inflation was contained at a reasonable rate. It was not, of course, a "free ride" for wealth. The business community demonstrated its perception of self-interest by supporting bourgeois political parties, which eventually displaced the Social Democratic government. Business reacted swiftly to the new political situation. In bargaining negotiations with the trade-union movement in the spring of 1977, the Swedish employers confederation (SAF) took a harsh and rigid stand, unprecedented since the late 1920s, not only with regard to wage demands but also on issues that had been legislated rather recently in parliament. Traditionally, these matters had been outside the accepted range of collective bargaining. Among other things, SAF demanded revisions in the legislated system of income benefits during illness, and of legislated provisions on working and vacation time.

The new government is not taxing the business community as severely as the Social Democratic government did. It is, in a general way, trying to improve the market situation for free enterprise and shows little taste for applying selective regulations on business. Yet these new policies have done little to improve the business climate. In addition to the impact of the abnormally prolonged international recession, the domestic situation has deteriorated a great deal, particularly in respect to relations between labor and capital. Gloom and disenchantment were obvious at midterm.

The solutions proposed by increasingly hawkish business leaders would ultimately dismantle some still significant welfare institutions. They would increase incentives for private capital accumulation and investment, allowing the market to operate with more complete freedom. Such a policy may indeed strengthen the position of capital. But the increasing strength that Swedish business may be gaining through further capital concentration, through the growing influence of investment companies and through investment abroad rather than in Sweden, may prove to be hollow. In its net effect, this strategy exposes the basically antisocial nature of capitalist relations of production, particularly at a time of prolonged recession when the most attractive asset of capitalism—its capacity for economic growth—is left in doubt.

Some less hawkish and more pragmatic business leaders may be aware of the hazards of allowing business criteria to show themselves in this naked and brutal manner. They may also anticipate the forceful reprisals to be expected from the powerful Swedish trade-union movement, and from the Social Democratic Party if it is returned to governmental power in the next general elections. But such pragmatism leads nowhere—except perhaps to a strategy of muddling through, which may work for a while in politics but will breed further stagnation in economic life.

When a crisis situation has deteriorated to a point where problems no longer are seen as exciting challenges but as a depressing tedium—as an occasion to find irrelevant scapegoats—then it is time to reconsider the very terms in which our problems have been perceived and defined. The pervasive chain of gloom and stagnation cannot be broken unless we discover that our problems can no longer be dealt with efficiently one by one, but only by tackling the social structures that have generated these problems in the first place, and that must be transformed in order to release new forces of social development. This may sound forbiddingly abstract or theoretical, but there is no way around it if we wish to escape what seem to be intractable difficulties and social boredom.

Structural Contradictions

Let us pause here to restate some of the aspects of Marxist thought in terms that can readily be understood by nonbelievers. The Marxist perspective recognizes a basic contradiction in that the industrial forces of production become increasingly societal, while the decision-making machinery implied in capitalist relations of production virtually excludes consistent and effective considerations of the wide-ranging societal responsibilities of production.

What is implied by an expression such as "the increasingly societal character of productive forces"? Industry depends more and more on society and state for infrastructural, productive, regulative, and planning inputs. Yet it manages its own internal decisions in a manner primarily conditioned by the narrow and often short-term needs of single-firm profitability. Simultaneously, the growing transnational market of commodities and capital significantly reduces the ability of society and state to influence and control the effects of their intervention. As productive forces grow they become increasingly international in character. "Outcomes" of industry in activity such as variations in productivity, capital-intensity, and related employment levels, and in the production of negative by-products (such as environmental effects) impose wide-ranging consequences on society as a whole.

The resource-accumulating, decision-making, and resource-allocating processes within capitalism—that is, the social relations of capitalist production—cannot match this increasingly societal and international character of the productive forces. Most of the piecemeal problems mentioned earlier derive from this basic problem of modern capitalism. They are generated by the structural contradictions of capitalism. But these contraditions of capitalism could be examined, not only with respect to the incompatibility of two overarching structures — the forces and social relations of production — but also in some other respects.

There are also more specific processes of internal and external contradiction unfolding as we take a closer look at concrete aspects of the modern capitalist economy: the competitive market, the interventionist state, and the incentive behavior of investors and labor.

A competitive market, in practice if not in the idealized models of neoclassical economic theory, operates in a self-destructive manner. The market is "self-contradictory" over time. The success that bred further success in what was originally a strictly competitive market succumbs, in time, to oligopolistic or monopolistic structures. These, in turn, reduce or eliminate the very competition that is supposed to be the unique vehicle of optimal resource allocation in a free-enterprise economy.

This contradiction coupled with recessions and crises, and the inability of capitalism to resolve them quickly, has promoted the demand for state intervention in all the advanced capitalist countries. Sweden was one of the first to introduce state intervention, to fight the business cycles, and, later, to mitigate market imperfections. It was the Social Democratic Party that was responsible for these early attempts to improve the functioning of the capitalist order, and it did so with the support of such liberal politicians as the leader of the Folkpartiet, Bertil Ohlin.

But even when the capitalist order, intelligently controlled by the state, operates reasonably well both in terms of growth and of distribution, and by improving the standards of living for most of the population, as it did for many postwar decades in Sweden, new contradictions emerge. The growth of affluence hurts the very mainspring of the capitalist system: its reliance on monetary incentives and rewards.

Several studies have suggested that a majority of Swedish employees, including the lower-paid, just a few years ago were less interested in increasing their private consumption than in improving the quality of working life and safeguarding an environment threatened by industrial pollution. This new attitude found an expression in demands for monthly salaries instead of backbreaking piece rates, despite the fact that monthly salaries frequently meant less money in the pocket by the end of the month. Wildcat strikes, as well as regular union activities, have now brought about a shift from piece rates to monthly salaries for large groups of Swedish workers.

Trade unions that have operated within the parameters of the capitalist order still demand higher wages, of course, since that is the job they have learned to do. But they have increasingly asked for other things as well: legislated authority to control health hazards at work, workers' codetermination, and worker-controlled capital funds that would give labor an increasing power over capital accumulation and investment. Monetary incentives are no longer seen as sufficient. No wonder that capitalist spokesmen complain about the loss of incentive to work. The only incentive they offer — monetary reward — no longer functions quite the way it did; and they are unwilling to offer the incentives of codetermination and power over capital now in demand.

As the unprecedented postwar years of economic growth and widespread affluence are grinding to a halt, other contradictions of the capitalist order emerge, especially as the puzzle of stagflation remains unsolved. Distrust in the system infects not only employees but also investors (see, for instance, an illuminating article by former President Ford's advisor Allen Greenspan in the *Economist* of August 6, 1977). Incentives for speculative and unproductive investments in art collections, diamonds, luxury houses, and idle land are often displacing productive investments in industry. This trend is as discernible in Sweden as elsewhere.

Liberal versus Socialist Perceptions

Leading liberal economists in Sweden have arrived at ideas that roughly, but far from completely, correspond to Marx's concept of the contradiction between the forces and the relations of production under capitalism. Progressive liberals are not unaware of what Marxists call the increasingly societal character of the productive forces, as contrasted with the narrow focus of business decisions.

Progressive liberal economists make an important distinction between the concept of business economics that emphasizes only private costs and benefits, and a broader concept of economics that embraces social or societal costs and benefits. These liberal economists are quite aware that there is no longer an "invisible hand" that will bring about an automatic harmony between private and social economic considerations. Though this perception may resemble Marxian theory, it differs significantly from a socialist conception based on a Marxist diagnosis of capitalism.

In Marxist terms, the structural contradiction of capitalism is not only a theoretical construct guiding the best-informed decision makers in government and private enterprise but also a reality that expresses itself in the exploitation of those who have nothing to sell but their labor. Some Marxists realize that this exploitation no longer can be defined exclusively, or even predominantly, as an appropriation of surplus value; it is an exploitation that defines the quality of working life and also the quality of leisure, since both have been shown to be closely correlated. Problems of family life and child rearing, alienation of working-class youth in school, work, and leisure are all manifestations of exploitation in the contemporary capitalist order.

There is, to be sure, a precise class content in Marxist analysis that is absent in corresponding liberal notions. In effect, it points to a third actor on the stage beside the interventionist state and private enterprise — namely, the working class as organized in trade unions and not only in political parties. The formation of social classes, which act out societal contradictions through measures of strike activity, political action, and so forth is an element missing in the liberal understanding of the divergencies between private and social economies. Of course, the existence of working-class organizations as social facts is obvious to everyone. What matters is that social liberals cannot relate effectively to this "social fact" evidenced by the deteriorating relationship between labor and government in our present bourgeois regime.

Nor do they seem particularly interested in theoretically considering the possibility of mobilizing this class under a liberal banner, since class action cannot be accommodated within the individualist framework of liberal theory. The failure of Swedish social-liberal politicians to relate at all to organized labor (in contrast to the experience of the United States) has left them in a predicament where they have access only to one actor—the interventionist state—to tackle all the problems gnawing at capitalism. This predicament is all the sharper because these Swedish social liberals, during the long era of Social Democratic government, relentlessly attacked the role of the state and the actions of the central governmental bureaucracies. Now that they are themselves in government, they cannot avoid using far-reaching state intervention, just as in other European states run by bourgeois governments. This is part of the internal inconsistency of bourgeois social liberalism. Another inconsistency may be found in its refusal to make use of specific government interventions proposed by the Social Democratic opposition, limiting themselves, instead, to generalized measures supplemented by appeals to the "social responsibility" of private enterprise. But, by definition, private enterprise cannot be socially responsible; in fact, it is not.

Though the policies of the Social Democrats in their 44 years of governmental power also were essentially social liberal—that is, using state intervention within the context of a so-called mixed economy—their "social liberalism" could be pressed much more consistently and energetically than the bourgeois social liberals would have dared undertake, given their ideological hangups regarding the role of the state.

Furthermore, the Social Democrats, because of their close collaboration with the trade unions, could involve more than the state in coming to grips with the problems of capitalism. The voice of organized labor was clearly heard in Social Democratic headquarters, and unions were usually willing to collaborate with the Social Democratic government. Now that this combination of capitalism, state interventions, and union collaboration seems to have reached its limits in negotiating the uphill stretch of economic policy, it is not too difficult for Social Democrats to change gears. The largely unused reservoirs of power, knowledge, and drive in the trade unions will be able to assert themselves in a new combination of labor and state once the Social Democrats recover their government posts.

But would not a political incorporation of the new issues of working-class power recently introduced by trade unions lead to more serious class confrontations, and thus threaten the creative national effort needed to get Sweden out of its present impasse? This has been suggested, for instance, by a leading management expert, Ulf af Trolle, who recently said: "We have created problems that cannot be solved in an atmosphere of confrontation." This statement is typically liberal in its idealistic belief that "confrontations" based on objective fact can be dissolved by wishes and good intentions. Policy formations based on mere good will are likely to intensify the contradictions they are meant to soften. There is no alternative to squarely facing the issues at stake, and allowing them to be articulated in political debate. Who will win forthcoming elections and on what platform? What is the likelihood of structural transformations in the relationships between capital and labor in the near future?

Who is Losing Ground?

On the stage of social change, there are several other actors besides the political parties formulating state policy, the business community and the trade unions among them. I will limit myself here to the relative strength of the political parties and the prospects of a Social Democratic comeback.

Seasoned political commentators are already predicting a Social Democratic victory in our next elections, with another relatively long period of Social Democratic government. The three bourgeois parties now represented in the government have been unable to deliver on most of their campaign promises. Inflation in 1977 was twice as high as before, taxes have not decreased except for certain higher-income groups, private enterprise has not shown itself more capable of improving its performance, and the nuclear power program, which the Center Party promised to abolish, is still being pursued, if at a somewhat slower rate. Important and urgent decisions in this and other areas where the three parties in government could not agree have been postponed, and thus have given the Social Democratic opposition an opportunity to argue that our present government is incapable of ruling. In the one area where the government admittedly is following the policies of the previous Social Democratic government in fighting unemployment, they have been somewhat more successful. All in all, it is not surprising that public-opinion polls show a decline in support for bourgeois parties.

However, all this could be a passing phenomenon. Viewed in a long-term perspective, it could be argued that a Social Democratic Party deriving most of its support from the working class will inevitably lose ground since the working class is diminishing in size. Certainly, the percentage of industrial workers is decreasing; today the proportion is only about a third of all those gainfully employed. But, at the same time, lower white-collar strata are being "proletarianized," which may compensate for the decreasing proportion of industrial workers. Operating machinery as "unskilled" labor, and performing routine tasks without access to the privileged knowledge embodied in this technical machinery, has become increasingly common among so-called nonmanual white-collar workers. Furthermore, the position of white-collar employees is more vulnerable than it used to be; unemployment is as much a threat to them as to blue-collar workers. It seems necessary, then, to redefine the working class, as many have proposed in Europe and the United States, to include clerical or service operations, which require no intellectual labor in the true sense. Under this definition, about three-quarters of all those gainfully employed in Sweden would be counted as part of the working class.

If the numerical strength of this working class were sufficient for constituting an electoral majority on behalf of a party prepared to initiate structural reforms leading to the abolition of the capitalist system, then Sweden would already have taken giant strides toward socialism, which it has not. The Swedish Social Democratic Party in recent years has been receiving only between 43 and 52 percent of the electoral vote, and the small Communist Party has obtained no more than about 4 or 5 percent. Not all members of the working class, as I have here defined it, vote labor. Factors beyond class position obviously affect the electoral vote. One such factor is the degree of unionization. Whereas more than 90 percent of all blue-collar workers in Sweden are organized in the LO (the central federation of blue-collar unions), unionization, until recently, has been much lower among white-collar employees. The trend, however, is clear; whereas only about 50 percent of white-collar employees were unionized in 1950, about 70 percent were unionized by 1975. Moreover, the collaboration between the TCO (the federation of white-collar unions) and the LO has become more and more intimate in recent years. Though the TCO is careful to indicate that it is unattached to any political party, its stand on several crucial issues with regard to workers' codetermination, labor-controlled capital funds, and other questions places it very close ideologically to the LO.

But Swedish labor is not only very highly organized and unified, it also has tended to become bureaucratized and centralized. The spread of wildcat strikes in the late 1960s and early 1970s can be interpreted as directed against this "centralistic" trend in trade unions, and not only against management. The fact that quite a number of wildcat strikes have been fairly effective in attaining their ends, plus the emergence of demands for a more responsive trade-union leadership, has, in my judgment, and however paradoxically, increased the strength of organized labor. The same union leaders who officially condemn wildcat strikes have privately condoned them as significant reactions to underlying problems. They see in them, off the record to be sure, hopeful signs of worker mobilization and sources of strength, a collective resource to be tapped in future union work. The rise of a new generation of union leaders is significant in this respect.

To understand why the size of the working class and the strength of its organizations so far have not assured greater electoral support for a labor party committed to structural changes, we must take a closer look at the ideological components of class relations, and the subjective consciousness displayed by different strata within the working class.

I referred earlier to sociological studies by Allardt and Scase, which show that Swedes generally exhibit a stronger sense of conflict, inequity, and injustice than people in comparable countries, and this despite Sweden's superior welfare programs. The Swedish working class displays a higher level of such social consciousness than the population as a whole. According to these studies, there is no evidence for an ideological "embourgeoisement" of the Swedish working class. Pursuing this theme, Goran Ahrne and I have carried out surveys probing the people's images of society, its threats and contradictions. We asked a series of questions regarding unemployment, inflation, nuclear power, and the like. These we called "piecemeal"

threats. If respondents combine a perception of these threats with a perception of threats considered as systemic aspects of society — the influence of
capitalism, the increasing mechanization of work, the growth of big
business, and others — we classify such respondents as exhibiting an
awareness of the structural problems that go beyond piecemeal issues. We
also asked questions about more "traditional" working-class identification.

We found that clerical workers with lower levels of skill, these new en-
trants into the extended working class, do not identify themselves as readily
with the labor movement and the working class as do industrial workers.
But they do exhibit an awareness of the structural threats of capitalism as
frequently as industrial workers; their increasing degree of unionization
would seem to promise a continued expansion of their ideological perception, since the awareness of structural defects is correlated with unionization. It is also interesting to note that this ideological awareness extends
beyond the working class far into the upper middle strata, although it is not
as frequently found there as in the working class itself. Consequently, the
extended working class might be able to find a significant number of
middle-class allies in support of structural reforms to reduce the flaws inherent in the capitalist order.

Finally, it is pertinent to emphasize that the emergence of this new type
of structural social consciousness is not correlated with leisure-time consumption of mass-media and consumer commodities. Rather it is linked to
the objective nature of the work situation, as well as to the degree of
unionization. Conjunctural swings in values related to leisure-time consumption are unlikely to affect this degree of social consciousness.

This social consciousness, however, merely sets the stage for the future.
It implies no more than a certain definition of the problems of capitalism.
The definition of a problem may be generally accepted long before adequate solutions come to be accepted by an electoral majority. But recently
the process of defining such problem solutions, and making them acceptable, has picked up speed in Sweden. The speed of this process depends not
only on the objective conditions of work and unionization mentioned
above, but also on the responsiveness of political leadership and the tempo
of political decision making. Our assessment of the political forces that push
toward more socialist solutions will therefore be concluded with a few
observations about the Social Democratic Party.

Three Stages

Looking back at the performance of the Social Democratic government
during the 1972–76 electoral period, when its position in parliament was
rather weak, we find a quite remarkable list of legislative accomplishments
on relations between labor and capital; for instance, acts on board
representation for employees in joint stock companies, on management
obligations to report on certain planning matters to trade unions, on greatly
expanded powers for union-appointed safety stewards, on employment
security, on the right of trade-union representatives to carry on union
business at the work place, and on the negotiability of most issues (which

previously were the prerogative of management) within a scheme of workers' codetermination. The party was under heavy pressure from below, particularly from the trade unions, and it certainly proved itself responsive to these demands.

Sociologically speaking, the most important aspect of many of these new legal acts is that they were intended to counteract the centralism that has been pervasive in Swedish society, without destroying the power of the national federation of trade unions, LO. Genuine, not fake, local controls are being placed in the hands of workers in local unions. One possible effect of these laws, apart from changing somewhat the power relationships between labor and capital, is to create a new social climate that will encourage new ways of thinking and acting about the relations of production.

Among proposals for new legislation one in particular deserves attention, since it may bring about more profound changes in the relationship between capital and labor, at least if the Social Democratic Party is returned to power. I am thinking here of the proposal for worker-controlled capital funds, originally initiated by the Federation of Metal Worker Unions. This proposal explores the possibilities of gradually transferring company profits to a capital fund controlled collectively by the trade unions. This would not only give trade unions a decisive proportion of the shares in these companies over a period of time but would also imply a corresponding transfer of decision-making power from the traditional holders of capital to labor. The Social Democratic Party was not prepared to make this an issue in the 1976 election campaign but is presently on the campaign trail to promote such a reform in the near future. The original proposal is now being revised to take into account the results of further studies and debates within the party and the trade-union movement.

The limited laws now in effect already reduce the decision-making power of capital within the existing order of private or company property. According to a voluntaristic interpretation of power, which assigns power to the majority will of decision makers, the legislation already in force, if pursued further, could lead to a more complete economic democracy if it did not change the basic features of the capitalist system.

Those who hold a structuralist interpretation of power may argue, however, that even if labor hypothetically achieves majority decision-making power, under capitalist relations of production, this could not significantly influence the movement of capital in the capital market. As long as there is a capital market, the movement of capital will be subject to market mechanisms and not to democratic decision making. The capital market is a structural arrangement that, among other things, separates capital and labor into different spheres of operation. Since the movement of capital in the present economic crisis is often geared more to profitable speculation than to production and labor, the dynamic of the capital market leads to a worsening of the predicament of labor. On the other hand, the labor-controlled capital funds proposed by the LO, the TCO, and the Social Democratic Party may significantly reduce the role of the capital market in capital accumulation and investment and may also help to reduce the contradiction of capital and labor. These funds will thus supplement the decision-making reforms provided in other laws at the point where these laws have shown their greatest weakness, and will make it possible to address more effectively the basic problems of capitalism.

Social Democratic historians now describe the development of the Swedish party in three periods. The first period was the struggle for universal suffrage and democracy undertaken together with liberal politicians some 70 years ago. In the second stage, the main issues were economic growth and social welfare redistribution. In the third phase, which has barely begun, the main issue is economic democracy, which implies a step-by-step but still complete overhaul of power relationships between capital and labor. From the point of view of professional academic historians, as well as that of Communist writers to the left of social democracy, this sequence of periods may seem a bit too neat to be historically true. In any case, my point is that this "periodization" of Social Democratic history is itself an indication of a changing ideological mood within the party.

But is the Social Democratic Party likely to become strong enough in electoral support and parliamentary votes to implement a program of structural reforms? Space limitation preclude here a thorough discussion of why the party lost in 1976 beyond a few observations buttressed by recent public-opinion polls.

Several statistical analyses of the 1976 election establish beyond doubt that the outcome rested on a single issue—the question of nuclear power. One of the bourgeois parties, the Center Party, promised to abolish nuclear power, and its leader even went so far as to promise that he would rather give up a ministerial post than compromise with his stand on this issue. There were, to be sure, other issues—a negative attitude to state bureaucracy and "socialism," for example—but these had arisen in earlier elections that were nevertheless won by the Social Democrats. Slightly more than half of the voters who shifted their allegiance from the Social Democratic Party to the Center Party seem to have based their switch on the nuclear-power issue. This same issue may appear again in later elections, though it is not likely to attain the same importance, for there is widespread disillusionment with the Center Party as the largest party in the 1976 government coalition.

While, normally, the parties that have gained the most in an election keep on gaining public support for a while, this time the Social Democratic Party has been growing remarkably after its defeat to a point where, since March 1977, public-opinion polls give it an absolute majority.

Whether or not predictions of a big Social Democratic victory in forthcoming elections prove true, it is clear that the Social Democratic Party has not moved closer to the center. The party leadership, as it enters its "third phase" of development, seems convinced that raising the issue of economic democracy, the real problem of Swedish society, corresponds with the mood of the electorate. The forces moving in a socialist direction are certainly more articulate and well organized than ever before, though perhaps more visible through the prism of sociological analysis than in explicit political pronouncements. But that is the Swedish way, low-keyed and reformist rather than expressive and rhetorical.

Forces opposing or trying to constrain structural changes in a socialist direction are certainly also considerable in Sweden, but they are less united. Most important, they lack a comprehensive and consistent diagnosis of the obvious weaknesses of the present system.

The outcome of a struggle between these opposing forces within the framework of a democratic policy is by no means certain. Some Marxist commentators have voiced apprehensions that the Swedish capitalist class may turn fascist. This seems farfetched to me. There is no evidence to support such a prediction; it rests purely on deductions from a highly simplified theory of class struggle, and on analogies of countries very different from Sweden, such as Allende's Chile. I keep my fingers crossed; it could still turn out to be at least partially true.

However, my own analysis — tentative as it is and relying on "fingertip" evidence — leads me to believe that Sweden, within a period of a decade beginning in the very near future, will become the first country in the world to have taken decisive and virtually irreversible steps toward socialist relations of production in a democratic and reformist manner. I see the following scenario: the business community is torn between its dependence on an interventionist state and its internal needs to minimize private costs and maintain or increase its profitability. After further electoral defeats of the bourgeois political parties, they will pragmatically decide, "If you can't beat them, join them." Burnham-type managers, separated from the ownership of capital and primarily concerned with doing a good job, will become increasingly common in the business community and, to their surprise, will find it as stimulating to work for labor as capital.

The greatest obstacle to taking these steps toward socialism will not be domestic. Our place in the international capitalist economy is not so easily resolved. Space prevents a full discussion of this point, but I would say it is very much a matter of timing and sequence. Certian changes, such as workers' control of capital accumulation and investment, can be realized while we still are part of this international capitalist order. Other, more far-reaching socialist changes are virtually impossible without at least the initiation of change in this international economic order. Close collaboration with working-class organizations in other countries is therefore essential. The building of a full-fledged democratic socialist society is certainly not something to be accomplished within ten years.

Liberalism Under Socialism

If the bourgeois parties stay in government long enough, we can expect more consistency in private interests and the economic policy pursued by the government. The conflict between labor and capital, on the other hand, could become more intense. However strange this may seem, the basic contradictions of Swedish capitalism would be dealt with less effectively by a bourgeois than by a Social Democratic government.

This does not mean that victorious return of a Social Democratic government would not have its problems. One particularly interesting problem concerns the future role dominated by worker-controlled capital funds and company decision making dominated by trade unions. Under present conditions, where the interests of labor and capital stand in clear opposition, the direction of trade-union policy is plainly on the side of labor. However, under conditions of worker-controlled "capital-fund socialism," the unions would have to operate on both levels—on the side of management and on the side of the workers. This double focus within the trade-union movement will require organizational innovations yet to be formulated in a way that will satisfy democratic criteria, articulate opposing interest, and still assure efficiency in production.

Should such a situation arise, part of the solution may rest with progressive liberalism. Unable today to place itself unambiguously on the side of either capital or labor, it might demonstrate a less ambiguous role under socialism, because it can then concentrate on its classical function as critic and as defender of individual human rights. We have to recognize here that problems of bureaucratic ossification and neglect for individual rights will exist in a democratic socialist society—just as they exist in our present type of capitalism. In a society that has arrived at a socialist order through democratic means and parliamentary legislation, the liberal posture could be maintained with more consistency and less ideological confusion. Once economic democracy based on workers' control and self-management has been made constitutional, these controversial issues, which now divide and confuse the social liberals, will be removed from day-to-day political preoccupations, just as political democracy stopped being controversial in Sweden long ago. Social liberals can then concentrate on a creative concern for individual rights and related issues.

Our Social Democratic leadership has repeatedly proclaimed that the Swedish style of socialism would not impose a one-party political system. In a future democratic socialist system adjusted to the specific historical requirements of Swedish society, with new and better relations of production having been legislated, opposing interests would still have to be represented by different political parties in parliament. Liberals may even find a role to play in trade-union elections where today they are seen as completely irrelevant. Paradoxical as it may sound, progressive liberalism would be more relevant in a system of democratic socialism than it seems to be in what we now call a liberal democracy.

10 Some Obstacles in Building a Mass Socialist Left in the United States

BOGDAN DENITCH

There have always been theories of American "exceptionalism." Even at the beginning of this century many theorists, Marxist and non-Marxist, have tried to answer what seems to be an obvious question: Why, given the many objective conditions favoring such a development, is there no mass socialist movement in the United States? There are a number of theories and answers ranging from the influence of the myth of the frontier, the special role of racism and immigrant labor, to the deeply rooted resistance of what is after all the bastion of world capitalism. This resistance has operated in both the objective and subjective spheres, again ranging from massive attacks on Left parties and organizations to a broad-fronted anti-socialist socialization in the schools, political and social institutions, and mass media. However, even if *objective* circumstances may explain why no massive working-class Left of a European type exists at this time in the United States, they cannot explain, in my view, the absence of at least substantial organized parties and groups of the Left. Put in another way, objective circumstances may explain why there is not an organized Left numbering in the millions, but not why there is not an organized Left numbering in the hundreds of thousands. Here, I believe, one should look for *subjective* reasons, reasons that are under the control of the present socialist and Marxist activists.

There are many circumstances that today make the task of organizing an active socialist political presence in the United States easier than at any time since the World War II. It is commonplace to speak of the general loss of legitimacy of the socioeconomic system. This is a phenomenon hailed by some and deplored by most of establishment, but its existence is un-challenged. The current cycle of inflation and high unemployment, catastrophic for the young and the urban blacks, has destroyed the old faith that a welfare capitalism is possible, that Keynes and his followers have tamed the capitalist cycle. The political institutions have never recovered from the impact of Watergate and the long, brutal imperialist war in In-dochina. Massive exposure of the role of the Central Intelligence Agency in shoring up corrupt reactionary regimes has all but destroyed the self-image of a United States that was a liberal democratic counterweight to an ex-panding Soviet bloc. The old easy optimism that racism could be dealt with within the framework of the system is long gone, and the activist policies of the New Deal and Fair Deal have been replaced with a growing neoconser-vativism within the Administration and Congress. President Johnson's Great Society was one of the most obvious victims of the war in Vietnam.

The organized trade-union movement is increasingly restive, and a major attack on the conservative policy of the AFL-CIO has developed within the trade-union leadership. This can be seen in the active political role of the more progressive unions; the United Automobile Workers (UAW) the Machinists (IAM), the Oil and Chemical Workers, and the fast growth of unionism among state, county and municipal workers (AFSCME). An extreme symbol of this trade-union discontent is the fact that the president of the million-member machinists' union is now the vice chairman of the U.S. affiliate of the Socialist International, the Democratic Socialist Organizing Committee. It is symbolic because, since the Great Depression of the thirties, there has been no major trade-union leader publicly identified as a member of an organized socialist group. Perhaps even more significant is the fact that the leadership of this union, traditionally heavily represented in the armament industries, now campaigns *against* increased spending for arms and instead calls for social ownership and planning. This is hardly radical in European terms but the move even to traditional social democratic politics is a major step forward within the American labor movement. The significance of the move has been grasped by the unions, which had been previously close to the American Communist Party, and many of the former Communist and Progressive Party activists in the unions have now been reactivated in a new framework. Socialist proposals have come out of the closet into which the years of the Cold War had driven the traditional Left.

The developments within the trade unions have numerous parallels. Strong socialist and Marxist elements can be found in the feminist and women's organizations and publications. The leadership of the women's organizations in the unions (CLUW) is democratic socialist, as are many of the local community activists. There was even an explicit socialist caucus openly functioning at the last Democratic Party issues conference. At least one major black Congressional leader, Ron Dellums of California, held a press conference to announce his membership in the fastest growing socialist organization, the DSOC. In this he has joined a growing list of notables, Nobel Prize winners, academics, and former activists of the New Left and student movement.

Perhaps the most marked revival of Marxist and socialist activity and presence is found in the universities. Hundreds of previous student civil-rights and peace activists of the mass student protests of the 1960s are now members of faculties, and their presence has had a major impact on the academic professional organizations. In the major social science and humanities associations, particularly of economists, political scientists, historians, and sociologists, Marxist and socialist caucuses function and have increasing influence. Their presence is accepted as legitimate, and their books and articles contribute to what is a remarkable revival of Marxist and socialist ideas. In many departments and disciplines, they are now the dominant current.

What strikes an observer and participant in radical politics in the United States, however, is the gap between the possibilities and reality. Put in a different way, what is striking today is the weakness of the organized Marxist and socialist Left, given the increasingly better objective environment for growth. To be sure, there has been growth but it does not begin to meet the opportunities that exist. A second intriguing fact is the relative vitality of a high-level theoretical and intellectual press, or rather journals, of a broad range, again combined with organizational weakness. The socialist and Marxist journals in the United States—*Monthly Review, Telos, Dissent, Socialist Review, Radical America, Science and Society,* to name only the most prominent—as well as the two weekly papers *In These Times* and *National Guardian,* all share at least a formal independence from any socialist or Marxist organization. They are also remarkable in that they are, irrespective of their point of view, by and large equal or *superior* to the journals published by the mass working-class parties of Western Europe. For example, there is to my knowledge no social democratic or socialist journal published by any of the European parties that approaches *Dissent* in quality, although they share the same range of politics. *Telos, Radical America,* and *Socialist Review* are all more substantial than their European counterparts. This is explicitly recognized in the case of *Monthly Review,* which is as a consequence translated into a number of languages.

Why this should be so represents an interesting problem, perhaps arising out of great gap between the objective tasks of a broad socialist movement and the subjective impatience of the theorists and activists in the United States. After all, the classic original sin of the American Marxist Left has been sectarianism, and the positive side of a sectarian tradition is a preoccupation with ideas and theories that are not relevant to the task of building a mass movement in one's own country.

In this essay, I will try to deal with a few of the problems that illustrate the gap between the subjective and objective needs in formulating a strategy for a mass socialist Left in the United States. This is a consciously limited essay, and one in which no pretense to objectivity is made, since I write as a participant in the debate. My underlying assumption is that, given the specific conditions and opportunities in the United States, what is objectively possible and desirable is to attempt to build a mass democratic socialist movement of a new type. It would be a movement that consciously seeks to contain within itself a broad range of views and diverse historical traditions. It would, however, also be a movement that seeks its roots in that which is healthy in the native American grass-roots tradition. That grass-roots tradition which is being rediscovered is one of sharp class conflicts and major struggles for women's and black rights, but there is also a tradition of democracy and the early development of formal institutions of popular sovereignty which were, as Marx and Engels noted, well in advance of Europe in their time.

After the Old and the New Left

The attempt to reconstitute a broad popular socialist movement in the United States occurs under peculiar circumstances. The fragments of the previous Old and New Left movements still remain, bringing their political heritages to contemporary politics. Broadly speaking, the most significant Old Left formation in the United States since the 1930s has been the Communist Party U.S.A., which at its peak had close to 100,000 members in its ranks and held sway over a variety of organizations involving perhaps as many as a million members. It was also by far the most significant explicitly radical organization operating within the American trade-union movement, and controlled a number of entire trade unions and sections of almost all industrial unions.

Since World War II no organization other than the CP has exceeded the size of a sect, although some, like the Socialist Party U.S.A., had historic claims to being the representative of the broad democratic socialist Left. At no point since World War II did any socialist organization have as many as 15,000 actual members. However, the Socialist Party did have large foreign-language affiliates, which, if counted, would have sharply increased the number of members, but these were relatively isolated from the mainstream of political life.

The effect of this relationship of forces was to make the CP and its periphery the most massive source of recruitment for all progressive and radical activities in the years after World War II, and for the CP heritage, sometimes in attenuated forms, to be the most significant usable past available to the New Leftists in the student antiwar movement. Of course, by the time the New Left developed, the CP was organizationally shattered and, while remaining the largest of the organizations, was merely a shadow of its old self. Nevertheless, it had left behind a tradition and certain norms with which, in one way or another, some kind of a reckoning had to take place.

A part of this heritage consisted of a hostility to the social democracies in advanced countries and a general unfocused sympathy with various Third World regimes that claim to be socialist or which appear to be in alliance, albeit somewhat precarious, with the U.S.S.R. This sentiment is still present today even among those former New Left activists who have nothing in common with the CP and who are quite critical of the practice and reality of Soviet-style "socialism." Somehow it is as if the "real" socialism and the "real" parties are those which come out of the Communist tradition, while the parties of the Socialist International are almost beyond the pale.

This can be seen in the preoccupation of much of the American Left with internal disputes within the Communist movement, the fascination with Euro-Communism combined with hostility or contempt for European socialism, and the repeated searching for a "real" socialist country or experience, ranging as it did from the Soviet Union to Cuba, to China, and for some even to Cambodia, Albania, and North Vietnam, but always the orbit of the parties and movements that come out of the Leninist tradition (no matter how modified).

Even broad socialist journals give more detailed coverage to the developments within the Communist movements of Europe than to those within the much larger and more significant socialist parties, and devote what seems an inordinate amount of attention to the debates between China and Vietnam, and Vietnam and Cambodia. There is something peculiarly archaic about this fascination because, whatever one's assessment of the situation in the Third World or Western Europe, it seems reasonably clear that a sentimental preoccupation with or attachment to a Communist past and a Third World present is inapplicable to the present strategic problems facing the American Left, and the Lefts of the advanced industrial societies as well.

The problem in the United States hardly seems to be one to be expressed in terms of the old dichotomy between reformist and revolutionary socialism, or, for that matter, between one-party regimes calling themselves socialist and advanced welfare states governed by socialist or social democratic parties. One of the burdens of the American Left is precisely this gap between the real possibilities and the desire of many of the remaining activists of the new left: between, in short, the subjective desires and objective possibilities.

The question one must ask is, What would or should a broad popular socialist movement in the United States look like? What would be its closest organizational and political analogies? What are the political tasks that it would have, and how would it relate to other movements in advanced industrial countries? My own argument is that, with appropriate modifications flowing from the American political tradition and with a sensitivity to the specific traditions from which many thousands of activists and participants in such a movement would come, that movement in the United States would belong within the framework of the present Socialist International. This is not to say that it would be uncritical of the real failures of social democracy when it dealt with theoretical questions, or that it would not seek to stress themes and demands that are characteristic of left-wing rather than right-wing socialists in Europe, but simply to locate the range of politics and, therefore, sympathies of such a movement within what is today broadly conceived of as democratic socialism.

Now, it is true, in specific cases in Europe, that that living democratic socialist tradition may well be represented as well as if not better by a Communist party than by the local socialist party. I personally regard the Communist parties of Italy and Spain as democratic mass workers' organizations, whose self-exclusion from the Socialist International is justified only by their specific historical tradition. But, even in these exceptional cases, one can note that the Italian Communist trade unions have broken with the Communist trade-union federation and operate as a part of the socialist-dominated Western European trade-union grouping. In point of fact, on most matters of general strategy, the Italian and Spanish Communists are indistinguishable from currents that already exist within the Socialist International. The specific historical experience that leads these parties to maintain an independent existence is a part of the special role and regard that those parties have in their own societies, and not of a desire to maintain a separate existence for the sake of positing a movement in competition to or as an alternative to the existing parties of the Socialist International. In

Spain, for that matter, the stated goal of the CP is to move toward the formation of a Spanish party of labor that would probably be affiliated with the Socialist International and that would include both of the present mass workers' parties.

The Socialist International and its parties organize at this time the vast majority of the European working class, as well as the vast majority of middle-class technicians and young people who regard themselves as socialists. Within that framework are found both right-wing and left-wing socialist views, and it is within that framework that most of the more novel strategic and theoretical analysis is occurring. It is, after all, in those parties, not the CPs, that a socialism based on decentralization, workers' control, and an attack on the central state bureaucracies exists. This fact has been noted not only by traditional apologists for social democracy but, in most European countries, by grouplets, parties, and individuals of the revolutionary Marxist Left who find the broad, loose, and democratic life of the socialist party far more congenial to internal debate and the development of new strategies than the CPs. The European analog of community activists, feminists, antiwar militants, and fighters for the democratization of the over-bureaucratized centralized states and for workers' control when organized by the Left, is found in the Socialist and not the Communist parties.

It is precisely the absence of a tradition of a total world view and a detailed, fully formulated program within the socialist parties that is an asset today. To put it in a slightly different way, what makes a party Marxist is not whether or not it has that term in its constitution and bylaws, but is determined by the activities, program, and the social base of those parties.

Given the realities of modern industrial societies, the whole issue of reform and revolution has been changed beyond recognition from the original issues. The present issue within the mass working-class parties of Europe is not whether the party calls itself "revolutionary" or "reformist." It is, rather, whether the party is committed to a fundamental transformation, no matter how gradual, of its society and economy to socialism or merely to administering an advanced welfare state with no further goals beyond minor incremental changes in the direction of egalitarianism. The problem with many of the social democratic parties is not that they are reformist but that they have ceased to be even reformist. Thus, much of what passes for the "left" wing of the British Labour Party or the German social democracy represents traditional socialist reformism, while the right wing has totally given up those aspirations.

This dichotomy within socialist politics is the cause of the crisis of present-day European socialism and the present immobility of European societies. It is probably also the reason that, despite the enormous opportunities that have opened up in Europe in the past half decade, the Left has not been able to advance but has, on the contrary, in some places even suffered setbacks. The stale, old program of classic post–World War II European social democracy neither inspires the activists nor reaches out to the masses of the new, better-educated workers entering the work force. As a consequence, a new revival of left-wing energies and programs is occurring within these parties, pushing them steadily to the left.

Changes in European Unions

A major and significant new phenomenon of European socialist politics is the reversal of the traditional relationship between the trade-union and parliamentary wings of the labor and socialist parties. Until a decade ago, it was taken for granted that the trade unions were the moderate right wing of the movement, while the parliamentary party and the constituency groups were considered leftist. Because of profound transformations of the European work force, this relationship is now exactly reversed in most European countries. In Sweden, Germany, France, Holland, even Italy and Great Britain to a certain extent, the push to the left now comes from the trade-union battalions. Given the great dependency of those parties on the organized labor movement, this means that, for the first time, fundamental structural challenge to the existing status quo has a stable, organizational mass base. The reaction to the recent setbacks will, in most cases, push the parties to a reexamination of their traditional politics.

Within this framework, it seems reasonably clear that an ideological crisis affects the Communist as well as the socialist movements. There is no ready guide in either tradition as to what is an appropriate strategy for an advanced industrialized society with deep internal stresses and an economic downturn but no crisis of regime—or, in other words, no revolutionary situation. Revolutionary scenarios, when applied to present-day Europe or the United States, have a profound unreality. It is as if one argued that a working class and a general Left electorate hesitant to give a majority to a reformist program would rally instead to a more advanced revolutionary struggle. It is as if substantial forces existed outside of the organized Left that were "to the left" of the existing CPs and SPs. There is no evidence that that is the case, except for marginal intellectuals, sometimes with a small following among the unemployed, students, and younger workers.

The real political problem is how to retain the traditional Left base in the face of an industrial society that has gradually destroyed the basis of an independent working-class culture. The new voters for the parties of the Left can no longer be recruited on the basis of a living working-class tradition but must be won over politically.

To win political adherence to the mass socialist and Communist parties does require settling certain historical accounts. The most obvious one in Europe, and to a certain extent in the United States, is the problem of what the Soviets call "real" socialism. It does no good simply to state that socialists, or for that matter Euro-Communists, deplore the violations of human rights in Eastern Europe and the Soviet Union, call for democratic restructuring of those societies, and even, in many cases, deny them the name "socialist." That last is a finesse which the mass media, unfortunately, have made all but irrelevant. The fact is that, in the mind of the general public, the bureaucratic and repressive state socialisms of Eastern Europe and the Soviet Union are linked with the socialist and working-class parties in Western Europe. There is *some* relationship. We all feel it when discussing socialist politics in the United States; if not the first, then the second question invariably is, how will "our" socialism differ from the existing systems calling themselves socialist.

Behind that question lies a more serious one: How will we assure that "our" socialism will not degenerate into a bureaucratic, albeit more humane, copy of state socialism? After all, it was not the subjective intent of the leaders of the East European societies to build societies that would be abhorrent to their own workers and would require heavy doses of repression to survive. Simply to say that we have a parliamentary tradition and are committed to democracy is nice, but not convincing, and it becomes less convincing when we maintain nostalgic and sentimental links with regimes and parties that are at least ambivalent on the question of democracy.

Another way of addressing this general issue is to say that for the socialists to regain their élan and relevance, and for a socialist movement to be able to draw on that which is best in the American tradition, democracy must be made the centerpiece and not the peripheral ornament of socialist politics. It is making democracy the centerpiece that gives a cutting edge to the demands for workers' self-management, for the extension of popular power into the economy and society, for the assault on patriarchal and racist values, for the unleashing of the energies of the rank and file in the trade unions, for an assault on imperialist and interventionist policies by the United States around the world, and ultimately for the democratic control and ownership of the economy and society by the masses of people.

In short, the consistent, relentless insistence on democracy *is* the socialist program. All of our economic demands rest ultimately on that issue, and in that, we are not merely drawing on the genuine democratic traditions that exist within our society but are utterly consistent with that vision of socialism and of the movement that had to struggle for it that informed the thinking of our revolutionary forebears — Marx, Engels and Luxemburg. Socialism was born as a modern mass movement, not out of the musings of Fabian bureaucrats but as the Left revolutionary wing of radical democracy in nineteenth-century Europe. The Soviet experience, however evaluated, clearly put that tradition in question, and whether one thinks of it as a tragedy, an experiment gone wrong, or the historical penalty paid for not having followed the Bolshevik Revolution with revolutions in the advanced countries of Western Europe, the Soviet experience demonstrated the possibility of a "socialism" where democracy was either secondary or irrelevant. There is no reason to expect that "socialism" and its spinoffs will be attractive to working classes that already have more rights, organizationally and politically, than their counterparts under state socialism.

The socialism we stand for must therefore be associated with more rather than less democracy than exists under capitalism and with a vast expansion of rights for the strata excluded from the decision-making levels of advanced capitalist democracies. If one has this orientation, then clearly Euro-Communism is a welcome development because it promises to bring back to its original roots working-class parties that had been in the shadow of the Soviet experience. It promises to reconstitute a unified socialist and workers' movement in the industrial heartland of capitalism, and the equivalent of that policy in the United States would be to build a broad democratic socialist movement within which former Communists and former social democrats could work, which would attract the activists of the 1960s and 1970s, and which could emerge as the intransigent defender of democratic rights and the extension of popular power.

The sentimental affair with state socialist systems and with Third World regimes calling themselves socialist is not a harmless pastime to be excused in Marxist activists. It is, on the contrary, in direct contradiction to what has to be done if a genuine American socialist movement is to be built.

There is something peculiar and archaic among American leftists who excuse violations of democracy in Third World countries. It is as if they regarded democracy as something that weakens a revolutionary regime. All great social revolutions, at the point when they are genuinely revolutionary, precisely strengthened themselves by expanding rather than limiting democracy, by expanding the participation of the hitherto excluded, and by permitting the creative energies from below to be released. It was not under the tutelage of parties with "correct lines" that revolutionary struggles were won; on the contrary, those parties consolidated power in the French and Russian revolutions after the victory of the revolutions. And we should, as socialists and revolutionary democrats, be clear on this. For us, democracy is the central weapon in the struggle for the expansion of popular power and not a reward to be given to a people or a working class after they have successfully accomplished tasks that have been set for them by their self-selected vanguard.

Index

About the Authors

BOGDAN DENITCH is professor of sociology at the Graduate School and Queens College of the City University of New York and Executive Officer of the CUNY Ph.D. Program in Sociology. His most recent works include *Legitimation of the Revolution: The Yugoslav Case* and *Legitimation of Regimes*.

FRANCO FERRAROTTI is professor of sociology at the University of Rome and has been a major figure in the development of Italian sociology since the end of the World War II. He is the author of many books, including *An Alternative Sociology*.

RAYMOND FRANKLIN is professor of economics at Queens College and professor of sociology at the Graduate School of the City University of New York. His interest centers on the problems of political economy.

ULF HIMMELSTRAND, professor of sociology at the University of Uppsala, is president of the International Sociological Association. He has published widely in political science, mass communications, and African development.

ROBERT LANE is Eugene Meyer Professor of Political Science, Yale University. He is past president of the American Political Science Association (1970-71) and is the author of *Political Man, Political Thinking and Consciousness,* and *Political Ideology*.

PETER LANGE is associate professor of government and a Research Fellow at the Center for European Studies, Harvard University. He has published extensively on the postwar strategy and organization of the Italian Communist Party and on the Italian political system. His most recent research has been focused on the Italian trade unions' response to the economic crisis of the 1970s as part of a larger multi-authored project on European trade unions in the 1970s sponsored by the Ford Foundation. His most recent publication is a collection of essays, *Italy in Transition* (London: Frank Cass, 1980), edited with Sidney Tarrow.

NANCY LIEBER is a Ph.D. in political science and the program director of the Institute for Democratic Socialism.

RICHARD LOWENTHAL is Professor Emeritus of International Relations at the Free University of West Berlin. He is author of *World Communism: The Disintegration of a Secular Faith* and other works on the theory of capitalism and socialism.

JOHN D. STEPHENS is a graduate of Harvard University. He is currently assistant professor of sociology at Brown University. He has contributed to various American journals on European and particularly Swedish politics. He is also active in American social democratic politics.